# Algorithms for Visual Design Using the Processing Language

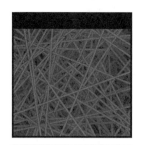

# Algorithms for Visual Design Using the Processing Language

## Kostas Terzidis

Wiley Publishing, Inc.

Algorithms for Visual Design Using the Processing Language

Published by
**Wiley Publishing, Inc.**
10475 Crosspoint Boulevard
Indianapolis, IN 46256
www.wiley.com

Published by Wiley Publishing, Inc., Indianapolis, Indiana

Published simultaneously in Canada

ISBN: 978-0-470-37548-8

Manufactured in the United States of America

10 9 8 7 6 5 4 3 2 1

Library of Congress Cataloging-in-Publication Data is available from the publisher.

*To my father, George*

# About the Author

**Kostas Terzidis** is an associate professor at the Harvard Graduate School of Design. His current GSD courses are Kinetic Architecture, Algorithmic Architecture, Digital Media I & II, Cinematic Architecture, and Design Research Methods. He holds a PhD in Architecture from the University of Michigan (1994), a Masters of Architecture from Ohio State University (1989) and a Diploma of Engineering from the Aristotle University in Greece (1986). He is a registered architect in Europe where he has designed and built several commercial and residential buildings.

His research work focuses on creative experimentation within the threshold between arts, architecture, and computer science. As a professional computer programmer, he is the author of many computer applications on form making, morphing, virtual reality, and self-organization. His most recent work is in the development of theories and techniques for algorithmic architecture. His book *Expressive Form: A Conceptual Approach to Computational Design*, published by London-based Spon Press (2003), offers a unique perspective on the use of computation as it relates to aesthetics, specifically in architecture and design. His latest book, *Algorithmic Architecture*, (Architectural Press/Elsevier, 2006), provides an ontological investigation into the terms, concepts, and processes of algorithmic architecture and provides a theoretical framework for design implementations.

# Credits

**Executive Editor**
Carol Long

**Senior Development Editor**
Tom Dinse

**Production Editor**
Angela Smith

**Copy Editor**
Foxxe Editorial Services

**Editorial Manager**
Mary Beth Wakefield

**Production Manager**
Tim Tate

**Vice President and Executive Group Publisher**
Richard Swadley

**Vice President and Executive Publisher**
Barry Pruett

**Associate Publisher**
Jim Minatel

**Project Coordinator, Cover**
Lynsey Stanford

**Compositor**
Craig Johnson,
Happenstance Type-O-Rama

**Proofreader**
Publication Services, Inc.

**Indexer**
Robert Swanson

**Cover Designer**
Michael Trent

**Cover Image**
© Kostas Terzidis

# Acknowledgments

This book was conceived as a first step towards open source development. I would like to thank the person who introduced me to the world of computer graphics back in 1986 at Ohio State University, Professor Chris Yessios. He gave me the knowledge and taught me the means of making my own tools to design and showed me how to share it with my colleagues.

Also, I would like to thank my doctoral student at Harvard University Taro Narahara for his help in formatting the text and images of this book. Tom Dinse, Angela Smith, and Carol Long also deserve thanks for their patience and helpfulness during the preparation of this book.

# Contents

# Introduction

How has design changed through the use of computers? Is it still valid to assume that a designer is in control of a design concept? What if there is a lack of predictability over what was intended by the designer and what came out on the computer's screen? Is computer programming necessary in design today?

This book is about computer programming. Programming is a way of conceiving and embracing the unknown. At its best, programming goes beyond developing commercial applications. It becomes a way of exploring and mapping other ways of thinking. It is the means by which one can simulate, extend, and experiment with principles, rules, and methods of traditionally human-defined theories. In developing computer programs, the programmer has to question how people think and how mental processes develop and to map them into different dimensions through the aid of computers. Computers should be acknowledged not only as machines for imitating and appropriating what is understood but also as vehicles for exploring and visualizing what is not (yet) understood. The entire sequence of specifying computer operations is similar (albeit not equal) to that of human thinking. When designing software, one is actually codifying processes of human thinking to a machine. The computer becomes a mirror of the human mind, and as such, reflects to a certain level our own way of thinking.

However, there is an unraveling relationship between the needs of a designer and the ability of a specific computer application to address these needs. Designers rarely know what the computer is capable of providing them intellectually and often designers overestimate the computer's capabilities. This can be attributed to at least two factors. First, designers are never really taught how to program (one should to look no further than the classic question/answer "What does computer programming have to do with design?"). In fact, in design schools today students are taught how to use CAD tools and how to experiment within the limits of the applications, but they are never taught how to channel their creativity through the language, structure, and philosophy of programming. Second, CAD developers rarely release source code. They may ask the users what they want, they may offer interfaces for customization, but they will never give access to their source code. For good reasons, code is proprietary information, and information is power. So, if a designer wants to experiment with the computational design, then he or she will need to write his or her own application, including the modeling, interface, display, optimization, and debugging modules, all on their own. How many people either have the time or the know-how to do this out there? When are we going to see a Linux-like CAD system? When are we going to see a community of designers-architects-programmers sharing common source code, for their own advancement?

It is possible to claim that a designer's creativity is limited by the very programs that are supposed to free their imagination. The motto "form follows software" is indeed a contemporary Whorfian hypothesis that still applies not only to language as a tool but also to computer tools. The reason for that is that there is a finite amount of ideas that a brain can imagine or produce by using a CAD application. If designers don't find the tool/icon that they want, then they are simply stuck. And, conversely, whenever they use a new tool provided for them by programmers, they think that they are now able to do something new and "cool." But are they really doing anything new? Or are they simply replicating a process already conceived by the programmer who provided the tool? Of course, if designers knew the processes, principles, and methods of the program behind the tool, then they would be empowered to always keep expanding their knowledge and scholarship by always devising solutions not tackled by anybody else. By using a conventional program, and always relying on its design possibilities, the designer/architect's work is sooner or later at risk of being imitated, controlled, or manipulated by CAD solutions. By cluttering the field with imitations of a type of particular software, one runs the risk of being associated not with cutting-edge research but with a mannerism of style.

In this context, there are many designers claiming to use the computer to design. But are they really creating a new design? Or are they just rearranging existing information within a domain set by the programmers? If it is the programmer who is considering all possible solutions to a design environment beforehand, who is really setting the parameters and the outcome of a design solution? We saw already the I-Generation (Internet-Generation) risen out of the information age. When are we going to see the C-Generation (Code-Generation) — the generation of truly creative designers who can take their fate into their own hands?

In the world of design today, computer programs have taken over many traditionally human intellectual tasks, leaving less and less tasks for traditional designers to do. From Photoshop filters to modeling applications, and from simulation programs to virtual reality animation, and even more mundane tasks that used to need a certain talent to take on, such as rendering, paper cutting, or sculpting, the list of tasks diminishes day by day only to be replaced by their computational counterparts. What used to be a basis to judge somebody as a talent or a genius is no longer applicable. Dexterity, adeptness, memorization, fast calculation, and aptitude are no longer skills to seek for, nor are they reasons to admire a designer as a "genius." The focus has shifted far away from what it used to be toward new territories. Computational tools allow not only manual, tedious, and repetitive tasks to be done quicker, cheaper, and more efficiently but also intellectual tasks that require intelligence, thought, and decision making. In the process, many take advantage of the ephemeral awe that the new computational tools bring to design, either manual or intellectual, by using them as means to establish a new concept, style, or form — only to have it revealed later that their power was based on the tool they used and not on their own intellectual ability. Of course, the tool that was used was indeed developed by somebody else, that is, a programmer, who discovered the tool's concept, mechanism, and implementation, and should, perhaps, be considered instead as the true innovator.

As a result of the use, misuse, and, often, abuse of computational design tools, many have started to worry about the direction that design may take in the next few years. As, one by one, all design tasks are becoming computational, some regard this as a danger, misfortune, or misappropriation of what design should be and yet, others regard it as a liberation, freedom, and power towards what design should be: conceptualization. According to the latter, the designer does not need to worry anymore about the mundane, tedious, or redundant tasks in the design process, such as construction documents, schedules, databases, modeling, rendering, animation, and so forth and can now concentrate on what is most important: the concept. But what if that is also replaced? What if one day a new piece of software appears that allows one to input the building program and then produces valid designs, that is, a plan, elevation, and sections that work? And, worse, what if they are better than the designer would have ever done by himself or herself? (Even though most designers would never admit publicly that something is better than what they would have designed, yet what if deep inside they would admit it?) What then? Are we still going to continue demonizing the computer and seeking to promote geniuses when they probably don't exist?

If that ever happens, then obviously the focus of design will not be in the process itself, since that can be replaced, but rather in the replacement operation itself. The new designer will construct the tool that will enable one to design in an indirect meta-design way. As the current condition indicates, the original design is laid out in the computer program that addresses the issues, not in the mind of the user. If the tool maker and the tool user is the same person, then intention and randomness can coexist within the same system and the gap can be bridged. Maybe, then, the solution to this paradox may not be found inside or outside the designer's mind but perhaps in the link that connects the two.

## Overview of the Book and Technology

This book offers students, programmers, and researchers the technical, theoretical, and design means to develop computer code that will allow them to experiment with design problems for which a solution is possible or for those for which it is not. The first type of problem is straightforward, where the methodology is to create an algorithm that will solve the problem in a series of steps. It is about the codification of ideas that are preconceived in the mind of the designer and await a way to manifest them in a physical form. Sample cases are given that address various problems such as geometrical, topological, representational, numerical, and so forth. In contrast, there is another set of problems, in which a solution is not preconceived, or even known. This book offers a series of procedures that can function as building blocks for designers to experiment, explore, or channel their thoughts, ideas, and principles into potential solutions. The computer language used in this book is a new, fascinating, and easy-to-use language called Processing, and it has been used quite extensively in the visual arts over the last few years. Although this book offers a quick and concise introduction to the language itself, the core of the book focuses on the development of algorithms that can enhance the structure and strategy of the design process. These algorithms and techniques are quite advanced and not only offer the means to construct new design tools but also function as a way of understanding the complexity involved in today's design problems. Such algorithms include Voronoi tessellation, stochastic search, morphing, cellular automata, and evolutionary algorithms.

## How This Book Is Organized

This book is divided into 11 chapters. It is assumed that the reader of the book has no previous knowledge of programming. Nevertheless, the topics of each chapter are organized so that successive chapters contain progressively more complex topics that are based on the previous chapters. Each chapter covers a discrete topic that allows you to build your knowledge not only by reading the chapters but also by applying the knowledge through relevant exercises.

This book introduces basic structures and processes of programming in Processing in order to clarify and illustrate some of the mechanisms, relationships, and connections behind the forms generated. This is not intended to be an exhaustive introduction to programming but rather an indication of the potential and a point of reference for assessing the value of algorithms.

- **Chapter 1** is a general introduction to the elements, operands, and operations of the Processing language. It covers basic concepts such as variables, arithmetic and logical operations, loops, arrays, and procedures. It also shows how to create basic geometry, how to affect their attributes, and how to interact with them. A series of exercises allows the reader to explore and test more possibilities.

- **Chapter 2** shows how to use points in order to construct curves or images, and how to use lines to construct shapes. It uses trigonometric functions as well as polynomials to determine the positions of points along a curve. Shapes are constructed by using trigonometric functions to place points along a circumference establishing equilateral polygons.

- **Chapter 3** introduces the concept of class and how classes can be used to organize code in hierarchical entities. This chapter introduces the classes of a point, a segment, a shape, and then a group. Each class contains methods that allow it to interact with other classes in a complementary, hierarchical, and object-oriented way. The advantage of this methodology is speed, organization, and interaction that allows objects or their subparts to be selected, modified, or deleted.

- **Chapter 4** introduces basic elements of a graphic user interface (GUI) such as buttons, choice menus, labels, and text fields. The objective is first to arrange them in the screen to provide an interactive environment, but more importantly to connect them with the classes introduced in Chapter 3. In such a way, the graphical user interface elements can determine the position, orientation, and size of geometrical entities such as vertices, edges, faces, or groups as well as their color.

- **Chapter 5** shows you how to process images. An image is a collection of colored pixels and can be changed by the application of certain functions that affect the color of specific pixels or their neighboring pixels. Grayscale, threshold, inversion, blur, or poster are some of the many image processing filters. However, you will look further into the structure of a pixel and see how it is represented in the computer's memory and then use this information to speed up the process so as to produce any possible filter. You will also look into interactive paint brushes and edge detection.

- **Chapter 6** is about motion. Motion is simply a visual phenomenon based on the speedy redraw of the screen. You will see how to produce motion using images or geometrical objects, how to constrain the motion within boundaries, and how to affect the direction or position of motion. You are introduced to the use of transformation operations and how they can be used to produce repetitive, recursive, or random patterns. Finally, you look into physics-based motion showing how to use friction, collision, and elasticity.

- **Chapter 7** is a collection of advanced graphics algorithms that can be used as techniques for design projects. These algorithms include Voronoi tessellation, stochastic search, fractals, hybridization, cellular automata, and evolutionary algorithms. Voronoi tessellation is shown as a method of subdividing the screen into multiple areas using pixels as finite elements. Stochastic search is a method of random search in space until a given or an optimum condition is met. Fractals are recursive patterns that subdivide an initial base shape into subelements and then repeat the process infinitely. Hybridization is a procedure in which an object changes its shape in order to obtain another form. Cellular automata are discrete elements that are affected by their neighboring elements' changes. Finally, evolutionary algorithms use biological Darwinian selection to optimize or solve a problem. Even though they are abstract, these algorithms have been used quite extensively to address or solve design problems and can function as metaphors or inspiration for similar design projects.

- **Chapter 8** introduces you to the concept of 3D space in the context of geometry. This is done through projections and transformation of three-dimensional points into two-dimensional viewing screens. Single or multiple objects can be viewed either statically or dynamically by rotating the scene. Formations of multiple objects are being studied as grids in space, spheres, or superquadrics.

- **Chapter 9** introduces basic concepts of solid geometry using the class structures introduced earlier in Chapter 3. Here you are introduced to classes for a point, a face, a solid, and a group. Each class contains the appropriate methods that allow it to interact with the other classes. Specifically, faces are arranged to form extruded polygons and then checked for visibility. Shading of faces is also introduced using vector geometry. Finally, objects or subelements can be selected and transformed in a user interactive environment.

- **Chapter 10** shows you the structure of files and how they can be used to save information or to input new information to a design project. You will cover basic file read and write operations and then look into the structure of universal file formats such as PDF, MOV, DXF, and VRML.

These will be used to interchange information between Processing and other applications, such as Acrobat, AutoCAD, Rhino, QuickTime, and so forth. The purpose is to take advantage of each application's tools and use them to enhance the initial processing form, or conversely, to input an application's file into Processing for further enhancements. You will also be introduced to client-server data transfer as a means of connecting to remote servers.

- **Chapter 11** shows you how to use Processing to produce physical motion in the environment. This will be done through electrical circuits and devices, such as photocells, motors, buttons, speakers, LEDs, and the like. You see how to process information coming in the computer and how to output information to the external physical world. You will be using a microcontroller called Arduino, which uses a computer language based on Processing. You will also see how input and output information can be connected in responsive and feedback systems and how this can be useful in a design or installation context.

Each chapter, apart from its theoretical and technical dimension, also contains a series of exercises that are meant to help the reader understand and explore possibilities beyond the chapter's content. For each exercise a solution is given in Appendix B so that the reader can try and then compare solutions.

## Who Should Read This Book

This book is aimed mainly at students (design, art, computation, architecture, etc.) and professionals (web developers, software developers, designers, architects, computer scientists). Since it addresses both a computer language and advanced algorithms, it can be seen as a textbook or a manual as well as a reference book.

From my experience as a professor and a software developer, there are many students, instructors, developers, and regular folks that cannot find a book that will teach them graphics software development in a simple, no-prerequisite, hands-on manner. Most of these people are ready to start writing software, and they are waiting for the chance. This book does it in a great and efficient way taking you much further than any other book.

## Tools You Will Need

The language used in the book is Processing, an open source, free-of-charge, powerful, and yet simple computer language that can be downloaded from the Internet. The version of Processing used in this book is the latest at this time, that is, version 1. You should also know that Processing is based on another language called Java, which is also available free of charge from the Internet. In the last chapter of this book, a physical device is introduced called Arduino that also uses a version of the Processing language called, appropriately enough, Arduino. The version used in this book is Arduino 0012.

## What's on the Web Site

All code shown in this book together with the exercises can be found at the book's web site at www.wiley.com.

## From Here

One of the main objectives of this book, compared to other computer graphics books, is to take away the fear of complexity or the assumption of prerequisites that most books have. There is a large audience of computer graphics–thirsty readers that simply cannot understand existing books because either they are full of mathematical formulas or assume that the reader already knows the basics. As a computer scientist and designer-architect, I have developed this book with this in mind. In addition, my experience with teaching computer graphics programming to design-oriented students with no programming experience guided me as well. The book is a bridge between the creative designer and the computer savvy.

# Algorithms for Visual Design
# Using the Processing Language

# Elements of the Language

Processing is a computer language originally conceived by Ben Fry and Casey Reas, students at the time (2001) at MIT. Their objective was to develop a simple language for use by designers and artists so that they could experiment without needing an extensive knowledge of computer programming. They began with Java, a popular computer language at that time, yet quite complicated for non-computer-science programmers, and developed a set of simpler commands and scripts. They also developed an editor so that typing, compiling, and executing code could be integrated. Specifically, the compiler used (called jikes) is for the Java language, so any statement in Java can also be included within the Processing language and will be consequently compiled.

Some of the characteristics of Processing (and Java) language are:

- **Multi-platform:** Any program runs on Windows, Mac OS, or Linux.
- **Secure:** Allows high-level cryptography for the exchange of important private information.
- **Network-centric:** Applications can be built around the internet protocols.
- **Dynamic:** Allows dynamic memory allocation and memory garbage collection.
- **International:** Supports international characters.

- **Performance:** Provides high performance with just-in-time compiles and optimizers.

- **Simplicity:** Processing is easier to learn than other languages such as a C, C++, or even Java.

The basic linguistic elements used in Processing are constants, variables, procedures, classes, and libraries, and the basic operations are arithmetical, logical, combinatorial, relational, and classificatory arranged under specific grammatical and syntactical rules. These elements and operations are designed to address the numerical nature of computers, while at the same time providing the means to compose logical patterns. Thus, it can be claimed that the Processing language assumes that a design can be generated through the manipulation of arithmetic and logical patterns and yet may have meaning attributed to it as a result of these manipulations.

The following sections examine basic structures and processes in Processing as they relate to graphics in two dimensions (2D) and three dimensions (3D). This is not intended to be an exhaustive introduction to Processing but rather an introduction to the elements and processes used in the context of 2D and 3D graphics. We will start with basic elements and processes, give examples, and then move into more complex topics.

# 1.1 Operands and Operations

The basic structure of a computer language involves operations performed with elements called operands. The operands are basic elements of the language, such as variables, names, or numbers and the operations involve basic arithmetic and logical ones such as addition, multiplication, equality, or inequality. The next section introduces the basic operands and operations used in Processing and their corresponding syntax.

## 1.1.1 Variable Types

*Variables* are used to hold data values. Variables can be of different types: if they hold whole numbers, they are called *integer* variables; if they hold true/false data, they are called *booleans*; if they hold fractional numbers they are called *float*, etc. In Processing, as well as in most computer languages, the syntax for declaring a variable is:

```
type name
```

For instance:

```
int myAge = 35
```

declares an integer variable called `myAge`. Depending on the type of data you want to store, you might use different variable types:

- `boolean`, which is 1-bit long and can take values of either `true` or `false`:

  ```
  boolean isInside = false;
  ```

- `char`, which is 16-bit long and therefore can store $2^{16}$ (= 65,536) different characters (assuming that each character corresponds to one number, which is its ASCII code):

  ```
  char firstLetter = 'A';
  ```

- `byte`, which is an 8-bit element and therefore can store $2^8$ (= 256) different binary patterns:

  ```
  byte b = 20;
  ```

- `int`, which is 32 bits long, can define integer (whole) numbers:

  ```
  int number_of_squares = 25;
  ```

- `float`, which is 32 bits long, can define real numbers:

  ```
  double pi  = 3.14159;
  ```

- `color`, which is a group of three numbers that defines a color using red, green, and blue. Each number is between 0 and 255:

  ```
  color c = color(255, 0, 0);
  ```

- `String`, which is a collection of characters used for words and phrases:

  ```
  String myName = "Tony";
  ```

  Be aware that a string is defined as characters within *double quotation marks*. It is different from `char` where we use *single quotation marks*.

Table 1-1 lists the variable types and their characteristics.

**Table 1-1:** Variable Types

| TYPE | SIZE | DESCRIPTION |
| --- | --- | --- |
| boolean | 1 bit | True or false |
| char | 16-bits | Keyboard characters |
| byte | 8 bits or 1 byte | 0–255 numbers |
| int | 32 bits | Integer numbers |
| float | 32 bits | Real fractional numbers |
| color | 4 bytes or 32 bytes | Red, Green, Blue, and Transparency |
| String | 64 bits | Set of characters that form words |

### *1.1.1.1 Cast*

A variable of one type can be cast (i.e., converted) to another type. For example:

```
float dist = 3.5;
int x = int(dist);
```

Here the value of the float variable `dist` can be cast to an integer `x`. After the casting, `x` will be 3 (i.e., the fractional or decimal part is omitted). The following command allows casting between different types:

```
boolean(), int(), float(), str(), byte().
```

For example:

```
float dist = 3.5;
String s = str(dist);
```

will create the string value "3.5" (not the float number 3.5).

## 1.1.2 Name Conventions

When you declare a variable (which is a made up name) you also need to tell what type it is and (if necessary) to give it an initial value. You use the following format:

```
type   name = value;
```

For example:

```
int myAge = 35;
```

declares an integer variable called `myAge` and assigns to it the data value 35, which is a whole number. All data types, if no initial value is given, default to 0. Booleans default to `false` and strings to `" "` (empty).

You choose a variable's name and, for the sake of readable code, it should make sense in the context of a problem. If you declare a variable that holds names, you should call it *names* or *newNames*, or something that makes sense given the context. Variables usually start with lower case, and when you want to composite more than one word, you use upper case for the next word. This is also referred to as *intercapping*. For example:

```
names or newNames or newPeopleNames
```

**WARNING** A name cannot start with a number, contain an empty space or contain any special characters except the underscore. For example, *1thing*, *x-y*, and *the plan* are invalid names, but *thing1*, *x_y*, and *the_plan* are valid names.

Booleans usually start with the prefix "is" For example:

*isLightOn* or *isItRaining*

As an example of initializing variables and data, let's define information about a circle. The following types, variables, and initializations can be used:

```
String    name    = "MyCircle";
int       location_x   = 22;
int       location_y   = 56;
float     radius   = 4.5;
boolean   isNurbs  = false;
```

In this case, we define information about a circle, that is, its name, its x and y pixel location on the screen (integer numbers), its radius, and an indication of its method of construction.

## 1.1.3 Arithmetic Operations

All the basic arithmetic operations, such as addition, subtraction, multiplication, and division are available in Processing using the symbols shown in Table 1-2.

**Table 1-2:** Arithmetic Operations

| OPERATOR | USE | DESCRIPTION |
| --- | --- | --- |
| + | op1 + op2 | Adds op1 and op2 |
| - | op1 - op2 | Subtracts op2 from op1 |
| * | op1 * op2 | Multiplies op1 by op2 |
| / | op1 / op2 | Divides op1 by op2 |
| % | op1 % op2 | Computes the remainder of dividing op1 by op2 |

For example, to get the sum of two numbers, you can write:

```
int sum;         // not initialized because we do not know how much
sum = 5 + 6;     // now sum is 11
```

Note that the addition operation occurs on the right side of the equal sign, and the result is assigned to the variable on the left side of the equal sign. This is always the case for operations, and it may seem odd, as it uses the opposite syntax to the statement 1 + 1 = 2. Note also the two slashes. They represent comments. Anything after // is ignored by Processing until the end of the line.

Therefore, `//` is for one-line comments. If you want to write multiline comments, use `/*` to start and `*/` to end. For example:

```
/* this statement is ignored
by processing even though I change
lines
*/
// this is ignored until the end of the line
```

The multiplication symbol is `*`, and the division is `/`. For example:

```
float result;
result = 0.5  +  35.2  /  29.1;    //this may be ambiguous
```

Since the result of this operation may seem ambiguous, you can use parentheses to define the parts of the formula to be executed first:

```
result = (0.5  +  35.2)  /  29.1;
```

This is obviously different from:

```
result = 0.5  +  (35.2  /  29.1);
```

However, there is a priority to the various symbols — if you can remember it, then you do not need to use parentheses. The sequence in which the operations will be executed follows this order: `(,),*,  /,  %,  +,  -`, as shown in Table 1-3.

**Table 1-3:** Precedence Operations Execution

| TYPE | SYMBOL |
| --- | --- |
| postfix operators | ( ) |
| multiplicative | * / % |
| additive | + - |

Finally, one useful operation is the remainder (`%`) operation. It is the remainder of the division of two numbers. Note that a remainder is always less than the divisor:

```
int moduloResult;
moduloResult = 10 % 2;  //the result is 0
moduloResult =  9 % 2;  //the result is 1
```

Processing provides convenient shortcuts for all of the arithmetic operations. For instance, x+=1 is equivalent to x = x + 1 or y/=z is equivalent to y = y / z. These shortcuts are summarized in Table 1-4.

**Table 1-4:** Equivalent Operations

| OPERATOR | USE | EQUIVALENT TO |
|---|---|---|
| += | op1 += op2 | op1 = op1 + op2 |
| -= | op1 -= op2 | op1 = op1 - op2 |
| *= | op1 *= op2 | op1 = op1 * op2 |
| /= | op1 /= op2 | op1 = op1 / op2 |
| %= | op1 %= op2 | op1 = op1 % op2 |

# 1.1.4 Logical and Relational Operations/Statements

Logical operations define the truthfulness of a conditional statement. Logical operations are tested with the word `if`, which represents a guess needed to be tested. In Processing, `if` statements have the following format:

```
if( condition )
      …;

    else
      …;
```

The conditions can be one of the following: equal, not equal, greater, or smaller. These conditions are represented by the following symbols:

```
if(a==b)       // if a is equal to b
if(a!=b)       // if a is not equal to b
if(a>b)        // if a is greater than to b
if(a>=b)       // if a is greater than or equal to b
if(a<b)        // if a is less than b
if(a<=b)       // if a is less than or equal to b
```

To combine conditions, we use the AND and OR operators represented by `&&` and `||` symbols. For example

```
if(a>b && a >c)     //if a is greater than b and a is greater than c
if(a>b || a >c)     //if a is greater than b or a is greater than c
```

Here is an example of a conditional statement:

```
String userName = "Kostas";
boolean itsMe;

    if( username == "Kostas") {
          itsMe = true;
          }
```

```
else    {
        itsMe = false;
        }
```

Note that the left and right curly brackets ({) and (}) are used to group sets of statements. If there is only one statement, we can omit the curly brackets, as in:

```
if( username == "Kostas")
        itsMe = true;
else
        itsMe = false;
```

Also, note that the semicolon (;) at the end of each statement indicates the end of the statement. Table 1-5 lists and describes the basic logical and relational operations.

**Table 1-5:** Logical Operators

| OPERATOR | USE | RETURNS TRUE IF |
|---|---|---|
| > | op1 > op2 | op1 is greater than op2 |
| >= | op1 >= op2 | op1 is greater than or equal to op2 |
| < | op1 < op2 | op1 is less than op2 |
| <= | op1 <= op2 | op1 is less than or equal to op2 |
| == | op1 == op2 | op1 and op2 are equal |
| != | op1 != op2 | op1 and op2 are not equal |
| && | op1 && op2 | op1 and op2 are both true, conditionally evaluates op2 |
| \|\| | op1 \|\| op2 | either op1 or op2 is true, conditionally evaluates op2 |

## 1.1.5 Loops

A loop is a repetition of statements. It allows statements to be defined, modified, or executed repeatedly until a termination condition is met. In Processing, as well as in most other languages, we have available two types of repetition statements: for and while. The for statement allows you to declare a starting condition, an ending condition, and a modification step. The statement immediately following the for statement (or all statements within a block) will be executed as a loop. The syntax is:

```
for(start condition; end condition; modification step){
....;
}
```

The *start condition* is the initial number to start counting. The *end condition* is the number to end the counting. The *modification step* is the pace of repetition. For example, a loop from 0 to 9 is:

```
for(int i=0; i<10; i=i+1){
    println(i);  // will printout the value of i
}
```

Here, the starting condition is `int i=0;` the end condition is `i<10;` and the step is `i=i+1`. The statement `println(i)` will print out the value of i in one line. The result is:

```
0123456789
```

The statement `i=i+1` can also be written as `i++`. It means add 1 every iteration through the loop. (`i--` means subtract 1 every time through the loop. These two statements can also be written as `i+=1;` and `i-=1;`.) The shortcut increment/decrement operators are summarized in Table 1-6.

**Table 1-6:** Increment/Decrement Operations

| OPERATOR | USE | DESCRIPTION |
|---|---|---|
| ++ | op++ | Increments op by 1; evaluates to the value of op before it was incremented |
| ++ | ++op | Increments op by 1; evaluates to the value of op after it was incremented |
| -- | op-- | Decrements op by 1; evaluates to the value of op before it was decremented |
| -- | --op | Decrements op by 1; evaluates to the value of op after it was decremented |

The `while` statement continually executes a block of statements while a condition remains true. If the condition is false, the loop will terminate. The syntax is:

```
while (expression) {
    statement
}
```

First, the `while` statement evaluates *expression*, which must return a boolean value. If the expression returns true, then the `while` statement executes the statement(s) associated with it. The `while` statement continues testing the expression and executing its block until the expression returns false. For example, in the loop:

```
int i=0;
while(i<10){
    println(i);  // will printout i
    i++;
}
```

the result is:

```
0123456789
```

Two commands are associated with loops: `continue` and `break`. The `continue` command skips the current iteration of a loop. The `break` command will force an exit from the loop. For example, consider the following loop:

```
for(int i=0; i<10; i++){
    if(i==5)continue;
    if(i==8) break;
    println(i);  // will printout the value of i
}
```

The result will be `0123467`. The reason is that when i becomes 5 the rest of the statements are skipped, and when i becomes 8 the loop is forced to exit (or break).

## 1.1.6 Patterns of Numbers

Loops can produce number patterns that can be used to produce visual patterns. By using simple arithmetic operations, one can produce various patterns of numbers. For instance:

```
for(int i=0; i<20; i++){
    x = i/2;
    println(x);
};
```

will produce the following pattern of numbers (notice that i is an integer so fractional values will be omitted):

```
00112233445566778899...
```

Similarly, the following formulas will result in the patterns of numbers shown in Table 1-7.

**Table 1-7:** Repetition Patterns

| FORMULA | RESULT |
|---------|--------|
| x = i/3; | 00011122233344455566 |
| x = i/4; | 00001111222233334444 |
| x = ($i+1)/2; | 01122334455667788910 |
| x = ($i+2)/2; | 11223344556677889910 10 |
| x = i%2; | 01010101010101010101 |
| x = i%3; | 01201201201201201201 |
| x = i%4; | 01230123012301230123 |
| x = (i+1)%4; | 12301230123012301230 |
| x = (i+2)%4; | 23012301230123012301 |
| x = (i/2)%2; | 00110011001100110011 |
| x = (i/3)%2; | 00011100011100011100 |
| x = (i/4)%2; | ~~00112233001122330011~~  *ooool ll l oool l l l l oooo* |

These patterns can be classified into three categories. Consider the three columns in Table 1-8: In the left column are division operations, in the right column are modulo operations. The middle column includes the combination of division and modulo operators. Note that divisions result in double, triple, quadruple, etc. repetitions of the counter i. In contrast, modulo operations result in repetition of the counter i as long as it is less than the divisor. Also, notice that the addition (or subtraction) of units to the variable i results in a shift left (or right) of the resulting sequences (column 1 and 2, row 4 and 5).

**Table 1-8:** Pattern Classification

| DIVISION OPERATIONS | COMBINATION | MODULO OPERATIONS |
|---------------------|-------------|-------------------|
| `for(int i=0; i<20;`<br>`   i++){`<br>`  int x = i/2;`<br>`  print(x);`<br>`};`<br>`//00112233445566778899` | `for(int i=0; i<20;`<br>`   i++){`<br>`  int x = (i/2)%2;`<br>`  print(x);`<br>`};`<br>`//00110011001100110011` | `for(int i=0; i<20;`<br>`   i++){`<br>`  int x = i%2;`<br>`  print(x);`<br>`};`<br>`//01010101010101010101` |
| `for(int i=0; i<20;`<br>`   i++){`<br>`  int x = i/3;`<br>`  print(x);`<br>`};`<br>`//00011122233344455566` | `for(int i=0; i<20;`<br>`   i++){`<br>`  int x = (i/3)%2;`<br>`  print(x);`<br>`};`<br>`//00011100011100011100` | `for(int i=0; i<20;`<br>`   i++){`<br>`  int x = i%3;`<br>`  print(x);`<br>`};`<br>`//01201201201201201201` |

*Continued*

**Table 1-8** *(continued)*

| DIVISION OPERATIONS | COMBINATION | MODULO OPERATIONS |
|---|---|---|
| ``` for(int i=0; i<20; i++){   int x = i/4;   print(x); }; //00001111222233334444 ``` | ``` for(int i=0; i<20; i++){   int x = (i/4)%2;   print(x); }; //00001111000011110000 ``` | ``` for(int i=0; i<20; i++){   int x = i%4;   print(x); }; //01230123012301230123 ``` |
| ``` for(int i=0; i<20; i++){   int x = (i+1)/2;   print(x); }; //011223344556677889910 ``` | ``` for(int i=0; i<20; i++){   int x = (i/2)%4;   print(x); }; //00112233001122330011 ``` | ``` for(int i=0; i<20; i++){   int x = (i+1)%4;   print(x); }; //12301230123012301230 ``` |
| ``` for(int i=0; i<20; i++){   int x = (i+2)/2;   print(x); }; //11223344556677889910 10 ``` | ``` for(int i=0; i<20; i++){   int x = (i%4)/2;   print(x); }; //00110011001100110011 ``` | ``` for(int i=0; i<20; i++){   int x = (i+2)%4;   print(x); }; //23012301230123012301 ``` |

## 1.2 Graphics Elements

The Processing language supports a number of graphics elements that can be used to design. Those elements can be grouped into geometrical elements (i.e., points, lines, curves, rectangles, ellipses, etc.) and their attributes (i.e., color, line weight, size, etc.). These elements can be invoked in the code as commands. A command is composed of a name and a set of parameters. So, for example, a point can be executed as the command "point" followed by the x and y coordinates as parameters. In the following sections, we will introduce these commands and explain how they fit within the structure of the Processing code.

### 1.2.1 Code Structure

The structure of Processing code is divided in two main sections: *setup* and *draw*. The setup section is used to define initial environment properties (e.g., screen size, background color, loading images or fonts, etc.) and the draw section for executing the drawing commands (e.g., point, line, ellipse, image, etc.) in a loop that can be used for animation. The structure of the code is:

```
void setup(){

}

void draw(){

}
```

The word `void` means that the procedure does not return any value back, that is, it returns void. The word `setup()` is the name of the default "setup" section, and the parentheses are there in case you need to insert parameters for processing; here they are empty, that is, `()`. The curly brackets `{` and `}` denote the beginning and end of the process and normally should include the commands to be executed.

## 1.2.2 Draw Commands

The `draw()` command contains almost all geometrical, type, and image commands with their corresponding attributes. The coordinate system of the screen (shown in Figure 1-1) is anchored on the upper-left corner with the *x*-axis extending horizontally from left to right, the *y*-axis extending vertically from top to bottom, and the *z*-axis (for 3D purposes) extending perpendicular to the screen towards the user.

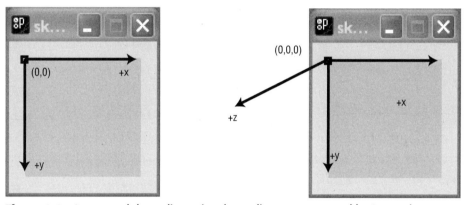

**Figure 1-1:** A two- and three-dimensional coordinate system used by Processing

## 1.2.3 Geometrical Objects

The main geometrical objects are:

- `point()` makes a point (i.e., a dot). It takes two integer numbers to specify the location's coordinates, starting from the upper-left corner. For example:

```
point(20,30);
```

will draw a point at the following location: 20 pixels right and 30 pixels below the upper left corner of the window, as shown in Figure 1-2.

**Figure 1-2:**
A point

- `line()` draws a line segment between two points. It takes four integer numbers to specify the beginning and end point coordinates. For example,

```
line(20,30,50,60);
```

will draw a line segment from point 20,30 to point 50,60 (shown in Figure 1-3).

**Figure 1-3:**
A line

And

```
line(20,30,20,50);
line(10,40,30,40);
```

will draw a cross at location 20,40 (see Figure 1-4).

**Figure 1-4:** Two lines
in the form of a cross

- `rect()` draws a rectangle. It takes as parameters four integers to specify the x and y coordinates of the starting point and the width and height of the rectangle. For example:

```
rect(30,30,50,20);
```

will draw a rectangle at location 30,30 (i.e., the coordinates of the rectangle's upper-left corner), as shown in Figure 1-5, with a width of 50 pixels and height of 20 pixels. If the command `rectMode(CENTER)` precedes the `rect()` command, then the first two coordinates (i.e., 30 and 30) refer to the center of the rectangle, not its upper-left corner.

**Figure 1-5:**
A rectangle

- `ellipse()` draws an ellipse. It takes four integers to specify the center point and the width and height. For example:

```
ellipse(30,30,50,20);
```

will draw an ellipse (shown in Figure 1-6) at location 30,30 (center point) with a width of 50 pixels and height of 20 pixels (also the dimensions of a bounding box to the ellipse).

**Figure 1-6:**
An ellipse

- `arc()` draws an arc. It takes four integers to specify the center point and the width and height of the bounding box and two float numbers to indicate the beginning and end angle in radians. For example,

```
arc(50,50,70,70,0,PI/2);
```

will draw an arc at location 50,50 (center point) with a width of 70 pixels and height of 70 pixels (bounding box) with an angle from 0 to $\pi/2$ degrees, as shown in Figure 1-7. Notice that angle is drawn in a clockwise direction.

**Figure 1-7:**
An arc

The syntax of the parameters is `arc(x,y,width,height,start,end)`.

- `curve()` draws a curve between two points. It takes as parameters the coordinates of the two points and their anchors. For example:

```
noFill();
curve(20,80,20,20,80,20,80,80);
curve(20,20,80,20,80,80,20,80);
curve(80,20,80,80,20,80,20,20);
```

will produce Figure 1-8.

**Figure 1-8:**
A curve

The syntax of the parameters is:

```
curve(first anchor x, first anchor y, first point x, first point y,
    second point x, second point y, second anchor x, second anchor y)
```

- `bezier()` draws a Bezier curve between two points, as shown in Figure 1-9. It takes as parameters the coordinates of the two points and their anchors. For example:

```
noFill();
bezier(20,80,20,20,80,20,80,80);
```

**Figure 1-9:**
A Bezier curve

The syntax of the parameters is:

```
bezier(first anchor x,first anchor y,first point x,first point y,
    second point x,second point y,second anchor x,second anchor y)
```

- `vertex()` produces a series of vertices connected through lines. It requires a `beginShape()` and an `endShape()` command to indicate the beginning and end of the vertices. For example, the number patterns shown earlier in this chapter can be visualized through simple algorithms. In that sense, the following code will produce a pattern of points shown in Figure 1-10.

```
for(int i=0; i<20; i++){
  int y = i%2;
  point(i*10, 50+y*10);
};
```

**Figure 1-10:** A
series of zigzag points

Whereas, the following code will produce a pattern of lines as shown in Figure 1-11.

```
beginShape();
for(int i=0; i<20; i++){
  int y = i%2;
  vertex(i*10, 50+y*10);
};
endShape();
```

**Figure 1-11:**
A zigzag line

## 1.2.4 Attributes

The following commands can modify the appearance of geometrical shapes:

- `fill()` will fill a shape with a color. It takes either one integer number between 0 and 255 to specify a level of gray (0 being black and 255 being white) or three integer numbers between 0 and 255 to specify an RGB color. For example:

```
fill(100);
rect(30,30,50,20);
rect(40,40,20,30);
```

will draw two dark gray rectangles, as shown in Figure 1-12.

**Figure 1-12:** Two
rectangles filled with gray

and

```
fill(0,200,0);
rect(30,30,50,20);
rect(40,40,20,30);
```

will draw two nearly green rectangles as shown in Figure 1-13. (Note that although you can't see the color in this book, the code does indeed produce green filled rectangles.) If the second parameter that corresponds to the green value was the maximum number 255, then the rectangles would really be filled with true green.

**Figure 1-13:** Two rectangles
filled with the color green

▪ noFill() will not paint the inside of a shape. For example:

```
noFill();
rect(30,30,50,20);
rect(40,40,20,30);
```

will draw only the bounding line but will not paint the interior surface, as shown in Figure 1-14.

**Figure 1-14:** Two
rectangles with no color

▪ stroke() will paint the bounding line of a shape to a specified gray or color. It takes either one integer number between 0 and 255 to specify a level of gray (0 being black and 255 being white) or three integer numbers between 0 and 255 to specify an RGB color. For example:

```
stroke(100);
rect(30,30,50,20);
rect(40,40,20,30);
```

will paint the boundary lines with a gray value, as shown in Figure 1-15.

**Figure 1-15:** Two
rectangles with gray strokes

- `noStroke()` will draw no boundary to the shape. For example:

```
noStroke();
rect(30,30,50,20);
rect(40,40,20,30);
```

will draw the shape in Figure 1-16.

**Figure 1-16:** Two
rectangles with no strokes

- `strokeWeight()` will increase the width of the stroke. It takes an integer number that specifies the number of pixels of the stroke's width. For example,

```
strokeWeight(4);
rect(30,30,50,20);
rect(40,40,20,30);
```

will draw the shape in Figure 1-17.

**Figure 1-17:** Two rectangles
with thick strokes

▪ background() specifies the gray value or color of the display background. It takes either one integer number between 0–255 to specify a level of gray (0 being black and 255 being white) or three integer numbers between 0–255 to specify an RGB color. For example,

```
background(200);
```

will paint the background dark grey, as shown in Figure 1-18.

**Figure 1-18:** A
grey background

## 1.2.5 Fonts and Images

Apart from simple geometrical objects and their attributes, the Processing language supports text and images. Those are invoked using more complex commands. These commands can either create new text and images or import existing fonts and image files. The following section shows briefly these commands, although images will be further elaborated in Chapter 5 of this book.

▪ createFont() creates a Processing-compatible font out of existing fonts in your computer. It takes the name of a font and the size. It returns the newly created font which needs to be loaded (textFont) and then displayed (text) at a specified location. For example,

```
PFont myFont = createFont("Times", 32);
textFont(myFont);
text("P",50,50);
```

displays Figure 1-19.

**Figure 1-19:** A text placed
at the center of the window

The first line creates a font out of the existing Times font at a size of 32. The command will return back the new font which is called here myFont. This font is then loaded using the `textFont` command, which can be displayed at any location in the screen using the `text` command.

■ `loadImage()` will load and display an existing image. It takes the location of the image and returns a `PImage` object that can be displayed using the image command. For example,

```
PImage myImage = loadImage("c:/data/image.jpg");
image(myImage, 0, 0);
```

will display an image at location 0,0 (i.e. the origin). Figure 1-20 shows an example.

**Figure 1-20:** An image placed at the upper left corner of the window

If a directory is not mentioned, then Processing will look for the image within the same directory that the code is (or inside the sub-directory "data"). The image will be drawn on the default $100 \times 100$ screen. If it is larger it will be cropped and if smaller it will be left with an empty margin (as in Figure 1-20).

## 1.2.6 Examples

This section introduced the basic graphics commands for geometrical objects, text, and images. These graphical objects are assumed to be static as paintings. The next section introduces motion and interactivity using the `draw()` command and by redrawing the screen to create an illusion of motion.

The follow code demonstrates most of the graphics commands introduced so far. Figure 1-21 shows an example.

```
size(300,200);  //size of the display
background(150); //set a dark background
PImage myImage = loadImage("c:/data/image.jpg"); //get an image
image(myImage, 100, 50);  //display it at the center of the screen

noFill();  //for an empty rectangle
strokeWeight(4);  //make a think line
rect(90,40, myImage.width+20, myImage.height+20); //make a rectangle
    frame
```

```
PFont myFont = createFont("Times", 32);    //create a font
textFont(myFont);    //load the font
fill(250);   //change the color of the text to almost white
text("What is this?",50,100);   //display the text
```

**Figure 1-21:** A combination of images, text, and a rectangle

The following code and figures provide examples of loops using graphics elements.

```
for(int i=0; i<50; i++){
  line(i*2,10,i*2,90);
}
```

```
for(int i=0; i<100; i=i+2){
  line(i,i,i,50);
}
```

```
for(int i=0; i<100; i=i+2){
  line(i,10,random(100),90);
}
```

```
for(int i=100; i>0; i=i-2){
  rect(0,0,i,i);
}
```

```
for(int i=0; i<100; i=i+5){
  rect(i,0,3,99);
}
```

```
for(int i=0; i<700; i=i+2){
line(i,50,i,sin(radians(i*3))*30+50);
}
```

```
for(int i=70; i>0; i=i-4){
  ellipse(50,50,i,i);
}
```

```
for(int i=70; i>0; i=i-4){
  ellipse(i,50,i,i);
}
```

## 1.3 Interactivity

So far, we have seen graphics elements displayed on the window as static entities. They appear to be stationary even though, as we will see, they are redrawn continuously on the computer screen. In this section, we will show how to take graphical elements and redraw them fast enough to produce the illusion of motion. This subject will be expanded further in Chapter 6.

### 1.3.1 Drawing on the Screen

As discussed earlier in this chapter, the structure of Processing code is divided in two main sections: the setup and draw section. The *setup* section is used to define initial environment properties (e.g. screen size, background color, loading images/fonts, etc.) and the *draw* section for executing the drawing commands (e.g. point, line, ellipse, image, etc.). The structure of the code is as follows:

```
void setup(){

}

void draw(){

}
```

By default, in Processing the draw area is executed repeatedly in a loop. The speed of this loop can be controlled by using the `frameRate` command to set the number of frames per second. For example, if we want to draw a vertical line that moves horizontally (as illustrated in Figure 1-22) then the following code can be used:

```
1    void setup(){
2       size(300,100);
3    }
4
5    int i=0;
6    void draw(){
7       line(i,0,i,100);
8       i++;
9    }
```

**Figure 1-22:** A moving line leaving a trace

The first three lines are used to set the size of the display. In line 5 an integer variable i is initialized to 0. It will be used as a counter. It is defined outside of the draw area. Line 8 increases the counter by 1 every time the screen redraws itself. So, then the line is being redrawn in increments of one pixel in the horizontal direction. In the resulting effect, the black line leaves a trace as it is redrawn that over time creates an increasingly black area.

The next example redraws the background every time the draw command is executed, creating an animating effect. This produces a line that seems to move from left to right one pixel at a time, illustrated in Figure 1-23.

```
1      void setup(){
2        size(300,100);
3      }
4
5      int i=0;
6      void draw(){
7        background(200);
8        line(i%300,0,i%300,100);
9        i++;
10     }
```

**Figure 1-23:** A moving line leaving no trace

Note that in line 8 we modulate the counter i by 300 so that when it reaches 300 it sets itself back to zero. Finally, in the last example, we replace the counter i with the mouse coordinates that are defined in Processing by mouseX and mouseY. In that way, we can get an interactive effect where the line is redrawn every time the mouse is moved, as illustrated in Figure 1-24.

```
1      void setup(){
2        size(300,100);
3      }
4
5      void draw(){
6        background(200);
7        line(mouseX,0,mouseX,100);
8      }
```

**Figure 1-24:** A line moved to follow the mouse's location

## 1.3.2 Mouse and Keyboard Events

A mouse's or keyboard's activity can be captured by using the `mouseDragged`, `mouseMoved`, `mousePressed`, `mouseReleased`, or `keyPressed` events. In each case, a series of commands can be activated every time the corresponding event is triggered. The structure of the code is:

```
void setup(){

}

void draw(){

}

void mousePressed(){

}

void keyPressed(){

}
```

In specific, these events are used in the following way:

- `mousePressed()` is called when a mouse button is pressed. For example,

```
1    void draw(){
2    }
3
4    void mousePressed(){
5       rect(mouseX,mouseY, 10,10);
6    }
```

produces the result shown in Figure 1-25.

**Figure 1-25:** Randomly located rectangles by the press of the mouse button

▪ `mouseDragged()` is called when a mouse is dragged. For example,

```
1      void draw(){
2      }
3
4      void mouseDragged(){
5        rect(mouseX,mouseY, 10,10);
6      }
```

will result in Figure 1-26.

**Figure 1-26:** Rectangles following
the location of the mouse

▪ `keyPressed()` is called when a mouse is pressed. For example,

```
1      void draw(){
2      }
3
4      void keyPressed(){
5        int x = int(random(0,100));
6        int y = int(random(0,100));
7        rect(x,y, 10,10);
8    }
```

will result in Figure 1-27.

**Figure 1-27:** Randomly located rectangles
by the press of any keyboard key

The example above uses a random generator to produce x and y coordinates. This is done by calling the `random()` function; we pass two numbers that correspond to the lower and upper limit (i.e. 0,100). Then we cast the resulting random numbers to integers. This is done because the random function always returns float numbers.

# 1.4 Grouping of Code

Computer code can be seen as language statements that convey a process to be executed by a computer. As a linguistic structure, code can be grouped into sentences, paragraphs, sections, etc. In the following sections we will examine basic structures of code that can store information (arrays), be referred to (procedures) and be self-referential (recursion).

## 1.4.1 Arrays

An array is an ordered set of data. It appears as a variable that can hold multiple values at the same time, but essentially it is a pointer to the memory addresses of where that data are held. We assign or extract the data values of an array by pointing at the index of the array, i.e., a number indicating the sequential order of the element of the array. For example, we may refer to the fifth or sixth element in an array. We can have arrays of any type, i.e., booleans, integers, strings, etc. We define an array by using the `[]` symbol. For example:

```
String [] names = {"Kostas", "Ivan", "Jeff", "Jie Eun"};
float []  temperatures = {88.9, 89.1, 89.0, 93.4, 95.2, 101.2};
int [] num_of_transactions = new int[50];
boolean [] isOff;
```

The above arrays define 4, 6, 50, or no elements, respectively, either populated or not. The word `new` is used to create and initialize the array (or, in technical terms, allocate memory for it). The term `populate` means that we are assigning specific values to the array, i.e. populating its content. In this case, we initialized the array `num_of_transactions` to 50 integer values. While creating an array we can fill it with data and then have access to them by pointing to an index number. For example, the following code:

```
for(int i=0; i<4 i++){
    println( names[i]);
}
```

will produce the following output:

```
Kostas
Ivan
Jeff
Jie Eun
```

This will extract the data from the array. Note that arrays start at 0. So, in order to access the second element of the array, we use the expression:

```
String person = names[1];   //arrays start at 0 so 1 is the second
    element. In this case it is Ivan
```

The above statement will return the second element (which should be the name Ivan). If we have a two-dimensional array we initialize it as:

```
int twoDArray[][] = new int[5][100];
```

It will initialize an array of 5 rows and 100 columns and we access its elements in the following way:

```
int someElement =  twoDArray[2][18];
```

The above statement will return the element at the third row and the nineteenth column. Arrays are very useful for storing a set of data under the same name. For example, float coords[][] can hold all the values of data residing at x and y coordinates of a grid.

While arrays may start with a specific number of positions, it is possible that they need to be expanded in order to receive new data values. Also, it is possible that they need to be shortened as the data values are much less than the positions. Consider the problem of a butterfly hunter who starts the day with a set of jars. What if she finds more butterflies than the available jars? What if she finds fewer and carries around empty jars? Processing (as well as Java) has dynamic memory allocation, i.e. memory allocated whenever it is necessary. So, in the case of the butterfly hunter, there is no need to pre-estimate the number of jars. She goes out with no jars, and every time a butterfly is caught, a jar is fetched from the camp. So, for convenience, there are, at least, five important methods associated with arrays:

- array.length: returns the number of elements of an array
- sort(*array*): sorts the elements of an array in alphabetic order
- append(*array,data*): expands an array by one element and adds data value
- subset(*array,offset,length*): creates a subset of an array at offset for a specified length
- expand(*array,size*): expands an array by a total size position retaining the existing data values

The following code shows how an array can be created, populated, sorted, and then shortened and expanded:

```
1        String [] s = new String[0];  //new empty array
2        s = append(s,"Kostas");
3        s = append(s,"Nashid");
4        s = append(s,"Jie Eun");
5        print(s.length);   //should be 3
6        for(int i=0; i<s.length; i++)
7           print(s[i] + ", ");
8        // should be: Kostas, Nashid, Jie Eun,
```

```
9       s = sort(s);
10      for(int i=0; i<s.length; i++)
11          print(s[i] + ", ");
12      // should be: Jie Eun, Kostas, Nashid,
13      s = subset(s,1,2);
14      print(s.length);    //should be 2
15      for(int i=0; i<s.length; i++)
16          print(s[i] + ", ");
17      // should be: Kostas, Nashid,
18      s = expand(s,5);
19      print(s.length);    //should be 5
20      for(int i=0; i<s.length; i++)
21          print(s[i] + ", ");
22      // should be: Kostas, Nashid, null, null, null,
```

In the first line of code, we declare an empty array of strings called s. Note that we are allocating 0 positions for this array so that we can expand it. In other words, it is not sufficient to just declare it without using the new command for memory allocation. Once, the array s is defined, we can printout its size and its members (line 7), sort it in ascending order (line 9), get a subset of the first two elements of the sorted array (line 13), and expand it to contain 3 more elements (i.e. a total of 5). Note that since we did not assign values to the expanded position, they will printout as null.

## 1.4.2 Procedures and Functions

When we write code in Processing, we occasionally may want to group a series of statements that do something useful. Then we can use these statements to perform repetitive tasks by making reference to that group of statements.

For example the following lines of code produce a series of 15 lined up long rectangles that start at location 10,10.

```
1       size(500,400);
2
3       int x = 10;
4       int y = 10;
5       int nrects = 15;
6       for(int i=0; i<nrects; i++)
7               rect(x+(i*10),y,10,50);
```

If we want to make more of these rectangle groups, we will have to use the same code again, changing only the number of rectangles and their starting location, as shown in the code and Figure 1-28.

```
8       x = 100;
9       y = 200;
10      int nrects2 = 12;
```

```
11        for(int i=0; i<nrects2; i++)
12                rect(x+(i*10),y,10,50);
13
14        x = 300;
15        y = 200;
16        int nrects3 = 18;
17        for(int i=0; i<nrects3; i++)
18                rect(x+(i*10),y,10,50);
```

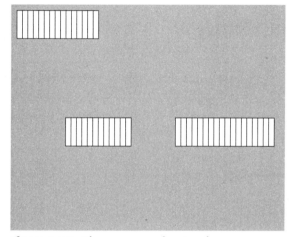

**Figure 1-28:** Three groups of rectangles

A simple observation of the code above shows a repetitive pattern where each group of rectangles is produced through the same code structure by altering only the number of rectangles and their starting location. The problem with this method of copying and pasting code is that it is specific, redundant, and repetitive. Further, it is limited to small repetitions. What if we need to produce the same pattern 1,000 times? The solution to this problem is the development of generic code that follows the same steps given different parameters (i.e. location and number of rectangles). The following code illustrates this point:

```
1  void stairs(int x, int y, int nsteps){
2    for(int i=0; i<nsteps; i++)
3        rect(x+(i*10),y,10,50);
4  }
```

In line 1 we define a process (also called a procedure) which we call here stairs. This name can be anything we want and should express the nature of procedure or its result. We then define the three parameters that are needed for the procedure (i.e. in this case the x and y starting location and the numbers of steps). These are enclosed in parentheses and are separated by commas. Note the word void at the beginning of the procedure's name; this means that the procedure does not return anything, i.e. it returns "void." The next paragraph covers this in more detail. Finally, we enclose the actual set of code lines that perform the procedure within curly brackets. The code itself is simply a generic version of the previous code and it uses the parameters that are passed through the procedure in line 1. Once we define a procedure, then we can call it by using the following code:

```
1        void setup(){
2        size(500,400);
3            stairs(10,10,15);
4            stairs(100,200,13);
5            stairs(300,200,10 );
6        }
```

Lines 3, 4, and 5 make calls to the procedure defined earlier in lines 1 through 4. These calls are placed within the `setup()` section which is also a procedure and evident from the word `void`. In this way, the procedure `stairs` and the procedure `setup` are groups of code that reside within the same program. The result of this program is exactly the same as in Figure 1-28.

Similarly, we can define a procedure that can perform a task and then returns a value. This type of procedure is also referred to as a function. For example, let's say we want to create a method that can calculate the area of a rectangle given its two sides and return the result as a float. Here is how it can be done:

```
float getArea(float w,  float h){
int myResult = w * h;
return myResult;
}
```

In the above example, we have declared a method called `getArea` and we use two float numbers `w` and `h` as parameters for the width and height of the rectangle. Within the method we define a variable called `myResult`, and we assign to it the result of the multiplication of the two parameters `w` and `h`. The procedure then returns the result. To invoke the method from another part of the code we write:

```
float a = getArea(3.5,  2.6);
```

The method `getArea()` will do the calculation. This can be very useful in organizing code through statements and commands that call one another. For example, if you want the surface area of a sphere you can call:

```
float sa = getSurfaceArea(float r);
```

The method `getSurfaceArea` will do the math with or without your knowledge or supervision. Sometimes methods can be very complex such as `morph(object a,object b)` or very simple such as `getArea(float w,float h)`.

## 1.4.4 Recursion

A recursion is a repetitive procedure in which part of the repetition involves a call to the procedure itself. In other words, the procedure is not only a group of code that serves an external-to-itself purpose, but it also involves its own existence in the grouping of the code. Let's examine a simple case of recursion used to calculate a factorial of a number. Please recall that a factorial of a number is the product of all the positive integer numbers less or equal to itself. For example, the factorial of 5 is 120 which is the product 1*2*3*4*5. In the following two columns we show two procedures that calculate the factorial of a number using iteration (left) and recursion (right).

```
1    void setup(){                      1    void setup(){
2       println(factorial(5));          2       print(factorial(5));
3    }                                   3    }
4    int factorial(int n){              4    int factorial(int n){
5       int fact = 1;                    5       if(n<=1)
6       for(int i=n; i>=1; i--)          6          return 1;
7          fact *= i;                    7       else
8       return fact;                     8          return n * factorial(n-1);
9    }                                   9    }
```

In the right column, we define a procedure called factorial which takes as a parameter an integer n. Then it examines n: if n is less or equal to 1 then it return 1; otherwise it returns the product of n with the result of the procedure itself passing the parameter n-1. This process is shown below for factorial(3): the first call to factorial breaks into the product of 3 times factorial(2); then factorial(2) breaks into 2 times factorial(1); then factorial(1) returns 1, which is then multiplied by 2, which is then multiplied by 3, resulting 6.

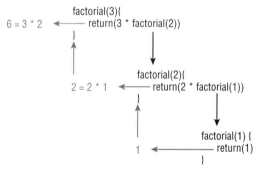

**Figure 1-29:** The deployment of the recursive procedure factorial()

Recursion can be used to produce graphical objects, as in the case of a series of nested circles constructed through the code shown below:

```
1    void setup(){
2      RecCircle(80);
3    }
4    int RecCircle(int r){
5      ellipse(50,50,r,r);
6      if(r<=10)
7        return(10);
8      else
9        return(r * RecCircle(r-10));
10   }
```

This algorithm will produce the following result:

**Figure 1-30:** Recursion used to place nested concentric circles

## 1.4.5 Importing Processing Classes

A number of sets of procedures (also known as classes) have already been developed within the Processing language or are provided by software development companies. These classes are inside compressed files called packages. For example, `processing.net.*` is a package that includes classes related to network communication (the `*` stands for "all files under the directory processing/net"). In Processing, these packages are located in the directory where Processing exists, that is, wherever its language was installed. To use those packages, we need to include them in the code and that is done through the statement

```
import processing.net.*;
```

which should always be the first line of the Processing file. So when we import, for example, `processing.net.*` we can include any class that exists in that package (i.e. Server) or the methods under those packages (i.e. `read()`, `write()`, etc.).

## Summary

This chapter introduced you to data types, arithmetic and logical operations, loops, arrays, methods, and classes. At this point you should know how constants and variables are declared, how conditional statements are made, how to loop with a counter and use it within the loop, what arrays are and how we declare, fill, and access their members, what are procedures and how they are called, and finally how recursions are formed. We also used these concepts to draw simple shapes on the screen and then explained the mechanisms of generating simple drawings in Processing.

## Exercises

**NOTE** Answers to the exercises are provided in Appendix B.

1.  Memorize the symbols/types and their meaning:

| | | | |
|---|---|---|---|
| boolean | for | >= | % |
| int | ( | <= | && |
| char | ) | + | \|\| |
| " | { | ++ | [] |
| String | } | += | class |
| "" | = | - | . |
| ; | == | -- | import |
| if | != | -= | // |
| else | > | * | /* */ |
| while | < | / | |

2.  Which is safe to use as a variable name in PROCESSING?

    A.  3D_Point

    B.  3DPoint

    C.  Point-3D

    D.  three_Dimensional_Point_3

3.  How many *bits* does the "boolean" primitive have?

    A.  2 bits

    B.  1 bit

    C.  8 bits

    D.  32 bits

4.  What is the result of the following program?

```
int a=0;
for (int i=0; i<5; i++){
      a++;
      a += i;
}
```

    A.  a = 10

    B.  a = 15

    C.  a = 21

    D.  a = 0

5.  Consider two integer variables, x and y. If you want to swap their value from x and y to y and x respectively, which program below is correct?

    A.
```
x = y;
y = x;
```

    B.
```
tempX = x;
tempY = y;
x = tempX;
y = tempY;
```

    C.
```
y = x;
tempX = x;
x = tempX;
```

    D.
```
tempX = x;
x = y;
y = tempX;
```

6.  Produce the following pattern using *only one loop*.

```
for(int i=0; i<15; i++){

  int x = _____;

  int y = _____;

  rect(x,y,10,10);
}
```

7. Write the code that will produce a pattern like this:

8. A golden ratio is defined as $1/\varphi$ where

$$\varphi = \frac{1+\sqrt{5}}{2} \approx 1.618033989$$

Write the code that will create a rectangle that has the golden ratio proportions.

9. Write the shortest possible procedural code that can generate the following number pattern using only standard arithmetic operations (+, -, *, 0, and %) :

    11101110111011101110

10. Write the code that will snap the mouseX to a $10 \times 10$ grid (i.e. if mouseX is 57 it should snap to 60, or if mouseX is 32 it should snap to 30).

    Hint: The round(value) function calculates the integer closest to the value parameter.

11. Write the code that will generate a random **even integer** number between -100 and 100.

12. What architectural element does the following pseudo-code below do:

```
element(float x_location, float y_location, intnumber_of_components){
   for(n=0; n<number_of_components; n++){
     MakeCube;
     Scale at (length 5, width 0.2, height 1.);
     Move at (x_location, y_location, n);
   }
```

13. Write the code that will produce the following patterns:

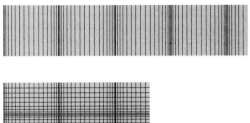

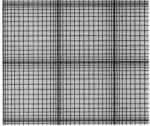

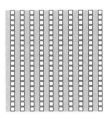

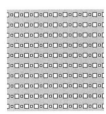

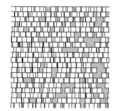

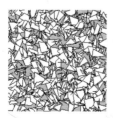

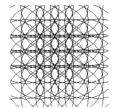

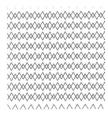

# Points, Lines, and Shapes

Geometry is the study of properties, measurement, and relationships of points, lines, angles, surfaces, and solids. Whereas Euclidean geometry is concerned with intuitive definitions of elements and their relationships, analytical geometry is concerned with the quantitative study of the relations and the properties of geometrical elements. The notion of quantity as a means of representing or displaying geometric information is key to computer graphics applications. In addition to conceiving geometrical elements as abstract entities, it is also necessary to represent and handle them as quantifiable information using flat screen displays populated with finite sized pixels. In that sense, abstract mathematical concepts such as infinity, eternal, or continuous can be replaced with those of finite, ephemeral, or discontinuous.

The dominant mode for representing geometric objects in computer graphics still adheres to the hierarchical sequence of points-lines-surfaces-solids. Yet, a point is simply a pixel on the screen, a line is a sequence of pixels, and a shape is an area of pixels. In that sense, a computer graphics programmer is offered a repertoire of finite-sized light intensities bounded to a finite length screen with a finite amount of colors. Within this finite domain, the most amazing forms, scenes, or animated pictures can be produced. The purpose of this chapter is to show how it is possible to create geometric entities and how such elements can be combined into complex shapes.

## 2.1 Sine and Cosine Curves

*Trigonometry* is the study of the relationships among the angles and sides of a triangle. In the right triangle shown in Figure 2-1, the *sine* of angle a is the ratio of BC/AB, and the *cosine* is the ratio AC/AB (It's a *right* triangle because one of the angles is 90 degrees, or a "right angle").

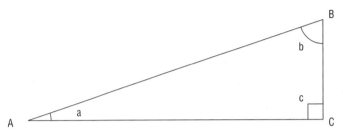

**Figure 2-1:** A right triangle

A sine or a cosine can take values between –1 and 1. The progress of sine or cosine values for a changing angle, say in the form of a counter from 0 to 360, is along the path of a curve. So, an interesting feature of sines and cosines is that, when we calculate their value for rotating angles, we get a "circular" behavior. Consider the following code:

```
1    for(int i=0; i<500; i++){
2        int x = i;
3        int y = int(50. * sin(PI/180.* i)  );
4        point(x, y+50);
5        println("x = " + x + " y = " + y);
6    }
```

As a reminder, 180 degrees is equal to PI radians. So, to convert $x$ degrees to $r$ radians, we use the formula $x = PI/180*r$ radians. Since `sin()` and `cos()` take for angles radians, we always need to convert degrees (0–360) to radians (0.0 – 3.14159). Conveniently, the Processing language offers a command called `radians()`, which converts degrees to radians (there is also the opposite command called `degrees()`, which converts radians to degrees).

In the code preceding, we loop from 0 to 180, and for $x$ we use the counter $i$. This ensures that we have a linear progress of one pixel in $x$. Similarly, for $y$ we get the cosine of the counter i (converted to radians), then exaggerated by 50.0. Since the result is a double, we cast it into an int to assign it to y:

```
int x =  i;
int y =  int(50. * sin(radians( i))  );
```

Then we draw the result using the point() command. So, as x moves on a linear increment based on the looping counter i (with values 0,1,2,3,4,5, . . . ,499), y moves in the y direction, up and down. Note that we also move the whole scene 100 pixels lower in the y direction to center it on the window (see line 4). The result is shown in Figure 2-2.

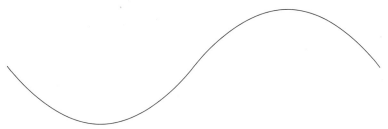

**Figure 2-2:** The output of a sine representation

So, the result is a set of dots (".") starting at (0,100) and then as x goes from 0,1,2,3,4, . . . 500, y produces cosine values. Since we know from trigonometry that a cosine will always be between –1 and 1, we multiply by 50 to make y a value between –50 and 50. Obviously, the resulting numbers place the points along the path of a curve. These numbers are sample values that result from the x and y parameters. The more we decrease the distance between consecutive i values, the more precise the path is. If we want to shorten the curve in the x direction, then we need to do the following adjustment to the x coordinate:

```
1    for(int i=0; i<5000; i++){
2        int x =  i/10;
3        int y =  (int)(50. * cos(PI/180.* i)  );
4        point(x , y+50);
5    }
```

The resulting points will be placed along a full circle when i goes from 0 to 360, so, in our case, 5000 will result in 5000 / 360 = 13.8 full circles. We don't want x to go to 5,000 because the screen is only 400 pixels long and it will be drawn outside of the visible screen. So we divide i by 10, and therefore x will go to only 500, resulting in an image like that shown in Figure 2-3.

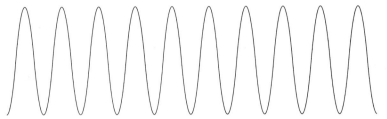

**Figure 2-3:** The output of a cosine representation

If we reverse the values of x and y, as is done in the following code, then we can obtain a rotated curve, as shown in Figure 2-4.

```
1    for(int i=0; i<5000; i++){
2        int x =   (int)(50. * cos(PI/180.* i)   );
3        int y =   i/10;
4        point(x+50 , y);
5    }
```

**Figure 2-4:** Reversing the direction
of a cosine representation

Now, if we combine the two, alternating sine and cosine, as in the following code:

```
1    for(int i=0; i<5000; i++){
2        int x =   (int)(50. * cos(PI/180.* i)   );
3        int y =   (int)(50. * sin(PI/180.* i)   );
4        point(x+50 , y+50);
5    }
```

this will result in the unexpected (perhaps) output shown in Figure 2-5.

**Figure 2-5:** The output of the combination of a sine and cosine representation

A circle! We will use this technique later on to rotate objects in the screen, because basically what we are doing here is forcing x and y to move on the perimeter of a circle. Or, to be precise, we force x and y to rotate around a center 13.8 times, since the counter goes from 0 to 5,000. If the counter is going from 0 to 180, as shown here:

```
1    for(int i=0; i<180; i++){
2      int x =  (int)(50. * cos(PI/180.* i)  );
3      int y =  (int)(50. * sin(PI/180.* i)  );
4      point(x+100 , y+100);
5    }
```

we would have created a half-circle (see Figure 2-6), because i is the number of degrees of the rotation angle.

**Figure 2-6:** A half-circle

The equations used to construct a circle or portions of it are defined through the following formulas:

```
x=r*cos(i), y=r*sin(i)
```

where i is the counter or any parameter that changes in an orderly fashion. Thus, such a set of equations are referred to as *parametric,* where the parameter here is i and, consequently, the resulting circle is a parametric one. However, in analytic geometry, the equation for generating a circle is different:

$$x^2 + y^2 = r^2$$

Such an equation denotes that for every point on a plane, only the points that satisfy the above equation are part of a circle of radius $r$ and center (0,0). The following code generates such a circle (shown on the left in Figure 2-7):

```
1       for(int x = -50; x<50; x++)
2         for(int y=-50; y<50; y++)
3           if(x*x + y*y == 25*25)
4             point(x+50,y+50);
```

Line 3 in the above code can be replaced with the following statement:

```
3       if(x*x + y*y > 25*25 && x*x + y*y < 26*26)
```

In this case, a circle is produced by selecting a series of points that fit the preceding two inequalities. This circle has a radius that ranges between 25 and 26 (shown on the right in Figure 2-7).

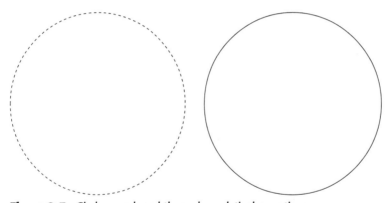

**Figure 2-7:** Circles produced through analytical equations

By taking a closer look to the two algorithms (i.e., parametric versus analytical) from a computational efficiency point of view, we may observe the following: the parametric algorithm involves 360 iterations, whereas the analytical involves 100 * 100 = 10,000 iterations. In addition, the parametric algorithm produces a much more precise set of points. Thus, parametric representation is preferable over the analytical, especially if such representations involve animation. In the next section, we will use parametric equations to produce curves.

## 2.2 Bezier Curve

As we have seen, a curve can be generated by sampling points from a parametric equation. In the case of the parametric equation $x = \sin(a)$, we derive points' coordinates based on the increments of the angle $a$. In a similar way, we can use more complex parametric equations to derive x and y coordinates of complex curves based on a changing parameter, $t$. So, by using a parametric equation of the form

$$p(t) = \sum_{i=0}^{n} p_i f_i(t)$$

where $t$ lies between 0 and 1, we can replace the function $f(t)$ with a Bernstein polynomial $B_{i,n}(t) = t^i (1 - t)^{n-1}$. This polynomial can be constructed based on the number of points (or degrees) given. So, for 3, 4, 5, and 6 points the polynomial becomes:

```
B3(t) = (1-t)²p₀ + 2t(1-t)p₁ + t2p₂

B4(t) = (1-t)³p₀ + 3t(1-t)²p₁ + 3t²(1-t)p₂ + t³p₃

B5(t) = (1-t)⁴p₀ + 4t(1-t)³p₁ + 6u2(1-t)²p₂ + 4t³(1-t)p₃ + t⁴p₄

B6(t)  = (1-t)⁵p₀ + 5t(1-t)⁴p₁ + 10t²(1-t)³p₂ + 10t³(1-t)²p₃ +
      5t⁴(1-t)p₄ + t5p₅
```

In the mathematical notation, a cubic Bezier curve is defined through the following equation:

$$\mathbf{B}(t) = (1-t)^3 \mathbf{P}_0 + 3t(1-t)^2 \mathbf{P}_1 + 3t^2(1-t)\mathbf{P}_2 + t^3 \mathbf{P}_3, t \in [0,1].$$

Where P0, P1, P2, and P3 are points in three-dimensional space, and the parameter $t$ can have values between 0 and 1. In the following code, we use the preceding equation to extract the coordinates of a Bezier curve based on four points:

```
float P0x = 10., P0y = 10.;
float P1x = 10., P1y = 40.;
float P2x = 40., P2y = 60.;
float P3x = 80., P3y = 20.;

for(float t=0.; t<1.; t+=0.01){
        float x = pow((1 - t),3)*P0x + 3*t*pow((1 - t),2)*P1x +
    3*pow(t,2)*(1 - t)*P2x + pow(t,3)*P3x;
```

```
        float y = pow((1 - t),3)*P0y + 3*t*pow((1 - t),2)*P1y +
3*pow(t,2)*(1 - t)*P2y + pow(t,3)*P3y;
        point(x,y);
    }
```

We then draw the four points together with the resulting sampled points (see Figure 2-8).

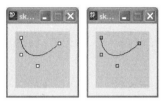

**Figure 2-8:** A Bezier curve based on four points

The resulting points (left) are the same as we would have obtained by using the `bezier()` command provided by Processing, as shown on the right and in the following code:

```
noFill();
bezier(P0x,P0y,P1x,P1y,P2x,P2y,P3x,P3y);
rectMode(CENTER);
rect(P0x,P0y,5,5);
rect(P1x,P1y,5,5);
rect(P2x,P2y,5,5);
rect(P3x,P3y,5,5);
```

# 2.3 Pointillist Images

Since we know how to create circles, or better, how to address "circular" behaviors, we will now use that knowledge to create images using simple mathematics. We will use the `point()` method to draw a point at a position (x, y) on the screen and then color it using the `stroke()` method. For example,

```
    point( 10, 20);
```

will draw a point at location (10,20). Now, if we replace 10 with a counter variable `i` we will have:

```
for(int x=0; x<100; x++){
  stroke(255, 0, 0);
  point( x, 200);
}
```

This, as expected, will draw a red line 100 pixels long. If we loop twice in both directions, we can get a red area of 100 × 100 pixels through the following code:

```
    for(int x=0; x<100; x++){
  for(int y=0; y<100; y++){
    stroke(255, 0, 0);
    point( x, y);
    }
  }
```

Suppose that we change the colors by using a random variable. Obviously, we will get a random colored image as shown in this code:

```
size(360,180);
for(int x = 0; x<360; x++)
  for(int y = 0; y<180; y++){

    int red   = int(random(255));
    int green = int(random(255));
    int blue  = int(random(255));

    stroke(red, green, blue);
    rect(x, y,1,1);
  }
```

The output is shown in Figure 2-9.

**Figure 2-9:** Random colored dots

Now, instead of random numbers, suppose that we use the sine and cosine methods we used earlier to affect the creation of the image by manipulating the way the color of the dots is produced. However, we must be aware of two things: RGB values must always be positive and less than 255. In the following example, we assign red to a sine value of the x coordinate, green to a cosine value of the y coordinate, and blue to the product of red and green. The result is shown in Figure 2-10.

```
1    size(360,180);
2    for(int x = 0; x<360; x++){
3      for(int y = 0; y<180; y++){
4
```

```
5          int red = (int)(255. * cos(  PI/180. * x) );
6          int green = (int)(255. * sin(  PI/180. * y));
7          int blue  = 0;
8
9          red   = abs(red) % 255;
10         green = abs(green) % 255;
11         blue  = abs(blue) % 255;
12
13          stroke(red, green, blue);
14          rect(x, y,1,1);
15       }
16     }
```

**Figure 2-10:** A color scheme as an
output of an algorithm

The image shows the color behavior of the combinations of sine and cosine of
the x and y coordinates. Blue is absent from the image, since we always assign
it 0. Now, if we involve blue in the picture by multiplying red and green, as in
the following code, we get the interesting result shown in Figure 2-11.

```
int red   = int (255. * cos(  PI/180. * x) );
int green = int (255. * sin(  PI/180. * y));
int blue  = red * green;
```

**Figure 2-11:** A color scheme as an
output of a constraint-based algorithm

We can "carve out" the preceding pattern, as shown in Figure 2-12, by setting
conditions in the code: for instance, any value above a certain color level could
be omitted (thus, setting a threshold):

```
size(360,180);
  for(int x = 0; x<360; x++){
```

```
for(int y = 0; y<360; y++){

    int red   = (int)(255. * cos(PI/180. * x) );
    int green = (int)(255. * sin(PI/180. * y));
    int blue  = red * green;

    red   = abs(red) % 255;
    green = abs(green) % 255;
    blue  = abs(blue) % 255;

    if(blue < 128)
      red = green = blue = 0;

    stroke(red, green, blue);
    rect(y, x,1,1);
  }
}
```

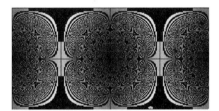

**Figure 2-12:** A color scheme as an output of a constraint-based algorithm

## 2.4 Polygons

A polygon as defined in the Processing language is a series of vertices that are connected with lines. The series of vertices are initiated by using the beginShape(POLYGON) method and terminating with the endShape() method.

```
beginShape(POLYGON);
    vertex(20,20);
    vertex(80,20);
    vertex(80,80);
    vertex(20,80);
    vertex(20,20);
endShape();
```

In the preceding code, we pre-compute the x and y values of the coordinates and then we assign them to the vertices. This method is called *hard-coding* because we are using fixed values. The result is a predictable square, shown in Figure 2-13.

**Figure 2-13:** A polygon in
the form of a square

Another way to create a polygon is through an array of x and y coordinates. An array is a set of memorized data values that can be accessed in an ordered way. The following code shows how to create a square using two arrays for the x and y coordinates. Instead of explicitly presetting the x and y coordinates using independent variables for each vertex point, we store them in an array that can be accessed in an ordered fashion for retrieval.

```
1    int n = 4;
2    int[] xArray = new int[n];  //allocate memory
3    int[] yArray = new int[n];
4    xArray[0] = 20;   //first point
5    yArray[0] = 20;
6    xArray[1] = 20;   //second point
7    yArray[1] = 80;
8    xArray[2] = 80;   //third point
9    yArray[2] = 80;
10   xArray[3] = 80;   //fourth point
11   yArray[3] = 20;
12   beginShape(POLYGON);
13   for(int i = 0; i < n; i++)
14     vertex(xArray[i],yArray[i]);   //retrieve in an ordered fashion
15   endShape(CLOSE);
```

First, we need to create two arrays with four integers each. Then we assign values to the array positions one by one. Finally, we draw the polygon using the `vertex()` method. The resulting polygon (shown in Figure 2-14) will look the same as that shown in Figure 2-13 (the difference is in the way it is constructed).

**Figure 2-14:** A polygon in the form
of a square constructed through arrays

In this example, we used the arrays to fill in the points and then we passed them to the `vertex()` method. The advantage of this method is that the arrays not only store information that can be reused later but can be changed and modified through the course of the session. However, it would be perhaps better if we could create a general algorithm that would fill the arrays with the necessary coordinates instead of pre-calculating and "hard-coding" the data. This problem is addressed in the next section.

## 2.5 Equilateral Polygons

In an equilateral polygon, vertex points are distributed along a circle in equal intervals. Earlier in this chapter you learned how to create circles using parametric equations (i.e., involving an angle and a radius). The next step is to create circular polygons, that is, polygons created through arrays that are obtained by distributing points equally on the perimeter of a circle. The following code demonstrates this method with a simple algorithm making use of our knowledge of the sine and cosine:

```
1    int n = 5;
2    float[] xArray = new float[n];      //allocate memory for 5 points
3    float[] yArray = new float[n];
4    void setup(){
5      float angle = 2 * PI / n;         //divide the circle in n sections
6      for(int i =0; i< n; i++){    //create points along a circle
7        xArray[i] = 50. + 30. * sin(angle*i);
8        yArray[i] = 50. + 30. * cos(angle*i);
9      }
10   }
11   void draw (){
12     beginShape(POLYGON);
13     for(int i = 0; i < n; i++)
14       vertex(xArray[i],yArray[i]);
15     endShape(CLOSE);
16   }
```

After creating the arrays of size n, you need to fill them with points. To do that, loop for n times and each time the x and y values are assigned. These values are calculated through the following algorithm:

- First, divide a full circle (2*PI) by n sections, which correspond to the number of the equilateral polygon's sides (or the size of the array), and name this ratio "angle".

- Then, store the coordinates of each polygon's vertex in the arrays by using the parametric equation of the circle.

- Use the stored values in the arrays to draw the polygon vertices.

The resulting shape is shown in Figure 2-15.

**Figure 2-15:** A central polygon implemented for five sides

## 2.6 Responsive Polygons

So far, the polygons that we have been constructing reside on the screen at a specific location, but they are not interactive. In other words, after a point is laid down, there is no way for the system to interact with it in order to rearrange it in another pattern or make it responsive to the user's actions. The following code develops a method of locating the coordinate positions for each point and then using that information to track and reposition them.

```
1    int n = 5;
2    float[] px = new float[n];
3    float[] py = new float[n];
4    void setup(){
5      float angle = 2 * PI / n;      //divide the circle in n sect
6      for(int i =0; i< n; i++){
7        px[i] = 50. + 30. * sin(angle*i);
8        py[i] = 50. + 30. * cos(angle*i);
9      }
10   }
11   void draw (){
12     background(200);
13     beginShape(POLYGON);
14     for(I nt i = 0; i < n; i++)
15       vertex(px[i],py[i]);
16     endShape(CLOSE);
17   for(int i=0; i<n; i++){
18       if(dist(mouseX,mouseY,px[i],py[i])<20)
19         stroke(255,0,0);
20       else
21         stroke(0,0,0);
22       rect(px[i],py[i],5,5);
23     }
24   }
25
```

```
26    void mouseDragged(){
27      for(int i=0; i<n; i++)z
28        if(dist(mouseX,mouseY,px[i],py[i])<20){
29          px[i] += (mouseX-pmouseX); //push only
30          py[i] += (mouseY-pmouseY);
31          px[i] = constrain(px[i],5,width-5);
32          py[i] = constrain(py[i],5,height-5);
33        }
34    }
```

In lines 2 and 3, we create two arrays, px[] and py[], that will store the x and y coordinates of the objects that we will place in the scene. Therefore, we allocate memory for five points here, that is, for as many as the variable n has. In lines 7 to 9, we populate the array with the coordinates of an equilateral polygon (created through the methods we discussed in the previous section). Those numbers are also used to place a rectangle at the end points of the polygon. Notice that we use rectangles instead of points only because they can be bigger and therefore more visible. In the draw() section, we draw these rectangles, but we also check to see whether the mouse is close enough so that we can highlight them as red. This is done in lines 18 through 21. First, we loop through all points and then compute the distance of each point from the mouse's location. If it falls less than a certain predefined tolerance (e.g., 20 pixels here), then we change the stroke color to red; otherwise, it defaults to black.

In the mouseDragged() section, we allow the user to interact with the selected (i.e., red) points. This is done in lines 26 to 34. We loop through all points and determine their distance from the mouse. If it falls within the range of 20 pixels, then we add an offset to it. This offset is the difference between the current position of the mouse (mouseX) and its previous position (pmouseX). This difference makes the rectangle move by an offset so that it appears that the mouse is pushing the rectangles. Lines 31 and 32 make sure that the modified points do not exceed the limits of the screen (within a frame of 5 pixels all around the window). Figure 2-16 shows the result.

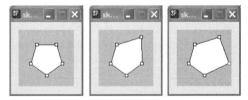

**Figure 2-16:** A polygon where points can be moved

## 2.7 Responsive Curve

In a similar fashion, a curve can become interactive by storing its control point coordinates and allowing the user to move them, affecting the shape of the curve. In the following code, we demonstrate this by using the code that generates Bezier sampled points, as discussed earlier in this chapter.

```
1    float [] px = {10.,10.,40.,80.};
2    float [] py = {10.,40.,60.,20.};
3
4    void draw(){
5       background(255);
6       for(float t=0.; t<1.; t+=0.01){
7          float x = px[0]*pow((1 - t),3) + 3*px[1]*t*pow((1 - t),2) +
3*px[2]*pow(t,2)*(1 - t) + px[3]*pow(t,3);
8          float y = py[0]*pow((1 - t),3) + 3*py[1]*t*pow((1 - t),2) +
3*py[2]*pow(t,2)*(1 - t) + py[3]*pow(t,3);
9          point(x,y);
10      }
11      for(int i=0; i<4; i++)
12         rect(px[i],py[i],5,5);
13   }
14
15   void mouseDragged(){
16      for(int i=0; i<4; i++)
17         if(dist(mouseX,mouseY,px[i],py[i])<20){
18            px[i] += (mouseX-pmouseX);
19            py[i] += (mouseY-pmouseY);
20         }
21   }
```

The first two lines predefine the coordinates of the control points. In lines 6, 7, and 8, we extract the x and y coordinates from the third-degree polynomials that define the Bezier curve (as discussed earlier in this chapter). Lines 11 and 12 draw the four control points. In the mouseDragged() section, we go through all control points and determine the ones that are closest to the mouse and we move them by an offset away from the mouse's position (it appears as if we are pushing the rectangles). This action results in a continuous redrawing of the screen that allows the user to modify the Bezier curve interactively, as shown in Figure 2-17.

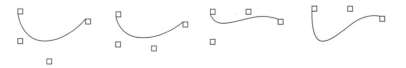

**Figure 2-17:** A Bezier curve where control points can be moved

## Summary

This chapter showed you how to draw simple shapes and text, get mouse feedback, use color, create random numbers, and use arrays. You were also introduced to some simple principles of trigonometry. The next chapter shows you how to create hierarchical structures of points, segments, shapes, and groups. This will allow a better understanding of the notions of classes, object-oriented programming, and inheritance.

## Exercises

**NOTE**  Answers to the exercises are provided in Appendix B.

1.  Write the code that will create the following shape:

    ```
    beginShape();

      for(int i=0; i<20; i++){

      float x =

      float y =

      vertex(x+50,y+50);

      }

      endShape();
    ```

    Hint: The coordinate points you need to create are:

    ```
       0.0          0.0
      10.0          0.0
      10.0         10.0
     -10.0         10.0
     -10.0        -10.0
      20.0        -10.0
      20.0         20.0
     -20.0         20.0
     -20.0        -20.0
    ```

```
 30.0        -20.0
 30.0         30.0
-30.0         30.0
-30.0        -30.0
 40.0        -30.0
 40.0         40.0
-40.0         40.0
```

2. Write the code that will connect each point with all others already drawn. A point should be created each time the user presses the mouse.

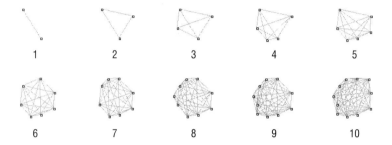

3. Write code that will draw a series of segments for every mouse click. If a key stroke is entered the polyline should end.

4. Write the code that will create the following brick pattern:

5. Write the code that will create the following stair pattern:

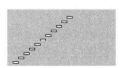

6. Modify the code to create the following staircase pattern:

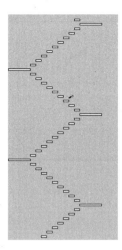

7. Write the code that will produce the following spiral pattern:

8. Modify the code so that it creates the following double spiral pattern:

9. Order and Randomness

   Objective:

   ▪ To demonstrate understanding of the use of loops, randomness, geometries, and attributes.

   ▪ To learn how to compose, run, and debug Processing.

   Description:

   ▪ Write the source code that will display a 2D pattern of shapes (size of your choice). The pattern should signify the notions of order and disorder within the same pattern.

10. Mathematical Image

    Objective:

    ▪ To demonstrate the use of mathematical functions.

    ▪ To learn how to compile, run, and publish a java applet.

    Description:

    ▪ Write the source code (with comments) for an applet that will display a $300 \times 300$ image created through `rect()`, as shown in the following code. Fill in the *c1, c2,* and *c3* variables using mathematical functions to create interesting patterns. For example *c1* may look like:

```
int c1 = int(255. * sin(radians(x)));
size(300,300);
for(int x=0; x<width; x++)
for(int y=0; y<height; y++){

int c1 = _____;
int c2 = _____;
int c3 = _____;

stroke(c1,c2,c3);
rect(x, y,1,1);

    }
```

11. Composition Tool

    Develop a program that will allow the user to create a composition. Provide options for controlling and/or altering the composition. The proposed system should be intuitive enough to not need a user's manual or any text description in the screen.

Objectives:

- To demonstrate understanding of the use of graphic elements, `draw()`, and key or mouse events.
- To address notions of composition, interaction, and response.

Process:

- Develop an idea of the tools and interactions.
- Make a diagram/sketch that represents a possible solution.
- Create a Processing script (with comments) that can implement the idea.
- Test the resulting code by reenacting a user.

Discuss the following questions:

- Does a tool maker of design tools need also to be a good designer?
- Is a tool maker responsible for the tool's misuses?

# CHAPTER 3

# The Structure of Shapes

Structure is the way in which parts are arranged or put together to form a whole; it is the interrelation or arrangement of parts in a complex entity. Complex structures often require hierarchical organizations in which groups of elements are successively ranked or graded, with each level subordinate to the one above. In that sense, a system with hierarchical groups can be more efficient in performing a task, since only the parts particular to the task need to be activated. At the same time, information can be divided into that which is related to the task itself (local) and that which concerns the control and accomplishment of the task as it relates to the whole (global).

Geometric structures are complex systems that can be arranged in hierarchical levels. For example, by extrusion, points can form lines, lines can form surfaces, and surfaces can form solids. In reverse, a complex geometric solid shape can be composed of surfaces that are composed of curves that are composed of control points. This chapter introduces a hierarchical geometric structure in which each hierarchical group maintains certain autonomy within its domain yet, at the same time, interrelates to the levels immediately above or below.

## 3.1 Introduction to Class Structures

So far, this book has dealt with single-file programs, that is, programs that reside in one single file with the same name. If we start adding more and more procedures in the file, it will become bigger, more complex, and less efficient to search, edit, and organize. To avoid such an accumulative complexity and to establish organization and clarity, we will break the one-file program structure into multiple files, and inside each file we will write the code for organized sets of variables and methods called *classes*. In that way, we will break the program into files, each of which will contain information relevant to those classes. These classes will perform functions or provide information and will be used later to build up complex programs. Each class will solve a particular problem, the specifics of which may not be understood outside of the class. In other words, a class may solve complex problems within its own domain, but from outside, that complexity is hidden. At a higher level, each class can be used for its functionality by making a reference to its own procedures (which will call methods).

To understand the structure of classes and their inherited values, consider an example from everyday life: building houses. Houses are constructed by workers, each of whom is specialized in a different business: plumbers, carpenters, construction workers, and so forth. You do not need to perform all the trades to build a house. Instead, you hire the appropriate person for each job, and each contributes to the overall home construction. You do not need to know what happens within the domain of expertise of each worker, that is, once the plumber is done you assume that all plumbing work is complete without knowing the specific details of the accomplishment.

Similarly, in geometry, solids are composed of faces, which are, in turn, composed of segments, which are, in turn, composed of points. Each geometrical element has its own functions and behaviors. The following sections break geometry into some of its constituent classes, starting with a basic element of geometry, the point.

## 3.1.1 Defining a Class Called MyPoint

First, we will create a new class called MyPoint. This new class will be used to store information about points and their related methods (i.e., create, plot, move, rotate, scale, etc.). The following is the code for this new class:

```
1    class MyPoint {
2    float x, y;  //members
3
4        MyPoint(float xin, float yin){  //constructor
5            x = xin;
6            y = yin;
7        }
8    }
```

The class name is defined in line 1. It is composed of two sections: the members (line 2) and the constructor (lines 4 through 7).

- Put all the variables that are associated with the class in the members area. Since, in this case, you are dealing with a point, you need to define the constituent members of a point, that is, its coordinates, which you define as two floats, named x and y.

- The second section is the constructor. In that area you construct a new point. This is done by assigning values to its members. So, in this case, to construct a MyPoint object, you need to pass two parameter variables, xin and yin, that are then assigned to the class's members x and y (lines 5 and 6).

In Processing, this new class is saved as a file, also called MyPoint, using the following method: in the upper-right side of the Processing editor, there is an arrow pointing right. If you press on it, a popup window appears. Select the new Tab command. A new tab will appear. The class code should be typed into that tab. Next, in order to use the newly defined class, you need to refer to it from outside its own class. So, you define another area using the tab defini-tion process or rename the original sketch tab. Name this new tab MyProject. The reference to the class MyPoint (also referred to as a "call" to a class) can be done as follows:

```
1    MyPoint p;
2    void setup(){
3       p = new MyPoint(10.,20.);
4       println("x = " + p.x + " y = " + p.y);
5    }
```

The first statement of the preceding code (typed up in the MyProject tab):

```
MyPoint p;
```

denotes that we are declaring a new object, p, of type MyPoint. Line 3 allocates memory, using the word new, to create a new MyPoint to which we pass as param-eters 10. and 20., which correspond to the x and y coordinates. Consequently, the statement invokes a call to the class MyPoint and uses the constructor to assign the values of xin and yin to the members x and y:

```
1    MyPoint(float xin, float yin){   //constructor
2          x = xin;
3          y = yin;
4    }
```

In other words, the input variable xin is 10. and yin is 20. Therefore, the x member is assigned the value 10, and the y member, 20. Now, when you want to print out the members of MyPoint, you use the statement:

```
println(" x = " + p.x + " y = " + p.y);
```

In this way, you obtain access to x and y of object p by using the "." opera-tor, which simply says "go to object p and give me the subordinate member x," that is, p.x. The same applies to y. In general, the dot operator is a reference to a member of a subordinate member (or operation) of a class. Figure 3-1 shows the structure of the MyPoint class as described in this section.

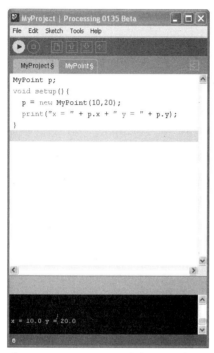

**Figure 3-1:** Structure of the MyPoint class

## 3.1.2 Adding Methods to a Class

Remember that the reason for creating a MyPoint class was to facilitate opera-tions on points by organizing and concentrating them in the class's area. Suppose that you want to draw a point on the screen, using the class's structure (or draw a tiny circle instead of a point only to make it stand out). You need to define a method called plot() within the MyPoint class that will draw an ellipse at the point's location, that is, at point x, y. The code added to the class is shown below in lines 10 through 13:

```
1    class MyPoint {
2        float x, y;  // members
3
4        //Constructor
```

```
5          MyPoint(float xin, float yin){
6              x = xin;
7              y = yin;
8          }
9
10         //Method
11         void plot(){
12             ellipse(x,y,5,5);
13         }
14     }
```

Back in the main code (i.e., MyProject), we will make reference to the new paint method by defining a point and then painting it on the screen as a tiny circle. So, we define x as a random number anywhere along the width of the screen, and y as a random number anywhere along the height of the screen. This is done in lines 3 and 4. In line 5 we plot the point invoking class's plot() method:

```
1      MyPoint p;
2      void setup(){
3          p = new MyPoint(random(width),random(height));
4          println("x = " + p.x + " y = " + p.y);
5          p.plot();
6      }
```

Note that even though the random numbers are of type float, they will be plotted as if they were integer values so that they can correspond to pixel values. In this way, you do not need to save the point's coordinates as integer values, but rather you can store them as floats, allowing them to have a higher degree of precision than their plotted location. Line 5 executes the plotting of the point by using the object p, then the dot operator, and then the method to invoke (i.e., p.plot()). You then print out x and y so that you can see the resulting random numbers, as shown in Figure 3-2.

**Figure 3-2:** A point's plot and printout of its random coordinates

Note that the constructor MyPoint does not take a "void" (unlike plot) because it is not a method. It is a constructor, and you simply declare it with the same name as the class (as displayed also in the tab) without any identifiers, except sometimes the identifier `public`, which means that the class definition (or any of its methods) can be referenced from outside the class. In Processing, this is the default case, so when a class is defined without the identifier `public`, it is assumed. The opposite case is the identifier `private`, which does not allow reference or changes from outside.

## 3.2 Organization of Classes

Any class is composed of three parts: members, constructors, and methods, as shown in Figure 3-3.

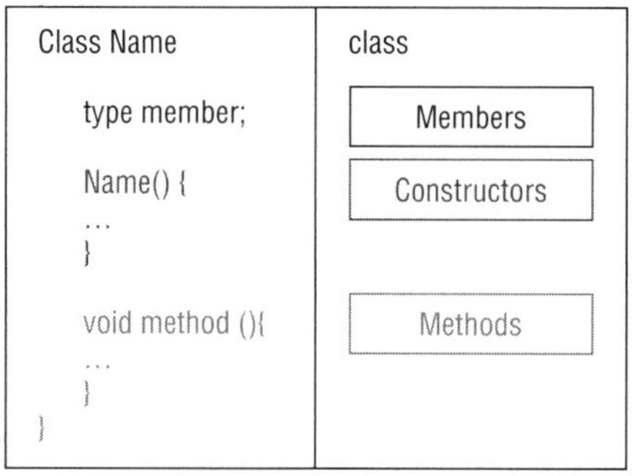

**Figure 3-3:** General structure of a simple class

In the `MyPoint` class, we have the following:

■ **Members:** Two floats named `x` and `y`
■ **Constructors:** Only one called `MyPoint`
■ **Methods:** Only one called `plot`

Members and methods can be accessed by external classes, using the "." symbol as in:

```
p.x or p.y or p.plot();
```

The constructors are accessed only once, that is, to create the class. We use the new command to allocate memory for the newly created class:

```
MyPoint p = new MyPoint(10, 20);
```

It is possible to have more than one constructor; we distinguish them from the number of arguments each one has. For example:

```
MyPoint(float xin, float yin){
        x = xin;
```

```
            y = yin;
            }
```

and

```
    MyPoint ( ){
            x = 0;
            y = 0;
            }
```

can both coexist within the same class `MyPoint`, except that when we call `MyPoint( )` it assigns 0 to both x and y as opposed to `MyPoint(10., 20.)`, which assigns 10. and 20. or whatever the values of xin and yin are. The same applies to methods, where we may have two or more methods with the same name. We distinguish them from the number of arguments that are being passed.

As mentioned earlier, classes are created in order to organize the code and minimize repetitive tasks. The definition of a class is based on its organizational identity. In other words, we usually define as a class a set of operations performed by an entity that has some kind of an identity and completeness. For example, if we are dealing with 2D shapes, it makes sense to define as classes the following entities: a point, a segment, a curve, a polyline, and a group. In that way, every time we want to create or modify a class we only have to create or modify its constituent parts. For example, the hierarchical scheme shown in Figure 3-4 uses a group-shape-segment-point hierarchy so that if we change a shape that will pass the change down to its segment, which, in turn, will inherit the change down to their constituent points.

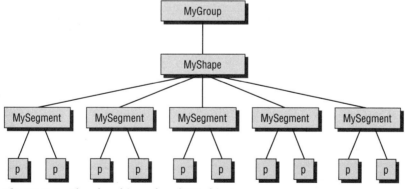

**Figure 3-4:** The class hierarchy of 2D objects

In the following section, we will create three classes that will illustrate the compositional tree of 2D class structures. Specifically, we will create the following three classes: `MyPoint`, `MySegment`, and `MyShape`.

### 3.2.1 Class MyPoint

This class is similar to the one we created in the previous section, but with the addition of one more method. First, we declare x and y to be numbers of type float because in real life locations can be fractional, that is, 0.35 meters or 2′ 4″, and the like. Second, we create two methods: plot and move. The move method adds an offset to its previous position.

```
1    class MyPoint {
2        float x, y;  // members of class
3
4        // Constructor
5        public MyPoint(float xin, float yin){
6            x = xin;
7            y = yin;
8        }
9        //Method1
10       public void plot(){
11           rect(x,y,5,5);
12       }
13       // Method2
14       void move(float xoff, float yoff){
15           x = x + xoff;
16           y = y + yoff;
17       }
18   }
```

### 3.2.2 Class MySegment

The next class is MySegment, which represents a line *segment*. Therefore, its members should be two points (a start and an end point). We construct a segment by passing two MyPoint(s), p1 and p2, which are assigned to its member's start and end. To move a segment, we simply call the move() method of its point members. Specifically, we are using start.move() and end.move(), which call the move method in the MyPoint class. Finally, to plot the points, we need to pass the x and y members of start and end, which are automatically converted to integers in order to be drawn as pixels on the screen. This conversion is done through the command line().

```
1    class MySegment {
2        MyPoint start;  // members of class
3        MyPoint end;
4
5        //Constructor
6        public MySegment(MyPoint p1, MyPoint p2){
7            start = new MyPoint(p1.x, p1.y);
```

```
8              end    = new MyPoint(p2.x, p2.y);
9          }
10
11         //Move
12         public void move(float xoff, float yoff){
13             start.move(xoff, yoff);
14             end.move(xoff, yoff);
15         }
16
17         //plot
18         public void plot(){
19             line(start.x, start.y, end.x, end.y);
20         }
21     }
```

## 3.2.3 Class MyShape

MyShape is a class that defines shapes (i.e., collections of segments). So, this class takes as its input segments. The problem, however, is that, unlike with a segment, which always takes two points, we do not know in advance how many segments are needed to construct a shape. It could be 3 (if it is a triangle), could be 24 (if it is a 24-gon), or could be 100 (for a complex shape). So we need to use an array of segments (MySegment[]), which we will call segs. The constructor MyShape takes two input variables: the number of segments and the array of segments. These two variables are assigned to the class members: numSegments and segs. To assign the values, we simply loop through the arrays, assigning the input value one at a time:

```
for(int i=0; i<numSegments; i++)
        segs[i] = inputSegments[i];
```

The move and plot methods are also straightforward. All we do is to invoke the segment methods move and plot of the segments one at a time:

```
1     class MyShape {
2         MySegment[] segs;  // members of class
3         int numSegments;
4
5         // Constructor
6         MyShape(int numInputSegments, MySegment[] inputSegments){
7             numSegments = numInputSegments;
8             segs = new MySegment[numSegments];
9             for(int i=0; i<numSegments; i++)
10                segs[i] = inputSegments[i];
11        }
```

```
12
13        // Move
14        void move(float xoff, float yoff){
15            for(int i=0; i<numSegments; i++)
16                segs[i].move(xoff, yoff);
17        }
18
19        // plot (or draw)
20        void plot(){
21            for(int i=0; i<numSegments; i++)
22                segs[i].plot();
23        }
24    }
```

In line 6, the constructor accepts the number of segments numInputSegments and an array in which to store the input segments inputSegments. These variables then assign their values to the class's variables called numSegments and segs. In particular, the array segs needs to be initialized, to allocate memory for it, through the statement:

```
segs = new MySegment[numSegments];
```

The move and plot methods simply invoke the methods of their constituent class's one level below, that is, segs[i].move(xoff, yoff);. Specifically, the hierarchical structure of these three newly introduced classes works as follows: when a method is called at the top, that method calls its corresponding method of the class one level below, and so on, all the way to the bottom classes. For example, a call to shape.move(x, y) will call the MySegment's method move, which, in turn, will call the MyPoint's method move, which will do the actual movement. Following is the main code (MyProject):

```
1     MyPoint p1, p2, p3, p4;                    //define four points
2     MySegment[] segment = new MySegment[2]; //define two segments
3     MyShape shape;                             //define a shape
4
5     //initialize variables
6      void setup(){
7
8         p1 = new MyPoint(10., 10.);  //make a point
9         p2 = new MyPoint(20., 20.);  //make a point
10        p3 = new MyPoint(20., 20.);  //make a point
11        p4 = new MyPoint(30., 10.);  //make a point
12
13        segment [0] = new MySegment(p1, p2); //make a segment
14        segment [1] = new MySegment(p3, p4); //make a segment
15
```

```
16              shape = new MyShape(2, segment);      //make a shape
17
18              shape.move(30., 35.);   //move the shape at (30.0,35.0)
19              shape.plot(); //draw the shape
20
21      }
```

First, we declare four points p1, p2, p3, and p4; a two-segment segment (actually, one array with two positions); and a shape. In the setup() method, we create all the objects: first, we create four points with fixed (a.k.a. "hard-coded") values, then we fill the two array positions, creating two segments, and finally we create a shape that needs the number of segments, that is, 2, and the array containing the segments. Once these objects are created, we call the move() and plot() methods of the MyShape class to move and plot. Indeed, in the plot method, all we do is to make one reference the shape class. Here is what is happening:

```
shape.move(30., 35.);
```

calls the move method of MyShape. That invokes the method:

```
void move(float xoff, float yoff){
```

which, in turn, loops and invokes the move method of the MySegment class,

```
for(int i=0; i<numSegments; i++)
    segs[i].move(xoff, yoff);
```

which, in turn, invokes twice the move method of the MyPoint class,

```
void move(float xoff, float yoff){
        start.move(xoff, yoff);
        end.move(xoff, yoff);
    }
```

which in turn assigns the moved offsets to the x and y members of the MyPoint class:

```
void move(float xoff, float yoff){
        x = x + xoff;
        y = y + yoff;
    }
```

The propagation of action from the shape's moving methods to the segments' moving methods down to the points' moving methods is illustrated in Figure 3-5 with a sequence of arrows.

```
shape.move(30.; 35.);

//********** Move (in MyShape)
void move(float xoff, float yoff){
    for (int i=0; i<numSegments; i++)
        segs[i].move(xoff, yoff);
}

        //********** Move (in MySegment)
        void move(float xoff, float yoff){
            start.move(xoff, yoff);
            end.move(xoff, yoff);
        }

                //********** Move (in MyPoint)
                void move(float xoff, float yoff){
                    x = x + xoff;
                    y = y + yoff;
                }
        }
```

**Figure 3-5:** Propagation of action though classes

The output of this two-segment four-point shape looks like Figure 3-6.

**Figure 3-6:** Drawing two segments through hierarchical calls

# 3.3 Standard Transformations (move, rotate, scale)

In the previous section, you created a method called move() that was used to move objects in a hierarchical manner. The move method belongs to a category of methods called *transformations*. Transformation is an alteration of the geometry of a shape. Transformations affect the location of the coordinates of a shape; there are three basic transformations: *translation* (or movement), *rotation*, and *scale*.

Translation is the alteration of the position of an object. It is accomplished by adding an offset value to the x and y coordinates. Specifically, we add an offset, xoff, to the existing value of x and an offset, yoff, to the existing value of y:

```
//Move
void move(float xoff, float yoff){
```

```
        x += xoff;   // or x = x + xoff;
        y += yoff;
    }
```

Scaling is the alteration of the size of an object. It is accomplished by multiplying each coordinate by a scaling factor xs and ys. Specifically:

```
    // Scale
    void scale(float xs, float ys){
        x *= xs;
        y *= ys;
    }
```

This will expand or shrink the size of the shape relatively to the (0,0) coordinate system. For example, (2,2) coordinate will become (6,6) if multiplied by 3. That will move (2,2) four units on each direction away from (0,0)).

However, in order to scale with respect to a reference point "ref" we need to:

1.  Move the coordinates to (0,0) (by subtracting ref).

2.  Do the scaling.

3.  Move them move back to the original position (by adding ref).

The following code demonstrates this process:

```
    // Scale with respect to a reference point
    void scale(float xs, float ys, MyPoint ref){
        x = (x-ref.x)*xs + ref.x;
        y = (y-ref.y)*ys + ref.y;
    }
```

*Rotation* is an alteration of the orientation of an object. It is accomplished by applying trigonometric functions to the values of the coordinates x and y. The functions are those of sine and cosine, and they will be needed in order to arrange things in a circular trajectory. In the previous chapter, we showed how to arrange points along a circle. Here, we do something similar: we multiply the x and y coordinates by both the sine and cosine of the rotation angle according to the following formula:

```
    //Rotate
    void rotate (float angle) {
        float newx =  x * cos(radians(angle)) + y * sin(radians(angle));
        float newy =  y * cos(radians(angle)) - x * sin(radians(angle));
        x = newx;
        y = newy;
    }
```

The preceding code will translate an object around the (0,0) origin. However, as in scaling, if we want to rotate around a reference point, we need to do the following:

```
//Rotate around point ref
void rotate (float angle, MyPoint ref) {
        float cosa, sina;
        cosa = cos(radians(angle));
        sina = sin(radians(angle));
        float newx = (x-ref.x) * cosa + (y-ref.y) * sina + ref.x;
        float newy = (y-ref.y) * cosa - (x-ref.x) * sina + ref.y;
        x = newx;
        y = newy;
    }
```

Briefly, we apply the following algorithm:

1.  Move the coordinates to (0,0) (by subtracting ref).

2.  Do the rotation.

3.  Move them move back to the original position (by adding ref).

All the above transformations can be generalized into schemes (called *matrices*) that can let you construct many more possible transformations. Using matrices is described in more detail in Chapter 8.

# 3.4 Implementing Transformations

After we create the basic transformation methods (move, rotate and scale), we place them into the `MyPoint` class.

```
1    class MyPoint {
2        float x, y;  // members of class
3
4        //Constructor
5        MyPoint(float xin, float yin){
6            x = xin;
7            y = yin;
8        }
9
10       //Move
11       void move(float xoff, float yoff){
12           x += xoff;
13           y += yoff;
14       }
15
16       //Rotate
17       void rotate(float angle, MyPoint ref){
18           float cosa, sina;
```

```
19              cosa = cos(radians(angle));
20              sina = sin(radians(angle));
21              float newx = (x-ref.x) * cosa - (y-ref.y) * sina + ref.x;
22              float newy = (y-ref.y) * cosa + (x-ref.x) * sina + ref.y;
23              x = newx;
24              y = newy;
25          }
26
27          //Scale
28          void scale(float xs, float ys, MyPoint ref){
29              x = (x-ref.x)*xs + ref.x;
30              y = (y-ref.y)*ys + ref.y;
31          }
32      }
```

Then we adjust the MySegment and MyShape classes to apply the transformation methods in a similar manner to the mySegment class. This is done as follows:

```
1   class MySegment {
2       MyPoint start;  // members of class
3       MyPoint end;
4
5       //Constructor
6       MySegment(MyPoint p1, MyPoint p2){
7           start = new MyPoint(p1.x, p1.y);
8           end   = new MyPoint(p2.x, p2.y);
9       }
10
11      //Move
12      void move(float xoff, float yoff){
13          start.move(xoff, yoff);
14          end.move(xoff, yoff);
15      }
16
17      //Rotate
18      void rotate (float angle, MyPoint ref) {
19          start.rotate(angle, ref);
20          end.rotate(angle, ref);
21      }
22
23      //Scale
24      void scale(float xs, float ys, MyPoint ref){
25          start.scale(xs, ys, ref);
26          end.scale(xs, ys, ref);
27      }
28
29      // plot
30      void plot (){
31          line(start.x, start.y, end.x, end.y);
32      }
33  }
```

In a similar manner, we apply the transformations to the MyShape class:

```
1    class MyShape {
2        MySegment[] segs;   // members of class
3        int numSegments;
4
5        //Constructor
6        MyShape(int numInputSegments, MySegment[] inputSegments){
7            numSegments = numInputSegments;
8            segs = new MySegment[numSegments];
9
10           for(int i=0; i<numSegments; i++)
11               segs[i] = inputSegments[i];
12       }
13
14       // Move
15       void move(float xoff, float yoff){
16           for(int i=0; i<numSegments; i++)
17               segs[i].move(xoff, yoff);
18       }
19
20       // Rotate
21       void rotate (float angle, MyPoint ref) {
22           for(int i=0; i<numSegments; i++)
23                segs[i].rotate(angle, ref);
24       }
25
26       // Scale
27       void scale(float xs, float ys, MyPoint ref){
28           for(int i=0; i<numSegments; i++)
29                segs[i].scale(xs, ys, ref);
30       }
31
32       // Plot
33       void plot(){
34           for(int i=0; i<numSegments; i++)
35               segs[i].plot();
36       }
37   }
```

Now in the main code MyProject, we create shapes and then transform them. The following code shows the process:

```
1            MyPoint p1, p2, p3, p4;
2            MySegment[] s = new MySegment[2];
3            MyShape shape;
7
3    public void setup(){
4
5            p1 = new MyPoint(0., 0.);
```

```
6                   p2 = new MyPoint(-10., -10.);
7                   p3 = new MyPoint(0., 0.);
8                   p4 = new MyPoint(10., -10.);
9
10                  s[0] = new MySegment(p1, p2);
11                  s[1] = new MySegment(p3, p4);
12
13                  shape = new MyShape(2, s);
14                  shape.move(30.,50.);
15
16          }
17
18          public void draw(){
19              background(200);
20              shape.plot();
21          }
22
23
24          MyPoint ref = new MyPoint(50., 50.);
25          void mouseDragged(){
26              int xoff = mouseX - pmouseX;  // get the offset
27              shape.rotate(xoff, ref);
28          }
```

The first part of the code, including the setup() method and the initialized variables, is the same as shown in the previous section of this chapter. The first difference is in the inclusion of a draw() section that handles the animation loop. The command background paints the window's background with a color that erases anything drawn on the screen. This gives the impression of movement as the screen continuously refreshes and a shape is redrawn in a slightly new position. We can add one statement to determine whether we want the screen to be redrawn or not. By default, the draw() method, when called, does not erase everything on the screen. If we add:

```
background(200);
```

then the method draw() redraws all the statements within the paint() method in their new position.

The rotate method takes an offset as the increment of rotation. For example, if an angle is at 40 degrees and we want to go to 45, we must pass 5 degrees to the rotate method because it adds it to the previous angle, that is, we do not pass the absolute value 45. The reason for that is that we pass the offset (or differential) of the mouse and not its absolute position. For example, in the mouse-Dragged method, we get the mouseX coordinate of the mouse and we subtract the first position of the mouse when it was clicked down (i.e., pmouseX). Then we get the difference, which we pass to the method rotate. This visual effect is shown to the right in Figure 3-7.

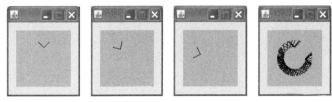

**Figure 3-7:** Redrawing the background while transforming (illusion of motion)

The `draw()` section of the code plots the shape repeatedly. The shape is redrawn, leaving a series of traces to imply motion. This effect can be altered to allow us to give the impression of movement as the screen continuously refreshes and a shape is redrawn in a slightly new position. We can add one statement to determine whether we want the screen to be redrawn or not. By default, the `draw()` method, when called, does not erase everything in the screen. If we add the statement:

```
background(200);
```

then the `draw()` method erases the screen before it redraws all the statements within the `plot()` method in their new position. In that way, the new graphics are not superimposed over the old ones. Here is the additional code:

```
void draw(){
background(200);
shape.plot();
    }
```

This visual effect is shown in the left-hand figures of Figure 3-7.

## 3.5 Creating Grids of Shapes

In the main code of `MyProject`, we created a V-like shape that we constructed by explicitly creating four points, then two segments, and then one shape. What if we want to construct a grid of 20x20 pentagons? Do we have to create all the points, then all the segments, and then all the shapes? It would take lines and lines of code, and most of it would be part of a redundant, repetitive, and unnecessary work pattern. Maybe instead we can create a simple method of constructing circular polygons and call that method repetitively within a loop. Since we already have constructed a method for computing points around a circle, let's use it. Here is what we have from Chapter 2:

```
Polygon makeNormalPolygon(int nsides){

int[] xArray = new int[nsides];
```

```
        int[] yArray = new int[nsides];

        //divide the full circle in nsides sections
        float angle = 2 * PI / nsides;

        for(int i =0; i<nsides; i++){
            xArray[i] = (int)(100. + 50. * sin(angle^i));
            yArray[i] = (int)(100. + 50. * cos(angle*i));
        }

        Polygon p = new Polygon(xArray, yArray, nsides);

        return p;
    }
```

We need to construct something that we can pass to the main program such as:

```
shape = new MyShape(numSides) ;
```

or to be more general:

```
shape = new MyShape(numSides, radius, xcenter, ycenter) ;
```

This must then be an alternative constructor of a shape that would look like this:

```
    MyShape(int numSides, float radius, float xoff, float yoff){

    numSegments = numSides;
    segs = new MySegment[numSegments];

    // divide the full circle in nsides sections
    float angle = 2 * Math.PI / numSegments;

    // create two points to store the segment points
    MyPoint p = new MyPoint(0.,0.);
    MyPoint pnext = new MyPoint(0.,0.);

    // loop to assign values to the points
    for(int i =0; i<numSegments; i++){
        p.x     = xoff + radius * sin(angle*i);
        p.y     = yoff + radius * cos(angle*i);
        pnext.x = xoff + radius * sin(angle*(i+1));
        pnext.y = yoff + radius * cos(angle*(i+1));
        segs[i] = new MySegment(p, pnext);
    }

    }
```

This constructor can coexist in the same class MyShape. It will be distinguished because of the different number and/or sequence of its parameters;

the older constructor had only two parameters; this one has four. In this new constructor, the first thing we need to do is to assign the number of sides and to allocate memory for the `segs[ ]` array:

```
numSegments = numSides;
segs = new MySegment[numSegments];
```

Then, we divide the full circle into sections:

```
float angle = 2 * Math.PI / numSegments;
```

Then we create two points, `p` and `pnext`, where we will put the two points necessary to create each segment. We initialize them to 0. Then we loop and compute the points around the circle and for each one we compute the one ahead; we need them in order to create the segments.

```
for(int i =0; i<numSegments; i++){
        p.x     = xoff + radius * sin(angle*i);
        p.y     = yoff + radius * cos(angle*i);
        pnext.x = xoff + radius * sin(angle*(i+1));
        pnext.y = yoff + radius * cos(angle*(i+1));
        segs[i] = new MySegment(p, pnext);
}
```

Once we compute the two points, `p` and `pnext`, we pass them to the `MySegment`, which constructs a segment, which is then assigned to the array `segs[]`, one at a time:

```
segs[i] = new MySegment(p, pnext);
```

All we need to do now is to call the creation of a 20×20 grid of pentagons in the main code:

```
1    MyShape[] shape = new MyShape[12*12];
2
3
4    void setup(){
5      size(350,350);   //make the screen big enough to see
6      for(int y=0; y<12; y++){  //for 12 steps in y
7        for(int x=0; x<12; x++){ //for 12 steps in x
8          //make a shape (calling the polygon constructor)
9          shape[y*12+x] = new MyShape(5, 10.,x*20., y*20.);
10         shape[y*12+x].move(10.*x, 10.*y);
11        }
12      }
13
14   }
15
16
```

```
17    void draw(){
18
19      for(int y=0; y<12; y++){  //for 12 steps in y
20        for(int x=0; x<12; x++){ //for 12 steps in x
21          shape[y*12+x].plot();  // plot the shapes
22        }
23      }
24
25    }
```

Take a note that the expression y*12+x is a way of counting from 0 to 144 (i.e., 12*12), using the two counters x and y. The result is shown in Figure 3-8.

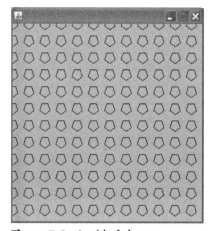

**Figure 3-8:** A grid of shapes

Once we have an array of shapes, we can then create a group-type class, which we will call MyGroup. Then we would only need to call group.move() and group.draw() to move and draw all the shapes together. This will be done in the next section.

## 3.6 Class MyGroup

MyGroup is a class that acts as a representative for a set of shapes. Its structure is similar to that of MyShape, except that it is one level higher:

```
1      class MyGroup {
2
3        // members of class
4        MyShape[] shapes;         // array of shapes
5        int numShapes;            //number of shapes
6
```

```
7
8           // Constructor
9             MyGroup(int numInputShapes, MyShape[] inputShapes){
10
11              numShapes = numInputShapes;
12              shapes = new MyShape[numShapes];
13
14              for(int i=0; i<numShapes; i++)
15                  shapes[i] = inputShapes[i];
16          }
17
18          // Move
19            void move(float xoff, float yoff){
20              for(int i=0; i<numShapes; i++)
21                  shapes[i].move(xoff, yoff);
22          }
23
24          // draw
25            void plot( ){
26
27              for(int i=0; i<numShapes; i++)
28                  shapes[i].plot();
29
30          }
31      }
```

Now, we do not need to create multiple shapes in the main code but, instead, call the creation of a group:

```
int numShapes = 12;  //num on side of grid of shapes
MyShape[] shape = new MyShape[numShapes*numShapes];
MyGroup group;

//*****************************************
void setup(){

  size(250,250);

  for(int y=0; y<numShapes; y++){
    for(int x=0; x<numShapes; x++){
      shape[y*numShapes+x] = new MyShape(5,9.,x*20., y*20.);
    }
  }

  group = new MyGroup(numShapes*numShapes, shape);
  group.move(10.,10.);
}
```

```
void draw( ){

  group.plot();

}
```

The result, shown in Figure 3-9, is the same, except that now we are in control of the whole group as one entity instead of 12×12 sub-entities:

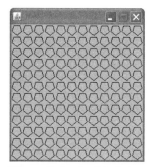

**Figure 3-9:** A grid of shapes

## 3.7 Selecting Objects

So far we are able to create shapes by calling the MyShape constructor. We store the shapes in an array of shapes, which form a MyGroup object, and then we draw them on the screen.

```
void setup(){

    for(int y=0; y<numShapes; y++){
        for(int x=0; x<numShapes; x++){
            shape[y*numShapes+x] = new MyShape(5,9.,x*20., y*20.);
        }
    }
    group = new MyGroup(numShapes*numShapes, shape);
}
```

Since these shapes are stored in an array, we should be able to *select* them. All we need is an x and y mouse point for picking and the array of shapes. What we do is simple: first we find which are the closest points to the x, y mouse point and then find to which shape do these points belong. Then, we could color the shape with a color, that is, red, to visualize it as picked.

To accomplish this, you need to create two more data members on each of the four classes we created (MyPoint, MySegment, MyShape, and MyGroup). You also need a boolean, to declare it picked, and a color to paint it. These are

```
boolean isSelected = false;
```

We also need to create a method called select (or pick). So in the case of the class MyPoint, we add the two new members, color and isSelected:

```
1      class MyPoint {
2
3          // members of class
4          float x, y;                    // the coordinates
5          boolean isSelected = false;    // is this point selected?
6
7
8          // Constructor
9           MyPoint(float xin, float yin){
10
11              x = xin;
12              y = yin;
13
14          }
15
16
17          // Move
18            void move(float xoff, float yoff){
19              x = x + xoff;
20              y = y + yoff;
21          }
22
23
24          // Select
25            boolean select(float xpick, float ypick, float tolerance){
26
27              if(abs(x - xpick) < tolerance  &&
28                 abs(y - ypick) < tolerance ) {
29                  isSelected = true;
30                  return true;
31                }
32              else {
33                      isSelected = false;
34                  }
35              return false;
36
37          }
38
39      }
```

The `select()` method gets two coordinates `xpick` and `ypick`, coming from the `myMousePressed`, and a tolerance of how far can a point be, in order to be selected. So, do the following: first, get the absolute distance of the `xpick` and `ypick` from the local `x` and `y` coordinates of the point and then check to see whether they are less than the tolerance value. If they are, then set the boolean `isSelected` to true; otherwise, set it to `false`. Next, the `select()` method returns whether the point was selected or not.

On the `MySegment` level, we do almost the same thing:

```
1    class MySegment {
2
3        // members of class
4        MyPoint start = new MyPoint(0., 0.);    // start point
5        MyPoint end   = new MyPoint(0., 0.);    // end point
6        color blue = color(0,0,255);            // default color
7        color red = color(255,0,0);             // selected color
8        boolean isSelected = false;        // is this segment selected?
9
10
11       // Constructor
12         MySegment(MyPoint p1, MyPoint p2){
13
14             start.x = p1.x;
15             start.y = p1.y;
16             end.x   = p2.x;
17             end.y   = p2.y;
18         }
19
20       // Move
21         void move(float xoff, float yoff){
22
23             start.move(xoff, yoff);
24             end.move(xoff, yoff);
25         }
26
27       // draw
28         void plot(){
29
30             if(isSelected)
31                 stroke(red);
32             else
33                 stroke(blue);
34             line((int)start.x, (int)start.y, (int)end.x, (int)end.y);
35
36         }
37
38       // Select
39         boolean select(float xpick, float ypick, float tolerance){
40
```

```
41                  if(start.select(xpick, ypick, tolerance)==true ||
42                      end.select(xpick, ypick, tolerance)==true)    {
43                      isSelected = true;
44                      return true;
45                  }
46                  else {
47                      isSelected = false;
48                  }
49                  return false;
50              }
51
52
53      }
```

At this level, the select() method gets the two coordinates, xpick and ypick (coming from the myMousePressed), and a tolerance distance value. It then transfers the process to the select() method of the two points start and end. If either one is yes, then set the boolean isSelected to true; otherwise, set it to false. Then return whether the segment was selected or not.

In addition, here, in the plot(..) method, you set the color to red if isSelected is true; otherwise, leave it with the default color.

At the level of the shape, you do almost the same thing as for the segment:

```
1       class MyShape {
2
3           // members of class
4           MySegment[] segs;              // array of segments
5           int numSegments;               // number of segments
6           boolean isSelected = false;    // is this shape selected?
7
8
9           // Constructor
10          MyShape(int numInputSegments, MySegment[] inputSegments){
11

      . . . . .
12          }
13
14
15          // An alternative constructor
16          // Creates
17          MyShape(int numSides, float radius, float xoff, float yoff){
18

      . . . . .
19          }
20
21
22          // Move
23          void move(float xoff, float yoff){
24
```

```
25              for(int i=0; i<numSegments; i++)
26                  segs[i].move(xoff, yoff);
27          }
28
29      // draw
30        void plot( ){
31
32            for(int i=0; i<numSegments; i++)
33                segs[i]. plot(g);
34
35        }
36
37      // Select
38        boolean select(float xpick, float ypick, float tolerance){
39            for(int i=0; i<numSegments; i++){
40                if(segs[i].select(xpick, ypick, tolerance)==true){
41                    isSelected = true;
42                    for(int j=0; j<numSegments; j++)
43                        segs[j].isSelected = true;
44                    return true;
45                }
46                else {
47                    isSelected = false;
48                }
49            }
50          return false;
51        }
52
53  }
```

Now, the select() method gets two coordinates, xpick and ypick (coming from the mouseDown), and a tolerance value. It then transfers the process to the select() method of the segments. If a segment returns true, then you set the boolean isSelected to true; otherwise, set it to false. If a segment was found, that means that the whole shape should be selected. Therefore you loop for all the segments of that shape and set their isSelected value to true.

At the level of MyGroup, it is almost the same structure. I omit it here, but it can be found in the source code on this book's web site. In the main code, you need to call the select() methods, passing the x and y coordinates of the mouse to determine whether a shape was selected within that tolerance:

```
void mousePressed(int x, int y){
    // Pick a shape
for(int i=0; i<group.numShapes; i++)
  if(group.shapes[i].select(mouseX-pmouseX, mousey-pmouseY, 10.)==true)
    println("Selected = " + i);


}
```

All we do is to go through all the shapes of the group and call the `select()` method passing the `x` and `y` coordinates of the mouse and the tolerance (in this case 10.). This will go all the way down into the shape, segment, and point classes and set the `isSelected` values to `true` (if picked). Anything selected will be drawn in red; otherwise, it will be drawn in blue (the default color). If we also want to move the selected shapes while dragging the mouse, we need to add the following code:

```
void mouseDragged(int x, int y){

    int xoff = mouseX - pmouseX;   // get the offset
    int yoff = mouseY - pmouseY;

    for(int i=0; i<group.numShapes; i++)
        if(group.shapes[i].isSelected)
            group.shapes[i].move(xoff, yoff);

}
```

We go through all the shapes, and if they are selected we move them. Figure 3-10 shows the result.

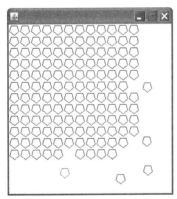

**Figure 3-10:** Selecting and moving objects

## Summary

In this chapter, you have learned about the point, segment, shape, and group hierarchy and their implementation as classes. You also learned about the basic transformations of movement, rotation, and scaling and how to pick and apply them at any level of the hierarchy. It is important to study the source code and, possibly, rewrite it on your own. This will allow you to understand the consistency, flow, and interdependency of the modules as well the potential for mistakes of any kind: spelling, syntax, or logical. The next chapter introduces some graphic user interface (GUI) techniques for additional user interaction.

## Exercises

**NOTE** Answers to the exercises are provided in Appendix B.

1. Construct a class called MyPixel that will contain all information needed to describe and manipulate a pixel. Then construct a class called MyScreen that will represent a computer screen.

2. The following program could not compile successfully. Explain why the program does not work well.

```
MyPoint [] p = new MyPoint[10];
void setup(){
  for(int i=0; i<10; i++)
    rect(p[i].x,p[i].y,5,5);
}
class MyPoint{
  float x, y;
}
```

3. The same problem occurs in this sequence of classes:

```
MySegment seg;
MyPoint p;
void setup(){
  seg = new MySegment();
  seg.a = p;
  println(seg.a);
}
class MyPoint{
  float x, y;
}
class MySegment{
  MyPoint a, b;
}
```

Even though the code compiles without any problems, when you print the value of seg, you get null. Why?

# Basics of Graphical User Interfaces

An interface is a point at which independent systems or diverse groups interact. Specifically, a computer interface is the point of interaction or communication between a computer and any other entity, such as a human operator. While the term interface implies action, control, or supervision, it also suggests reaction, response, and reply as a mutual consequence. An interface is understood as a pair of actions tied up in a feedback cycle. This interactive cycle is of significant value to human cognition because it engages the human mind in a relationship that involves both interaction and control. In that sense, computer interfaces can become intuitive means of merging oneself into an immersive interaction.

Often there is some intermediate component between two systems, which connects their interfaces, for example, a button or a lever. While certain symbols are associated with certain actions or responses, a challenge arises as to how to design new interface components that more accurately or intuitively represent the action to be performed. In this chapter, we will show a few ways of creating graphical user interfaces, using standard library components, and then connect them to geometrical actions.

# 4.1 Basic GUI (Buttons)

GUI (pronounced *gou-ee*) are initials that stand for graphical user interface and refer to all means of communication between the user and a computer system, such as, buttons, dialog boxes, menus, popup windows, and so forth. These elements are designed to convey information to the user about the status of a computer program and to exchange user-input information with the program. GUIs are a rich area of computer graphics, as they involve, apart from practical applications, many theories on how information should be manipulated or represented by a designer. The focus, however, of this book is on 2D and 3D environments, so we will not spend too much time on GUI cognitive theories. For practical purposes, we will use simple GUI elements and start by building a set of buttons and use them to implement transformation operations (i.e., move, rotate, or scale) and to select objects on the screen.

We define a button using a class called `Button` (a Java class):

```
Button b = new Button("Click Here");
add(b);
```

This will create a button and then display it on the screen, as shown in Figure 4-1. It is automatically placed in the center and top of the screen. To alter this layout, use the `setLayout(null)` command, then you can place buttons (or other GUI objects) using `b.setLocation(x,y)` or define their size using the `b.setSize(w,h)` command described in section 4.3.

**Figure 4-1:** A button
displayed on the screen

Although the newly created button is displayed, it is not yet responsive. To make it respond to a user click, we need to add the following lines of code:

```
b.addActionListener(new ActionListener() {
  public void actionPerformed(ActionEvent e) {
    println(b.getLabel());
  }});
```

The first line adds an action listener, which contains a method called actionPerformed, which, in turn, calls the print command to display the label of the button. This code is in Java and runs within the Processing environment.

The following code uses the same setup to construct three buttons within their own class:

```
1   class MyControl{
2     String status = "Move";  //initialize a variable status
3     Button bmove;   //three buttons
4     Button brotate;
5     Button bscale;
6
7     MyControl(){
8     bmove   = new Button("Move");  //create the buttons
9     brotate = new Button("Rotate");
10    bscale  = new Button("Scale");
11    add(bmove); //add them to the screen
12    add(brotate);
13    add(bscale);
14
15      bmove.addActionListener(new ActionListener() {
16      public void actionPerformed(ActionEvent e) {
17        status = bmove.getLabel();
18      }});
19      brotate.addActionListener(new ActionListener() {
20      public void actionPerformed(ActionEvent e) {
21        status = brotate.getLabel();
22      }});
23      bscale.addActionListener(new ActionListener() {
24      public void actionPerformed(ActionEvent e) {
25        status = bscale.getLabel();
26      }});
27    }
28  }
29  MyControl control = new MyControl();
```

So, in the code above, we define three Button objects: bmove, brotate, and bscale, labeled "Move", "Rotate", and "Scale", respectively. These are placed within a class called MyControl that will be used later as a method of grouping GUI elements in the structured code introduced in the previous chapter. In the constructor of the MyControl class, we create the buttons and add them to the main code. This will create three buttons on the screen, which will be placed sequentially, as shown in Figure 4-2. Of course, the buttons will be unresponsive, since they are not connected to any transformation events. Nevertheless, they do change the status variable to whatever their label is (see lines 17, 21, and 25).

**Figure 4-2:** Three
buttons displayed

Now we need to connect the buttons to actions. Specifically, we need to associate the three buttons with the transformation methods of move, rotate, and
scale. So far, the mouse responds to the `mousePressed()` and `mouseDragged()`
methods, using listeners. (A *listener* is a class that "listens", or interrupts, for
events during a session.) As mentioned earlier, there is a Java method that
allows GUI objects, such as buttons, to use listeners in order to return back
useful information to the main program without being placed in the `draw()`
section of the code. So, we add lines 15–26 to the end of the `setup()` method.
These methods invoke the method `ActionListener`, which "listens" for events,
in this case, "button pressed" events. These methods tell the system to listen for
actions associated with the buttons. If a button is pressed, then we can find out
which button was pressed by using the method `getLabel()`, which will return
the labels of that button, that is "Move," "Rotate," or "Scale" and, perhaps, print
out the value for debugging purposes.

Now, we can call the preceding `MyControl` class from the main code to handle
movement, rotation, or scale choices:

```
1    int numShapes = 12;  //num on side of grid of shapes
2    MyShape[] shape = new MyShape[numShapes*numShapes];
3    MyGroup group;
4    MyControl control;   //the control buttons
5
6    void setup(){
7      size(300,300);
8      for(int y=0; y<numShapes; y++){
9        for(int x=0; x<numShapes; x++){  //make a grid of shapes
10           shape[y*numShapes+x] = new MyShape(5,9.,30+x*20., 30+y*20.);
11         }
12       }
13     group = new MyGroup(numShapes*numShapes, shape);
14     group.move(10.,10.);
15     control = new MyControl();
16   }
17
```

```
18   void draw( ){
19      background(255);
20      group.draw();
21   }
22
23   void mousePressed(){
29      for(int i=0; i<group.numShapes; i++)
30        if(group.shapes[i].select((float)mouseX, (float)mouseY, 5.) ==
true){
31          println("Selected = " + i);  //for debug
32        break;   //if an object is found no need to continue
33        }
34   }
35
36   void mouseDragged(){
37      int xoff = mouseX - pmouseX;  // get the offset
38      int yoff = mouseY - pmouseY;
39      MyPoint ref = new MyPoint(0.,0.);
40      for(int i=0; i<group.numShapes; i++)
41        if(group.shapes[i].isSelected){
42          ref = group.shapes[i].centroid();  //this can be constructed
43          if(control.status.equals("Move"))   //Move
44            group.shapes[i].move(( float)xoff, ( float)yoff);
45          if(control.status.equals("Rotate"))   //Rotate
46            group.shapes[i].rotate(( float)xoff, ref);
47          if(control.status.equals("Scale"))  //Scale
48            group.shapes[i].scale((float)mouseX/(float)xfirst,
                                    (float)mouseY/(float)yfirst, ref);
50      }
53   }
```

A MyControl class is declared by the statement:

```
MyControl control;
```

which is defined in the beginning of the program outside of any methods, to make it globally accessible. It is initialized through the statement:

```
control = new MyControl();
```

Once the control class is created, its member "status" can be referenced by using the expression `control.status`. Specifically, if a shape was selected and the control status is equal to "Move", then the `move()` method is used (lines 43–44). The result of this code is shown in Figure 4-3.

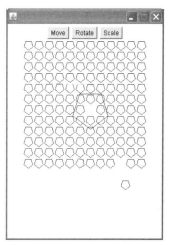

**Figure 4-3:** Basic transformation GUI

# 4.2 Choice, Label, and TextField

A Choice is a pull-down menu. In a `Choice` object, you can select from a list of choices only one at a time. We will create one with three choices, move, rotate, and scale, instead of the three buttons we used earlier. Here is the code:

```
Choice transform;   //definition
transform = new Choice();
transform.addItem("Move");
transform.addItem("Rotate");
transform.addItem("Scale");

 add(transform);
```

We first define the object transform, and then we create it. Next, we add the items of choice, and finally we add the object to the screen. In order to get feedback, we use the following code:

```
transform.addItemListener(new ItemListener() {
  public void itemStateChanged(ItemEvent e) {
    status = transform.getSelectedIndex();
    }
  });
```

The transform choice menu can add functionality to itself by using the `addItemListener`, which listens for item selection. If an item is selected, then the `itemStateChanged` will be activated and the selected item number will be returned through the method `getSelectedIndex`.

A `Label` and a `TextField` are also Java GUI objects that can be called to add extra functionality. Both GUI objects, `Label` and `TextField`, are created in a similar way similar to a `Choice` object:

```
Label coordsDisplay;   //definition
  TextField input;         //definition

  //Label setup
  coordsDisplay = new Label();

  //TextField setup
  input = new TextField("Welcome");

  //display
  add(coordsDisplay);
  add(input);
```

and the TextField action feedback looks like:

```
input.addActionListener(new ActionListener() {
       public void actionPerformed(ActionEvent e) {
             println("textfield = " + input.getText());
          }
    });
```

The input text field can add functionality to itself by using the `addActionListener`, which listens for text input. If an item is selected the `actionPerformed` will be activated and the input text number will be returned through the method `getText`.

## 4.3 Arranging GUI Objects on the Screen

By default, newly created GUI objects are arranged sequentially on the screen, starting from the top center. This is done because, by default, every applet (or application) has a method called `setLayout` that is responsible for setting the GUI elements in a horizontal linear top-down sequence. If we set `setLayout` to null (the default is `FlowLayout`), then we can arrange elements in our own way:

```
setLayout(null);
```

In this way, we have control over the position and size of each GUI element. This is done individually for every element, using their `setSize` and `setLocation` methods:

```
transform.setLocation(200, 0);
transform.setSize(100, 40);
```

In the following code, we will create four GUI elements and we will control their size and location:

```
1    class MyControl{
2       String status = "Move";
3       Button bexit;
4       Choice transform;
5       Label coordsDisplay;
6       TextField input;
7
8       MyControl() {
9        // Button setup
10        bexit = new Button("Exit");
11        bexit.setLocation(width-50, height-30);
12        bexit.setSize(40, 20);
13        // Label setup
14        coordsDisplay = new Label();
15        coordsDisplay.setLocation(10, height-30);
16        coordsDisplay.setSize(100, 20);
17        // TextField setup
18        input = new TextField("Welcome");
19        input.setLocation(10, height-60);
20        input.setSize(width-20, 20);
21        // Choice setup
22        transform = new Choice();
23        transform.addItem("Move");
24        transform.addItem("Rotate");
25        transform.addItem("Scale");
26        transform.setLocation(width/2-50, 0);
27        transform.setSize(100, 40);
28        // Screen setup
29        setLayout(null);  //use the user specified size and location
30        add(transform);
31        add(coordsDisplay);
32        add(input);
33        add(bexit);
34
35        transform.addItemListener(new ItemListener() {
36          public void itemStateChanged(ItemEvent e) {
37            status = transform.getItem(transform.getSelectedIndex());
38            control.input.setText(status);        }});
39        bexit.addActionListener(new ActionListener() {
40          public void actionPerformed(ActionEvent e) {
41            exit();
42          }});
43        input.addActionListener(new ActionListener() {
44           public void actionPerformed(ActionEvent e) {
45            println("textfield = " + input.getText());
46          }});
47      }
48    }
```

```
49   MyControl control;
50   void setup(){
51     size(400,300);
52     background(200);
53     control = new MyControl();
54   }
55   void draw(){
56     control.coordsDisplay.setText("x= " + mouseX +
                          "    y= " + mouseY);
57   }
```

First, we define four objects: a `Button`, a `Choice`, a `Label`, and a `TextField`. Each one is initialized using its corresponding constructor and then we set a location and a size to be displayed. This is done by canceling the automatic placement of objects in the scene with command `setLayout(null)` in line 29. The `Choice` object can invoke its selection by using the `getItem()`, which returns the string label of the selected choice, using `getSelectedIndex`, which returns the number of the choice. The button "Exit" will execute the `exit()` command, which will terminate the session (line 41). The `TextField` object will return any text typed by the user (after a return carriage is typed). Finally, within `draw()` in line 56 there is a method connected with the `MyControl` object `coordsDsiplay`, and it is used here to display the location of the mouse:

```
control.coordsDisplay.setText("x= " + mouseX + "    y= " + mouseY);
```

The resulting GUI is shown Figure 4-4.

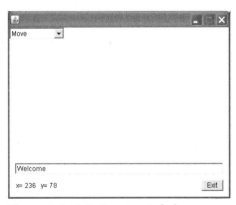

**Figure 4-4:**  A Button, two Labels, a
TextField, and a Choice object

If the new `MyControl` class is replaced in the main code in section 4.2, we are faced with a new (and functional) interface that will look like Figure 4-5.

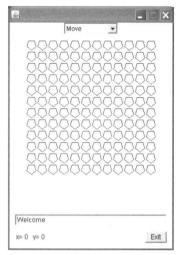

**Figure 4-5:** The new GUI in the old code

# 4.4 Selecting Points, Segments, Shapes, or Groups

In the code introduced in the previous chapter, we have been able to select shapes and move, rotate, or scale them. As a reminder, here is the part of the code that selects shapes:

```
void mousePressed(){
  xfirst = mouseX;  // remember this point
  yfirst = mouseY;
  // Pick a shape
  for(int i=0; i<group.numShapes; i++)
     if(group.shapes[i].select(( float)x, ( float)y, 10.) == true)
       control.input.setText("Selected = " + i);
     }
```

Since we have written our whole project in a point-segment-shape-group class hierarchy, it should be easy for us now to select any object at any level of that hierarchy. All we need to do is go through the levels and extract the classes that we want. So, for example, if we wanted to select a segment in the preceding code, we need to write:

```
// Pick a Segment
for(int i=0; i<group.numShapes; i++)
```

```
for(int j=0; j<group.shapes[i].numSegments; j++)
  if(group.shapes[i].segs[j].select(( float) mouseX,
                                (float) mouseY, 10.) == true)
    control.input.setText("You got Segment=" + j + " of shape="+ i);
```

As you see, we use the dot operator to point to a subclass of a class. For example, `group.shapes[i].segs[j].select` will address the select method of the `segs` object under the `shapes` object under the `group` object. So, to select a point we use the following code:

```
// Pick a Point
for(int i=0; i<group.numShapes; i++)
  for(int j=0; j<group.shapes[i].numSegments; j++)
    if(group.shapes[i].segs[j].start.select(( float) mouseX,
                                  (float) mouseY, 10.) == true)
      control.input.setText("You got Point=" + j + " of shape="+ i);
```

The same applies to moving or rotating a point or a segment. By arranging the graphical user interface, we can break down all the possible combinations of move/rotate/scale operations for any group/shape/segment/point to allow the user to interact in all possible ways. The GUI for this would be:

```
// Choice setup
transform = new Choice();
transform.addItem("Move");
transform.addItem("Rotate");
transform.addItem("Scale");

whatPart = new Choice();
whatPart.addItem("Select Point");
whatPart.addItem("Select Segment");
whatPart.addItem("Select Shape");
whatPart.addItem("Select Group");
```

This will show two choice buttons like those in Figure 4-6.

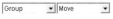

**Figure 4-6:** Two Choice interfaces

Next, we arrange their functionality to select points or segments or shapes or groups in order to move or rotate or scale. An implementation of this is shown in Figure 4-7.

**Figure 4-7:** Selecting groups, shapes, or segments

# 4.5 Color Setup

In our code so far we have been able to select shapes and move/rotate/scale them. But we always assume that all shapes are blue because that is how we define them in the default data member area of each class. If we want to assign a color, we need to create a method that will set the color to a specified input color. This should be put within each class. The method for this is the following:

```
void setColor(color inColor){
    color = inColor;
}
```

The code is the same for all classes (from `MyPoint` to `MyGroup`). Next, we need to draw the object, either with its assigned color or red (to indicate it being selected). So, at the level of `MyPoint`, we need to create a draw point method that will draw a point:

```
void draw( ){
    if(isSelected)
        stroke(255,0,0);  //red
    else
        stroke(0,0,255);  //blue
    rect((int)x, (int)y, 1, 1);
}
```

We use `rect()` to draw a rectangle 1×1 pixel wide that represents, on the screen, a point. At the level of a segment, we do the following:

```
void draw( ){
    if(isSelected)
        stroke(255,0,0);   //red
    else
        stroke(0,0,255);   //blue
    line((int)start.x, (int)start.y, (int)end.x, (int)end.y);

}
```

At the level of the shape (and the group), we do the following:

```
void draw(){
    for(int i=0; i<numSegments; i++)
        segs[i].draw();
  }
```

Now all we need is to set the color for the objects and draw them. For example, in the main code if we want to draw all the shapes green, we write:

```
for(int i=0; i<group.numShapes; i++)
        group.shapes[i].setColor(0,255,0);
```

Similarly, if we want to draw the segments with random colors, we write:

```
for(int i=0; i<group.numShapes; i++)
    for(int j=0; j<group.shapes[i].numSegments; j++)
```

Figure 4-8 shows the output for random-colored segments.

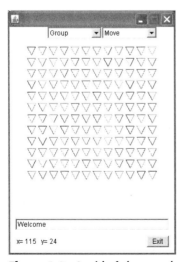

**Figure 4-8:** A grid of shapes where each segment is drawn with a different color

## 4.6 Putting the GUI Elements in Their Own Window

So far we have been mixing the workspace and the GUI elements in the same window. The problem is that the GUI elements may be placed on top of objects, obstructing one's view of them. It would probably be better to put all the GUIs into a floating window so that we can move it around in the screen and work uninterrupted in the drawing canvas area. Here is how this can be done.

First, we need to create a new window, which we will call "Tools" and where the GUI elements will be residing. At this point, we are adding all the GUI elements to the applet through the statement add(). So, we need to make a few modifications to the existing MyControl code:

```java
class MyControl extends Frame{
    Button bexit;
    ...

    MyControl(){

    super("Tools");
    setSize(300,400);
    setLocation(420,0);
    setVisible(true);

        // Button setup
        bexit = new Button("Exit");

        bexit.addActionListener(new ActionListener() {
public void actionPerformed(ActionEvent e) {
System.exit(0);
}
    });

        add(bexit);
    ...
    }
```

We first extend MyControl to be a Frame object, and we construct it by using the super() method. The super() method declares the name of a window that is dependent on the main window. Next, we set the size and location and then we show it. We then add any GUI elements we created to the MyControl class and not to the main window. This will produce the output shown in Figure 4-9.

Of course, the tool window can be moved and scaled to the user's convenience.

The main code knows about the GUI changes because it is notified of everything through flags, such as the status variable in MyControl, which is accessed as control.status in the main code.

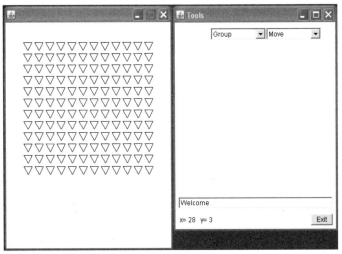

**Figure 4-9:** GUI objects are put in a separate window.


## 4.7 Mouse Wheel Control

Some mice have a middle wheel that can be rolled back and forth. The turns of the wheel can be recorded using the following code:

```
int wheel;
void setup(){
   addMouseWheelListener(new MouseWheelListener() {
      public void mouseWheelMoved(MouseWheelEvent e){
         println(wheel += e.getWheelRotation());
      }});
}
```

This code can be used to get the value of the wheel's rotations and can be further used to scroll the screen or to zoom in and out.


## Summary

In this chapter, you were introduced to the structure of the basic Java GUI elements: buttons, labels, text fields, and choice lists. Most importantly, their connection to the shapes and colors on the screen was pointed out.

# Exercises

**NOTE** Answers to the exercises are provided in Appendix B.

1. Read the Java documentation for the classes:

   ```
   Button
   ```

   ```
   Label
   ```

   ```
   TextField
   ```

   ```
   Choice
   ```

   Read about their constructor methods and their event listeners. Then create each one in a separate class and give it functionality (i.e., select, transform).

2. To display a `Button` with a size of $30 \times 30$ at position 100, 100 you need to do the following:

   ```
   Button b = new Button("Click Here");
   b.setSize(30, 30);
   b.setLocation(100, 100);
    add(b);
   ```

   What is missing?

3. Choose the method that Processing does not support:

   A. `mouseDragged ()`

   B. `mouseUp ()`

   C. `mousePressed ()`

   D. `mouseButton ()`

# CHAPTER 5

# Image Processing

An image is a two-dimensional reproduction of the form of an object. As a reproduction of something else, an image is associated with the notions of representation, interpretation, duplication, and sampling. While an image appears to be an exact copy of its target, for practical purposes an image contains only enough information to convey the impression of a copy. Sampling and resolution are parameters that determine the degree of resemblance between source and image.

Because of their representational nature, images are associated, often directly, with the objects they represent. While photographs or film may convey an almost perfect degree of resemblance to reality, paintings and drawings entail a certain degree of personal, private, and idiosyncratic interpretation of reality. Rather than representing reality as is, subtle alterations of the parameters of an image may affect the viewer's apprehension and stir emotions or convey indirect messages. Furthermore, juxtaposition, collage, superimposition, filtering, and other image-related operations can be used to shift between the limits of what something is and what something appears to be. This chapter shows you certain techniques for processing images to produce either an alteration of a local area or a global affect in the form of a filter.

## 5.1 Displaying Images

An image in Processing is an array of pixels. Displaying an image is straightforward. Processing (as well as Java) has built-in methods that read `.gif`, `.jpg`, `.tga`, and `.png` image file formats. The method is:

```
PImage myImage = loadImage("memorial.jpg");
```

where the only parameter needed is the path location of the image. If the image is called memorial.jpg and it is in the data directory of the Processing Sketch folder, then you would type it in the form of a string, that is, `"memorial.jpg"`. Otherwise, you would give the full path, that is, `"C:/images/memorial.jpg"` (use forward slashes). The following code demonstrates how to read an image and then display it:

```
1 PImage myImage;                         //define a PImage object
2 myImage = loadImage("memorial.jpg");   //load an image
3 size(myImage.width, myImage.height);   //size the window to the w and h
                                         //or the image
4 image(myImage, 0, 0);                  //display the image at 0,0 offset from
                                         //the window's upper left corner
5 save("copy of memorial.jpg");          //save the image as a file (copy for now)
```

The output is shown in Figure 5-1.

**Figure 5-1:** An image

# 5.2 Preset Image Filters

Processing offers a series of preset filters that can be applied to any image. The command filter() applies a filter to an image using the following syntax:

> filter(*MODE*);   or   filter(*MODE*, *level*);

where *MODE* is one of the following:

- THRESHOLD: Converts the image to black or white pixels, depending on whether they are above or below the threshold defined by the *level* parameter. The level must be between 0.0 (black) and 1.0 (white). If no level is specified, 0.5 is used.

- GRAY: Converts any colors in the image to grayscale equivalents.

- INVERT: Sets each pixel to its inverse value.

- POSTERIZE: Limits each channel of the image to the number of colors specified as the level parameter.

- BLUR: Executes a Gaussian blur with the *level* parameter specifying the extent of the blurring. If no *level* parameter is used, the blur is equivalent to Gaussian blur of radius 1.

- OPAQUE: Sets the alpha channel to entirely opaque.

The following code demonstrates how to display images to which filters are applied:

```
1    PImage myImage;                        //define an image object
2    myImage = loadImage("memorial.jpg"); //load it
3    size(myImage.width,myImage.height);   //size it to fit the window
4    image(myImage, 0,0);                   //display the image
5
6    int filter = 1;                       //choose a filter
7
8    switch(filter) {
9    case 1:
10     filter(THRESHOLD, .6); //every pixel below .6 becomes black
11     break;
12   case 2:
13     filter(GRAY); //all pixels get the average value of their rgb
14     break;
15   case 3:
16     filter(INVERT); //all pixels get the opposite value of their rgb
17     break;          // (i.e. 255-r)
18   case 4:
19     filter(POSTERIZE, 2); //limits each channel of the image to 2
20     break;                //  colors
21   case 5:
22     filter(BLUR, 1); // executes a Guassian blur with radius 1
23     break;
```

```
24  case 6:
25    filter(BLUR, 6); // executes a Guassian blur with radius 6
26    break;
27  }
28  save("memorial_filter_"+filter+".jpg");  // save the image
    // as a numbered file
```

After loading and displaying the image, an integer variable called `filter` is defined and set to 1 (see line 6). A series of cases are created to apply the filter modes. Notice that some filter commands take a second parameter that indicates the level to which the filter is to be applied, that is, `filter(BLUR, 6)`. In the last line (28), we save the image using the `save()` command and name it using the filter index. The various filters used are demonstrated in Figure 5-2.

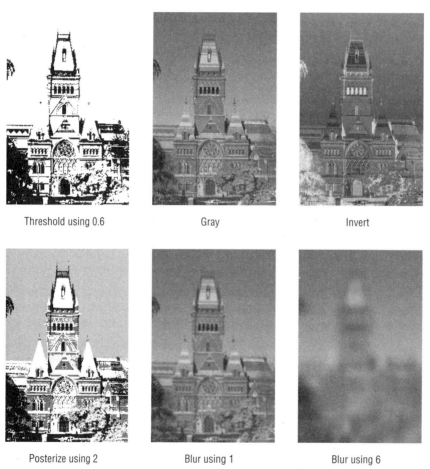

| | | |
|---|---|---|
| Threshold using 0.6 | Gray | Invert |
| Posterize using 2 | Blur using 1 | Blur using 6 |

**Figure 5-2:** A series of filters applied (from top left clockwise): threshold, gray, invert, blur (level 6), blur (level 1), and posterize

Every pixel's color can be queried or assigned by using the `get()` and `set()` methods. In that way, filters can be constructed by using these two methods for pixel color manipulation. The following code demonstrates a filter that inverts the pixel color value for every pixel in the image:

```
1    PImage myImage;                          //define an image object
2    myImage = loadImage("memorial.jpg"); //load it
3    size(myImage.width,myImage.height);  //size it to fit the window
4    image(myImage, 0,0);                     //display the image
5
6    for(int y=0; y<myImage.height; y++)  //for all pixels in y
7       for(int x=0; x<myImage.width; x++){ //for all pixels in x
8         color myPixel = get(x,y);        //get a pixel's color
9         int a = int(alpha(myPixel));     //extract the alpha value
10        int r = int(red(myPixel));       //extract the red value
11        int g = int(green(myPixel));     //extract the green value
12        int b = int(blue(myPixel));      //extract the blue value
13        color inverse = color(255-a,255-r,255-g,255-b);
                                 //make a color by inverting (255-value)
14        set(x,y,inverse);      //set the pixel's color in the image
15      }
16   save("memorial_inverted.jpg");          // save the image as a file
```

Lines 6 and 7 loop through all pixels in the image in both y and x directions to extract the color value of every pixel (line 8). We use the `get()` method, which takes the x and y coordinate of a pixel and returns its color. Next, in lines 9 through 12, we extract the alpha, red, green, and blue values of the pixel's color. Then we compose a new color by adding four channels using the `set()` command for alpha, red, green, and blue, except that we reverse their values by subtracting them from the maximum value of a byte, that is, 255. The result can be seen to the left in Figure 5-3.

While the filters provided by Processing are adequate for simple, basic image processing, this does not allow experimentation beyond that simple level. In contrast, the `get()` and `set()` operations can be used to produce interesting filters that can be used in many creative ways. For example, the following code builds upon the existing grayscale filter provided by Processing and further extracts edges by marking the difference between consecutive neighboring pixels:

```
1    PImage myImage;                          //define an image object
2    myImage = loadImage("memorial.jpg"); //load it
3    size(myImage.width,myImage.height);  //size it to fit the window
4    image(myImage, 0,0);                     //display the image
5
6    // convert the image to grayscale
7    filter(GRAY);
8
9    color white = color(255,255,255);    //define white
10   color black = color(0,0,0);          //define black
```

```
11   //extract edges
12   for(int y=0; y<myImage.height-1; y++)     //for all pixels in y
13     for(int x=0; x<myImage.width-1; x++){ //for all pixels in x
14       color thisPixel = get(x,y);     //get a pixel's color
15       color nextPixel = get(x+1,y);   //get the next pixel's color
16       int ra = int(red(thisPixel));   //extract the red value
17       int rb = int(red(nextPixel));   //extract the red of the next
18       if(abs(ra-rb)>6)                //if they are different
19           set(x,y,black);             //set the pixel's color black
20       else
21           set(x,y,white);             //else to white
22     }
23   save("memorial_edge.jpg");          // save the image as a file
```

After loading the image, we filter it so that it becomes gray by using Processing's filter. Then we extract every pixel's color from the image, using `get(x,y)`, and also the next pixel, using `get(x+1,y)`. We then extract the red part of both neighboring pixels and compare their values. If the difference is more than 6, then we set the current pixel to black; otherwise, to white. The result can be seen to the right in Figure 5-3.

**Figure 5-3:** An inverted image (left) and an image that contains only the high differential points in the x direction (right)

Instead of changing the color value of a pixel, it may be possible to change its location within an image. This can be done by coloring one pixel with the color of another pixel. The following code demonstrates this displacement operation, which results in a fairly interesting impression:

```
1    PImage MyImage = loadImage("memorial.jpg");
2    size(MyImage.width, MyImage.height);
3    image(MyImage,0,0);
4
```

```
5    for(int x=2; x<width-2; x++)   //for all rows
6      for(int y=2; y<height-2; y++){ //for all columns
7        color c = get(x,y);
8        //make sure the values fall between 0-255
9        int xx = x+int(random(-3,3));
10       int yy = y+int(random(-3,3));
11       set(xx,yy,c); //color the pixel
12       fill(c);
13       noStroke();
14       rect(xx-5,yy-5,4,4);
15     }
```

After extracting the color of a pixel (line 7), we create two random numbers and add them the values x and y. This displaced location is then used to draw a 4 × 4 rectangle at that location. The result of this operation is shown in Figure 5-4.

Original image                   Displaced image

**Figure 5-4:** The original image (left) and a displaced pixel image (right)

While the preceding code is still quite simple and straightforward, it is also slow in execution. This is because the set(), get(), int(), alpha(), red(), green(), and blue() methods add an extra overhead to the overall number of computations for all pixels in the image. In order to optimize the get(), set(), and color extractions for every pixel, we will use bit-level manipulations, which are demonstrated in the following section.

## 5.3 Bit Manipulation on Pixels

The value of a pixel is represented in Processing (and Java) as an integer. In that sense, an image is an array of integers. An integer is composed of 32 bits or 4 bytes. So Processing uses those 4 bytes to store information about the pixel's color. Specifically, the first byte (i.e., eight bits) are for the degree of *transparency* (also known as *alpha channel*), the second byte for *red*, the third byte for *green*, and the fourth byte for *blue*. Schematically, the bits of an integer, representing a pixel, look like Figure 5-5.

| Alpha | Red | Green | Blue |
|-------|-----|-------|------|
| 00000000 | 00000000 | 00000000 | 00000000 |

**Figure 5-5:** The bits of an integer representing a pixel.

To get access to a color, we need to do manipulation at the bit level to extract the proper 8 bits. This is done through bit-manipulation methods provided by Processing. In brief, the process is shown below. Suppose that we have a pixel called myPixel.

```
int myPixel;
int alpha    =( myPixel & 0xff000000)>>24;
int red      =( myPixel & 0xff0000)>>16;
int green    =( myPixel & 0xff00)>>8;
int blue     =( myPixel & 0xff);
```

The variables alpha, red, green, and blue contain the corresponding values for that pixel. To get the value of red, we AND (using the symbol &) with the hexadecimal number oxff0000, and then we shift the bits (using the symbol >>) by 16 positions. This will return only the second group of 8 bits that holds the value of red. So, for example, the color red is represented as:

```
00000000111111110000000000000000
```

In this bit sequence above, the first 8 bits are the alpha channel (i.e., transparency), the next 8 bits are the color red, and the rest of the bits are for green and blue. Now, we want to determine which bits are set to 1 in order to determine what color this sequence of bits represents. We are not interested in what decimal integer this is (which happens to be 16,711,680 or $2^{23}+2^{22}+2^{21}+2^{20}+2^{19}+2^{18}+2^{17}+2^{16}$). To extract the value of a byte, we use the bit-wise operations >> and << to shift bits right or left, respectively. For example, to extract the value of red from the above set of bits, we shift the bits by 16 positions right and then add the binary set:

```
00000000000000000000000011111111
```

or, in hexadecimal format 0xFF, to clean up any 1's that may exist in the first 24 to 8 bit range. So, for example, if we are given the color represented as:

```
00110110 00101110 10010100 00101111
```

and we want to find the amount of red, we first shift the bits by 16 positions:

```
00000000 00000000 00110110 00101110
```

and then we add `0xFF`:

```
    00000000   00000000   00110110   00101110
&   00000000   00000000   00000000   11111111
    00000000   00000000   00000000   00101110
```

Notice that in the & operator 1 & 1 = 1, 1 & 0 = 0, 0 & 1 = 0, and 0 & 0 = 0. So, the alpha byte becomes zero, and the red byte remains as is. The result of the operation yields an integer that is the value of red (i.e., in this case, it is 46). In the following example, a filter is applied to an image using bit-wise operations:

```
1    PImage myImage;                       //define an image object
2    myImage = loadImage("memorial.jpg");  //load it
3    size(myImage.width,myImage.height);   //size it to fit the window
4    image(myImage, 0,0);                  //display the image
5
6    loadPixels();                 //get access to the array of pixels[]
7
8    for(int index=0;index<width*height;index++)
9    {
10     int myPixel = pixels[index];  //get a pixel value
11     int r = myPixel >> 16 & 0xFF; // get red(myPixel)
12     int g = myPixel >> 8 & 0xFF;  // get green(myPixel)
13     int b = myPixel & 0xFF;       // get blue(myPixel)
14     int av= (g + b) /2;       // average only green and blue
15     if(av>128){  //e.g. if av is 00000000 00000000 00000000 11111111
16       r = av << 16;   // Binary: 00000000 11111111 00000000 00000000
17       g = av << 8;    // Binary: 00000000 00000000 11111111 00000000
18       b = av;             // Binary: 00000000 00000000 00000000 11111111
19       pixels[index] = r | g | b; //compose a color using bitwise OR
20     }
21   }
22
23   updatePixels();               // see the result
24
25   save("memorial_altered.jpg");  // save the image as a file
```

In line 6, the command `loadPixels()` loads the pixels in an array called `pixels[]`. Each pixel is then extracted by looping sequentially (line 10) through the number of pixels of the image (i.e., width*height). Each pixel is an integer called `myPixel`. In lines 11, 12, and 13 the red, green, and blue values of each pixel is extracted using the right shift bit operation (see the previous paragraphs). Once the RGB values are extracted, they are manipulated as integers (in this case, we average the green and blue values). Then, based on whether the average is above 128 or not, we compose an integer out of the RGB values: using `av` we shift its last 8 bits by 16 positions left to populate the red byte. Then we shift its last 8 bits by 8 positions left to populate the green byte. The blue byte occupies the last part of the integer, so it is left intact. Then we use the bit operation OR to compose the color that we put back into the `pixels[]` array. After completing these operations for all pixels, we update the screen with the new values placed in the `pixels[]` array. The result of this process is shown in Figure 5-6.

**Figure 5-6:** A custom-made "average-green-and-blue-over-128" filter

Image manipulation is a powerful tool. It allows us, as humans, to see and interpret the images further. However, for the computer, an image is simply a long array of numbers. So we, as human beings, need to create algorithms that take advantage of the computational power of the machine and allow us to explore images beyond what we can see with our eyes.

## 5.4 A Paint Brush Tool

One common problem with images is that even though they are viewed by human beings as two-dimensional grids, for a computer the pixel information is stored in a one-dimensional array. In other words, Processing provides us with a one-dimensional array (i.e., `pixels[]`) that corresponds to a two-dimensional image. So we need to go from two to one and from one to two dimensions (see Figure 5-7).

To address this problem, we use the following technique that allows us to extract the index of the one-dimensional array `pixels[]` from two counters `x` and `y`:

```
for(int y=0; y<height; y++)
    for(int x=0; x<width; x++)
        int myPixel = pixels[y*width+x];
```

```
pixels[0*w + 0]            (0,0)  (1,0)  (2,0)  (3,0)  (4,0)  . . .  (w,0)
pixels[0*w + 1]            (0,1)  (1,1)  (2,1)  (3,1)  (4,1)  . . .  (w,1)
pixels[0*w + 2]            (0,2)  (1,2)  (2,2)  (3,2)  (4,2)  . . .  (w,2)
pixels[0*w + 3]            (0,3)  (1,3)  (2,3)  (3,3)  (4,3)  . . .  (w,0)
pixels[0*w + 4]   <--->    (0,4)  (1,4)  (2,4)  (3,4)  (4,4)  . . .  (w,4)
  . . .                                        . . .
  . . .                                        . . .
pixels[y*w + x]            (0,h)  (1,h)  (2,h)  (3,h)  (4,h)  . . .  (w,h)
```

**Figure 5-7:** Mapping of a two-dimensional array to a one-dimensional one

In the next section, we will create a mouse-based user interaction with the pixels in the screen in the form of a simple paint brush. Here, the paint brush is a 20 × 20 pixel square that will be updated as the mouse is dragged around the image and the one-dimensional array pixels[] is also updated.

To add interaction to an image, we incorporate the image filtering in the mouseDragged() method:

```
1    PImage myImage;                            //define an image object
2
3    void setup(){
4      myImage = loadImage("memorial.jpg"); //load it
5      size(myImage.width,myImage.height);  //size it to fit the window
6      image(myImage, 0,0);                 //display the image
7      loadPixels();                        //load the pixels
8    }
9    //**********
10   void draw(){
11   }
12   //********* drag to simulate a paint brush
13   void mouseDragged(){
14     for(int y=mouseY-10; y<mouseY+10; y++) //for a 20x20 brush area
15       for(int x=mouseX-10; x<mouseX+10; x++){
16         int xx = constrain(x,0,width-1);   //do not exceed the screen
17         int yy = constrain(y,0,height-1);
18         pixels[yy*width+xx] = pixels[yy*width+xx]^0x0000FF;
19       }                                    //invert blue
20     updatePixels();
             //update to see the changes
21   }
22   //********** Save just in case it is needed
23   void keyPressed(){
24     save("memorial_inverted.jpg");
25   }
```

After defining, loading, and displaying an image, we use the loadPixels() command to populate the pixels[] array. The pixels[] array is the default system array that holds the colors of all pixels of an image. In the mouseDragged()

section, we loop within a 20 × 20 area (i.e., the area of the virtual paint brush). This is done by using the mouseX and mouseY coordinates and looping 10 pixels around it. The constrain() command makes sure that the mouse does not try to draw outside the canvas window. Next, we use the 2D to 1D conversion formula discussed earlier to extract the value of each pixel. This value is inverted at the blue byte and then assigned back to the image (line 18). After updating the image, we can see the effect of a brush that inverts the pixels in a 20 × 20 area. The result is shown to the left in Figure 5.8.

The "pixelating" effect occurs because we are reversing the pixels over and over within the same area. As the mouse is dragged, the 20 × 20 area is inverted, but as the mouse moves by one pixel the same pixel is inverted back to its original color. To avoid this situation, we need to make a copy of the original image and use it to extract colors but not write to it. In the following code this problem is addressed:

```
1    PImage myImage;   //define an image object
2    PImage cpImage;   //define a copy image
3
4    void setup(){
5      myImage = loadImage("memorial.jpg"); //load it
6      cpImage = loadImage("memorial.jpg"); //load the copy
7      size(myImage.width,myImage.height);   //size it to fit the window
8      image(myImage, 0,0);                  //display the image
9      loadPixels();                         //load the pixels
10   }
11   //**********
12   void draw(){
13   }
14   //********* drag to simulate a paint brush
15   void mouseDragged(){
16     for(int y=mouseY-10; y<mouseY+10; y++) //for a 10x10 brush area
17       for(int x=mouseX-10; x<mouseX+10; x++){
18         int xx = constrain(x,0,width-1);   //do not exceed the screen
19         int yy = constrain(y,0,height-1);
20         //read from the copy and update the image
21         pixels[yy*width+xx] = cpImage.pixels[yy*width+xx]^0x0000FF;
         //invert  blue
22       }
23     //copy the two images
24     myImage.copy(cpImage, 0,0,width,height,0,0,width,height);
25     updatePixels();                       //update to see the changes
26   }
```

In line 2 we define an image (cpImage) that will be the copy of the original image (myImage). This is loaded in the same way as the original. The difference from the previous paint brush code is in line 21; we read the pixel value of the copy image but update the original:

```
pixels[yy*width+xx] = cpImage.pixels[yy*width+xx]^0x0000FF;
//invert  blue
```

When finished with the 20 × 20 pixels, we copy one image into the other in order to update the changes:

```
myImage.copy(cpImage, 0,0,width,height,0,0,width,height);
```

The code that demonstrates this technique is shown above, and the effect is captured to the right in Figure 5-8.

**Figure 5-8:** Inverting the pixels, using a 20 × 20 paint brush

## 5.5 Edge Detection

An important part of image processing is the quantitative measurement of pixels to determine certain characteristics of the depicted object. In satellite image analysis, counting pixels can help determine amounts, ratios, or comparisons between various areas within an image or across images. One of them is edge detection. Edge detection is a method of finding pixels that have a high differential value in brightness value compared to their neighboring pixels. In other words, we compare neighboring pixels one by one and mark only the ones that have a subtraction difference that exceeds a certain threshold. The following code demonstrates how to detect edges in an image:

```
1   int [] xd = {0,1,1,1,0,-1,-1,-1,0}; //neighbors' x index cw (top)
2   int [] yd = {1,1,0,-1,-1,-1,0,1,1}; //neighbors' y index cw (top)
3   PImage MyImage = loadImage("stockholm.jpg"); //load an image
```

```
4   size(MyImage.width,MyImage.height);  //size to match the image
5   image(MyImage, 0,0);                  //display the image
6   int [][] MyCopy = new int[width][height];  // array equal to image
7   for(int x=1; x<width-1; x++)          //for all pixels (except border)
8     for(int y=1; y<height-1; y++){
9       int b=0;
10      int a=0;
11      for(int i=0; i<8; i++){
12        if(brightness(get(x+xd[i],y+yd[i]))<128)        //case 1
13          b++;
14        if(brightness(get(x+xd[i],y+yd[i]))<128 &&
15          brightness(get(x+xd[i+1],y+yd[i+1]))>128)     //case 2
16          a++;
17      }
18      if((b>=2 && b<=6) || a==1 )
19        MyCopy[x][y]=1;                  //mark these ones as edges
20      else
21        MyCopy[x][y]=0;
22    }
23
24  for(int x=1; x<width-1; x++)           //go through all pixels
25    for(int y=1; y<height-1; y++){
26      if(MyCopy[x][y]==1)                //if they are marked
27        set(x,y,color(0,0,0));           //paint them black
28      else
29        set(x,y,color(255,255,255));     //else white
30    }
31  save("MyImage.jpg");                   //save just incase
```

The first two lines of code define the x and y offset for every pixel P1 in order to determine their eight neighbors in a clockwise fashion, starting from the top (as shown in Figure 5-9 (a)). Lines 3, 4, and 5 are simply the loading and displaying of an image (in this case Stockholm.jpg). In line 6 memory is allocated for a copy of all the pixels in the image. This will be used later to mark the edge pixels. Then we go through all pixels and we consider two cases: In the second case we use a counter b to count the number of dark neighboring pixels (that is, pixels below a threshold of 128). In the first case, we use a counter a to count the number of consecutive dark pixels). So in the examples shown in Figure 5-9 (b), (c), and (d) the left pattern (b) would amount to b=2 and a=0, the middle pattern (c) to b=2 and a=0, and the right pattern (d) to b=3 and a=0.

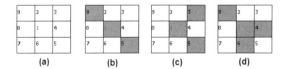

**Figure 5-9:** An eight-neighbor arrangement for a center pixel (a) and three cases (b), (c), and (d) where some neighboring pixels form patterns of gray and white

In line 18, we mark the pixels that have b between 2 and 6 and a as 1. These are edge pixels, which we later mark in the image in lines 24 to 30. This algorithm is one of many used in image processing. The result of this algorithm can be seen in Figure 5-10.

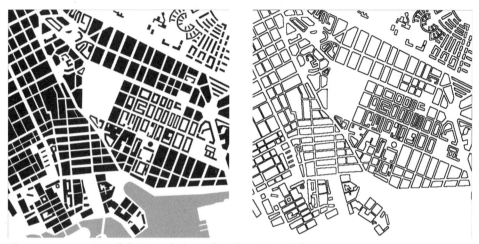

**Figure 5-10:** Original (left) and after edge detection (right)

## Summary

In this chapter, you were introduced to image reading, displaying, processing, and interaction. You are now able to display an image, filter its colors, and use the mouse to affect certain areas of the image. These operations are important for graphics because images are very strong visual elements. Any alteration to their content can affect their interpretation.

## Exercises

**NOTE** Answers to the exercises are provided in Appendix B.

1. Consider a two-dimensional integer array, which is a 4 × 3 and named "a." The data is

```
a[0][0]=0      a[0][1]=2      a[0][2]=4      a[0][3]=6
a[1][0]=8      a[1][1]=10     a[1][2]=12     a[1][3]=14
a[2][0]=16     a[2][1]=18     a[2][2]=20     a[2][3]=22
```

We want to make a new one-dimensional array named "b" in which to store a's data. In other words, the data of "b" should be:

```
b[0]=0    b[1]=2   b[3]=4   . . .   b[11]=22
```

Which is the correct program?

```
int[] b = new int[12];
for (int i=0; i<3; i++) {
    for (int j=0; j<4; j++) {
        //***** Choose one from A, B, C, and D.
    }
}
```

A. `b[i]        = a[i][j];`

B. `b[j*4 + i] = a[i][j];`

C. `b[i*4 + j] = a[j][i];`

D. `b[i*4 + j] = a[i][j];`

2. Modify the code at section 5.4 so that when the mouse gets close or beyond the boundaries of the image the inversion of pixels stops.

3. Write the code that will take an image and create a perforated pattern of circles based on each pixel's brightness, as shown in the following image:

4. You are given a 100 × 100 image called "spill.gif" (see the image at the left of the following figure; the background is in white and foreground is black). Write the code that would convert it so that the background becomes red and the foreground white, as it appears to the left in the

following figure. (Note that the figures in this book are black and white, but the original shows a red background.)

```
PImage MyImage = loadImage("spill.gif");
image(MyImage,0,0);

for(int x=0; x<width; x++)
  for(int y=0; y<height; y++){
}
```

5. Write the code that would produce an effect of pixel shrinking that will lead toward a skeleton, as shown in the following figure.

# CHAPTER 6

Motion is the act or process of changing position or place. While the perception of motion is based on the assumption that time is continuous, human vision per se is not continuous. Instead, as the distance between "before" and "after" diminishes, it reaches a point where both appear to blend in a continuous succession. The impression of motion is, therefore, only a reconstruction in the mind of a sequential display of static impressions.

Animation is the sequential display of images. While the connotations associated with animation points to films, movies, or cartoons, the root of the word "animation" stems from the Greek word "anemos," which means wind, as in the wind that blows life into lifeless forms. Animation is about the alive, lively, vibrant, vigorous, dynamic, and energetic. In its primordial sense, animation is a sign of life, an indication of a living organism. In this chapter, we will show how to create single and multiple animated objects as well as ways to simulate dynamic behavior.

## 6.1 Animation Basics

In our previous examples, we have created animation by repainting the graphics on every mouse movement. As you may have noticed, that was a controlled animation. Eventually, we may want to set an object in motion independently of the mouse's movement. To make things even more complicated, we may want to set a series of objects in motion and control their behavior through a common clock. This involves understanding of the basics of a computer clock. As you already know, computers have internal clocks that tick extremely fast, that is, for example, 1 GHz, which means a billion ticks per second. When we do animation, we need to use that clock as a guide of time. Sometimes we also need to keep track of two or more animations as they are deployed in parallel in the scene. For example, in a car race video game, there may be one car moving, and at the same time other cars that need to bypassed, not to mention moving obstacles on the road. It seems that these animations are happening in parallel. But practically that cannot happen because then we would need parallel processors, each taking care of one moving object. Instead, what we do is to divide the processor time in small time sections, called *threads*, each keeping track of an animated object in the scene. This is not too hard to do for the processor, since theoretically it can take care of 1 billion things every second!

In the following example, a maple leaf is drawn on a brown background and then redrawn after moving it by a random offset to produce the effect of trembling. The process is quite simple:

```
1    PImage leafImage;  //define an image object
2    PImage myBackImage;  //define an image object
3
4    void setup(){
5      leafImage = loadImage("maple_leaf.gif");  //load it
6      myBackImage = loadImage("ground.jpg");  //load it
7      size(myBackImage.width,myBackImage.height);
8    }
9
10   int x, y;  //the location of the cursor
11   void draw(){
12     image(myBackImage,0,0);  //draw the ground
13     image(leafImage,x,y);    //then the leaf
14     x += int(random(-5,5));  //random tremblings
15     y += int(random(-5,5));
16   }
17
18   void mouseDragged(){
19     x = mouseX-(leafImage.width/2);  //move the cursor
20     y = mouseY-(leafImage.height/2);
21   }
```

In the first two lines of the preceding code we define two images that are loaded in lines 5 and 6. The size of the screen is then set to the background image's size. Before we draw we define two integer variables $x$ and $y$ to hold the coordinate location of where to draw the leaf image[1] (line 13). These two coordinates are randomly moved by five units every time the frame is refreshed. The leaf image can be moved to any location in the screen simply by dragging it. A screen capture of the process is shown in Figure 6-1.

**Figure 6-1:** A leaf trembling on top of the ground

Suppose now that we want to draw multiple leaves that tremble at different speeds to produce an autumn scene. This process involves two modifications of the previous code. First, we need to create an object (i.e., a class) that would hold information about each leaf. Then we need to use the speed of the clock and draw each leaf one at a time. However, while those leaves that are redrawn at the speed of the clock will be the fastest, the ones that are redrawn at the same position twice or more will appear to be moving at half-speed and so on. For example, if the rate of redrawing an image is 4, that is, it is drawn at a new position only every four clock ticks that will make it appear to move at a quarter of the speed of another leaf with speed 1. So, in the definition of the class, we will use that principle to control the speed of each leaf. We define therefore a class called `Leaf`:

```
1    class Leaf {
2       int x, y;  //the leaf's position
3       PImage picture;  //an image object
4       int rate;  //rate of waiting to be redrawn
5
6       Leaf(){  //constructor
7         x = int(random(width));  //get an initial location
8         y = int(random(height));
9         picture = loadImage("maple_leaf.gif");  //get the image
10      }
11
12   int k=0;  //a counter
13      void draw() {
```

```
14        if(k==rate){  //if the counter is as the rate then draw
15          x += int(random(-5,5));  //random tremblings
16          y += int(random(-5,5));
17          k=0;  //reset the counter
18          }
19        k++;  //increate the counter; during every increment there is no draw
20          image(picture,x,y);  //now draw the image
21        }
22    }
```

The class Leaf contains the following variables: two coordinates, an image, and a rate. The rate is an integer number that indicates the number of times to wait before redrawing the image. Line 6 contains the constructor information about the leaf, that is, defining a random initial location and loading the image (maple_leaf.gif). Before drawing the image we define a counter k. This is used to skip drawing the image until the counter is equal to the rate (line 14). If they are equal, we draw the image at a randomly offset location; otherwise, we increase the counter k. This technique allows an image to be drawn at a variable rate resulting in a variable speed of trembling motion.

In the main code we define a number of leaves to be created that we put into an array myLeaf[]. Then, we loop through the number of leaves and create a Leaf object and assign it a random rate between 2 and 20 (line 10). Next, we draw all the leaves, but since each one has a different rate the overall result is a variable speed motion. We assume here that the frame rate is at a default 60 frames per second (fps). So, if the rate is 6 that means that a leaf will not be redrawn for six times, giving it a perceived frame rate of 10 fps (i.e., six times slower movement).

```
1     int numLeaves = 400;  //number of leaves to draw
2     PImage myBackImage;  //define a backgound image
3     Leaf[] myLeaf = new Leaf[numLeaves];  //define a Leaf object
4
5     void setup(){
6       myBackImage = loadImage("ground.jpg");  //load it
7       size(myBackImage.width,myBackImage.height);  //size screen to the image
8       for(int i=0; i<numLeaves; i++){  //for all the number of leaves
9         myLeaf[i] = new Leaf();  //create a Leaf object
10        myLeaf[i].rate=int(random(2,20));
11      }
12    }
13
14    void draw(){
15      image(myBackImage, 0,0);  //draw first the backgound
16      for(int i=0; i<numLeaves; i++)
17        myLeaf[i].draw();  //draw all the leaves
18    }
```

The result of this process can be seen in Figure 6-2:

**Figure 6-2:** Multiple leaves of variable trembling speed

## 6.2 Erratic Motion

In the previous section, you saw how an image can be used to produce the impression of animation simply by altering its position and redrawing the screen. If the process of redrawing the screen is fast enough (or less than a tenth of a second), then the image appears to move relative to its previous position. The same effect can be accomplished with geometrical entities by simply drawing to the screen and redrawing the background. For instance, in the following code we will redraw a small circle after moving it by a slight random location away from its previous position:

```
1   void setup(){
2     size(300,300);
3     frameRate(30);
4   }
5   float x,y;
6   void draw(){
7     background(255);
8       x = x + random(-3,3);
9       y = y + random(-3,3);
```

```
10      ellipse(x,y,10,10);
11   }
12   void mousePressed(){
13     x = mouseX;
14     y = mouseY;
15   }
```

In line 3 we set the frame rate, that is, the number of pictures to display per second. Each picture is displayed every time the screen is redrawn using the background() command. Then in the draw() section of the code we draw an ellipse at location x, y plus a random offset. The result of this random offset is a jittering erratic motion of a circle, as shown in Figures 6-3 and 6-4. Please note that in Figure 6.3 the background in not redrawn, so the circle leaves a visible trace. In the mousePressed() section, we assign x and y with the mouse's position in case the jittering circle starts to move off the borders of the window.

**Figure 6-3:** Jittering motion of a circle

An alternative way to ensure that the jittering circle does not move out of the visible screen is to insert the following lines of code before drawing the ellipse, that is, between lines 9 and 10:

```
x = constrain(x,0,width);
y = constrain(y,0,height);
```

or, if we want to constrain the motion within a 100 × 100 area at the center of the window, we can use the following code:

```
x = constrain(x,width/2-50,width/2+50);
y = constrain(y,height/2-50,height/2+50);
```

The result of this constraining motion is shown in Figure 6-4.

**Figure 6-4:** Constraint motion of circles within a 100 × 100 pixel area

## 6.3 Line Traces

In the following code, we will show how to create a series of lines that connect a set of random points:

```
1   void setup(){
2     size(300,300);
3     frameRate(60);
4   }
5   float x=150,y=150,xn=150,yn=150;
6   void draw(){
7       //background(255);
8       x = x + random(-5,5);
9       y = y + random(-5,5);
10      x = constrain(x,0,width);
11      y = constrain(y,0,height);
12      line(x,y,xn,yn);
13      xn = x;
14      yn = y;
15  }
```

In line 3, we set the frame rate to 60 frames per second. Next, in line 8 and 9, we generate points that are placed from their previous position by a random offset in a 10 × 10 pixel area (that is, 5 pixels in each direction), then we draw a line from the previous point to the next one. In lines 13 and 14, we preserve the values of $x$ and $y$ by assigning them to $xn$ and $yn$, respectively. The result of this erratic line traces can be seen in Figure 6-5.

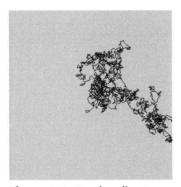

**Figure 6-5:** Random line traces

If we want to constrain the traces only in horizontal or vertical direction, that is, in orthogonal directions, then we need to replace the following lines of code instead of lines 8 and 9 of the preceding code:

```
11  if(random(1.)>0.5)
12        x = x + random(-10,10);
13     else
14        y = y + random(-10,10);
```

Line 11 produces a 50% chance by generating a random number between 0 and 1 and then selecting the numbers that are less than 0.5. So, in either case we increase the x or the y coordinate by a random offset (see lines 12 and 14. The result is shown in Figure 6-6 (left).

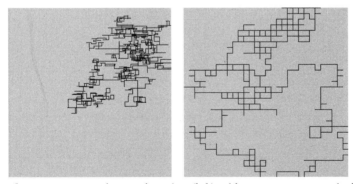

**Figure 6-6:** An orthogonal motion (left) with a snap every 10 pixels (right)

Further, if we want to snap the traces on a 10 × 10 grid, then we need to insert the following code between lines 9 and 10 of the preceding code:

```
11  x = round(x/10.)*10; //snap
12  y = round(y/10.)*10;
```

...d returns an integer number that is closest to the ..., by dividing x or y by 10, we obtain a float number ...sest integer which, in turn, is multiplied by 10. The ...own in Figure 6-6 (right).

## ...ansformations

... to move geometrical elements or images in order to ... motion. This is done by placing the element in a new ... the screen in a sequential manner. In the following ...slate() and rotate() commands to rotate two rect- ... and 50,50, respectively. Consider the following code:

```
...seX*3.6));
```

```
...seX*3.6));
```

...slate() command, which takes as parameter the coor- ...ove at. In line 3, we use the rotate() command, which ...gle to be rotated (in radians). So, we use the mouse's ...nd then convert it into radians. The reason that we use ...imension of the screen is 100, so the maximum angle ...n we use the rect() command to draw a rectangle at ...ted position. The result can be seen in Figure 6.7 (left): ...ound point 20,20 as expected, but the second rectangle ... not point 50,50. The reason is that the whole scene is ..., the second translation occurs as the addition of the ...n is explained in more detail in Chapter 8 in section ...e use the popMatrix() and pushMatrix() commands ...formation. So, the preceding code will be as follows:

```
       ...seX*3.6));
5      rect(0,0,20,10);
6      popMatrix();
7      pushMatrix();
```

```
8      translate(50,50);
9      rotate(radians(mouseX*3.6));
10     rect(0,0,20,10);
11     popMatrix();
12 }
```

The result of this code is shown in Figure 6-7 on the right.

**Figure 6-7:** Transformation without matrices' reset (left) and with (right)

In the next code sample, we will use multiple instances of transformations in a loop:

```
1  void draw(){
2    background(255);
3    for(float i=0; i<30; i++){
4      pushMatrix();
5      rectMode(CENTER);
6      noFill();
7      translate(50,50);
8      scale(1/(i/mouseX),1/(i/mouseX));
9      rotate(radians(i*mouseY));
10     rect(0,0,50,50);
11     popMatrix();
12   }
13 }
```

Within the loop, we use the pushMatrix() and popMatrix() to reset the scene and then draw a square after transforming it in three ways: first, we translate it to the center of the screen (at point 50,50), then we scale it by a fraction of the mouse's position, and finally we rotate it by the mouse's position, treating it as an angle degree. The result of this interactive transformation can be seen in Figure 6-8.

**Figure 6-8:** Interactive transformation of a square

Suppose now that we have a series of rectangles that are translated in random positions, and we want to rotate them around their center just by sliding the mouse right or left. Since each rectangle will be rotated around its center, we need to keep track of each rectangle's center, and its angle of rotation. So, we will use three arrays to hold this information. The code is shown here:

```
1   float px[] = new float[300];
2   float py[] = new float[300];
3   float pr[] = new float[360];
4   void setup(){
5     size(300,300);
6   }
7   void draw(){
8   }
9   void mousePressed(){
10    for(int i=0; i<mouseY; i++){
11       px[i] = random(width);
12       py[i] = random(height);
13       pr[i] = random(360);
14    }
15  }
16  void mouseDragged(){
17    background(255);
18    for(int i=0; i<mouseY; i++){
19      pushMatrix();
20      rectMode(CENTER);
21      translate(px[i],py[i]);
22      rotate(radians(pr[i] + mouseX));
23      rect(0,0,5,500);
24      popMatrix();
25    }
26  }
```

In the first three lines, we define three arrays that will hold the x and y coordinates and rotation angles for each rectangle. We define the maximum number of rectangles as 300, then in the `mousePressed()` section of the code we create random numbers that we use to populate the arrays. Please note that we are not using the maximum number of rectangles, that is, 300, but only a number equal to `mouseY`. This means that the number of rectangles increases or decreases, depending on the vertical motion of the mouse. Next, in the `mouseDragged()` section of the code, we go through all the rectangles in the scene and perform the transformations: we translate each rectangle to its center, which is stored in the arrays `px[]` and `py[]` and then rotate by an angle, which is the addition of the mouse's x direction and its previous rotation angle stored in the pr[] array. The result of this algorithm can be seen in Figure 6-9.

**Figure 6-9:** Interactive rotation of multiple rectangles

# 6.5 Double Buffering

When we draw on the screen we use the draw() method. Every time we call a graphics object, such as a line() or an image(), we are actually writing to the screen sequentially. Suppose that we have 1,000 lines to draw on the screen and use the following code:

```
for(int i=0; i<1000; i++)
    line(x1, y1, x2, y2);
```

We are actually sending line commands to the screen 1,000 times. This turns out to be an inefficient way of drawing that causes the whole system to slow down and the screen to, eventually, flicker. To avoid such a problem we do not draw straight to the screen but instead we draw to an off-screen image and then when done, we send the off-screen image to the screen as one action. This image is also referred to as an off-screen graphics or a buffer. Internally, a buffer is a memory area where we store temporary information. The method of indirect drawing is called double buffering. In the following code we will demonstrate a case of double buffering. First, we create an object of type PGraphics:

```
PGraphics pg;
pg = createGraphics(dim, dim, P3D);
```

Next, in the draw() section we draw to the buffer and then, when we are done, we display it as an image. The image and the buffer are associated, so any drawing on pg is, by association, drawn to the off-screen image. This process is initiated by using the beginDraw() and is terminated using the endDraw() methods of the PGraphics object. An example of code for double buffering looks like this:

```
1    PGraphics pg;  //define a buffer
2    int dim = 200; //screen dimension
3    void setup() {
4      size(dim, dim);  //size up the screen
5      background(102); //set the background
6      pg = createGraphics(dim, dim, P3D); //create a buffer
7    }
8
9    void draw() {
10     image(pg, 0, 0);  //draw the buffer
11   }
12
13   int x1,y1,x2,y2;  //coordinates of a line
14   void mouseDragged(){
15     pg.beginDraw();  //start writing to the buffer
16     pg.background(102);
17     pg.stroke(255);
18     for(int i=0; i<1000; i++){  //draw 1000 lines
19       x1 = int(random(dim)); y1 = int(random(dim));
20       x2 = int(random(dim)); y2 = int(random(dim));
21     pg.line(x1, y1, x2, y2);
22     }
23     pg.endDraw();  //end writing to the buffer
24   }
```

In the code above, we first define a PGraphics object called pg, which we initialize in line 6. The parameter P3D refers to the rendering mode that supports such actions; besides 2D, it also renders 3D graphics. Next, in line 10 we draw the pg buffer as an image on the screen. The pg buffer is filled with graphics commands (in this case, calls to the line() command) within the mouseDragged() method, starting at line 15 (pg.beginDraw()) and ending at line 23 (pg.endDraw()). In between these two graphics methods, we write every graphics command to the buffer. The result of this process can be seen in Figure 6.10.

The advantage of this technique is significant, since it allows the same scene to be viewed in a much more smooth and continuous way, using the same memory and clock speed. The solution is in writing to a memory location instead of straight to the screen.

**Figure 6-10:** Double buffering

# 6.6. Motion and Friction

Motion is not always based on linear movement, in which objects' locations are determined by an incremental change (usually an addition of subtraction of a counter). Physical motion is governed by laws that take under consideration collision, friction, and acceleration/deceleration. The effect of these laws can be described by mathematical formulas applied to the moving objects' material attributes. The following sections show three examples where motion is constrained by friction, collision, and by elastic forces, respectively. Both of these examples use an element or a spring as the object upon which forces are exerted.

```
1   class MyElement{
2     int diameter = 5;
3     float xpos = 0.; float ypos = 0.;  //position
4     float friction = 0.5;
5     float xspeed = 0; float yspeed = 0;  // speed
6
7     void move() {
8       xpos += (xspeed/friction);
9       ypos += (yspeed/friction);
10      if (xpos  > width) xspeed *= -1;
11      else if (xpos < 0) xspeed *= -1;
12      if (ypos > height) yspeed *= -1;
13      else if (ypos < 0) yspeed *= -1;
14      xpos = constrain(xpos, 0, width);
15      ypos = constrain(ypos, 0, height);
16      ellipse(int(xpos),int(ypos),diameter,diameter);
17      friction += 0.01;
17    }
18  }
```

Here, we define an object (or class) called MyElement. This is composed of a size, position, speed, and friction. The move() method will eventually draw a circle (line 16) and position it in the screen based on its speed slowed down by the increase in friction. Please note that this is a just simple version of friction that applies a change in speed intensity over time. Of course, in cases of physics simulations, other methods are being used. Lines 10 and 15 are just conditions to keep the element from exceeding the limits of the screen so that when it reaches the frame it reverses direction. This appears as if the ball is bouncing off the screen.

The main code is shown here:

```
1  MyElement e = new MyElement();  //define an element
2  void setup(){
3    e.xspeed = random(1);
4    e.yspeed = random(1);
5  }
6
7  void draw(){
8    background(200);
9    e.move();  //draws the element
10 }
11
12 void mouseDragged(){
13   if(dist(mouseX,mouseY,e.xpos,e.ypos)<20){
14     e.friction = .5;
15     e.xspeed = mouseX-pmouseX;
16     e.yspeed = mouseY-pmouseY;
17   }
18 }
```

We define an element and then draw it using the e.move() procedure. The speed of the element can be altered using the mouse's speed. To get its speed, we compute the difference between its first pressed mouse's position (i.e., pmouseX or pmouseY) minus its first dragged position (i.e., mouseX or mouseY). That difference becomes the element's speed, which we pass using the e.speed = mouseX-pmouseX expression.

The effect of the bouncing motion of the ball with the screen's frame is shown in Figure 6-11 (the motion is traced for visual purposes).

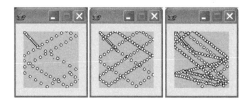

**Figure 6-11:** A bouncing ball with friction

A similar version of the preceding code can use two elements connected with a line to show a more dramatic effect of bouncing around the screen:

```
1   int nelements = 4;
2   MyElement [] e = new MyElement[nelements];
3   void setup(){
4     for(int i=0; i<nelements; i++){
5       e[i] = new MyElement();
6       e[i].xspeed = random(1);
7       e[i].yspeed = random(1);
8     }
9   }
10
11  void draw(){
12    background(200);
13    for(int i=0; i<nelements; i++)
14      e[i].move();
15    for(int i=0; i<nelements-1; i+=2)
16      line(e[i].xpos,e[i].ypos,e[i+1].xpos,e[i+1].ypos);}
17
18  void mouseDragged(){
19    for(int i=0; i<nelements; i++)
20      if(dist(mouseX,mouseY,e[i].xpos,e[i].ypos)<20){
21        e[i].friction = 0.5;
22        e[i].xspeed = mouseX-pmouseX;
23        e[i].yspeed = mouseY-pmouseY;
24      }
25  }
```

Instead of one element we define an array e[]. We draw four elements connected with a line (see line 16). Then we set the speed of all elements to random speeds. The resulting effect is shown (traced) in Figure 6-12.

**Figure 6-12:** Two bouncing balls connected with a line under friction

# 6.7 Collision

So far, we have shown how to create multiple objects that can be set in motion bouncing off the borders of the screen and slowing down because of friction. In this section, we will consider the possibility of objects colliding with one another. To do this, we first need to establish the position of each neighbor to an object in order to determine its distance. So, we need to modify the `MyElement` class by adding an array of neighbors and a method called `collide()`:

```
1 class MyElement{
2   int id;
3   int size = 10;
4   float xpos = 0.; float ypos = 0.; //position
5   float friction = 0.05;
6   float xspeed = 0;   float yspeed = 0;  // speed
7   MyElement[] others;
8
9   MyElement(int idin, MyElement[] othersin){
10    id = idin;
11    others = othersin;
12  }
13
14  void move() {
15    xpos += xspeed; ypos += yspeed;
16    if (xpos  > width) xspeed *= -1;
17    else if (xpos < 0) xspeed *= -1;
18    if (ypos > height) yspeed *= -1;
19    else if (ypos < 0) yspeed *= -1;
20    xpos = constrain(xpos, 0, width);
21    ypos = constrain(ypos, 0, height);
22    ellipse(int(xpos),int(ypos),size,size);
23  }
24  void collide() {
25    for (int i = id + 1; i < nelements; i++) {
26      if (dist(xpos,ypos,others[i].xpos,others[i].ypos) < 2*size) {
27        float angle=atan2(others[i].ypos-ypos, others[i].xpos-xpos);
28        float targetX = xpos + cos(angle)*2*size ;
29        float targetY = ypos + sin(angle)*2*size ;
30        float ax = (targetX - others[i].xpos) * friction;
31        float ay = (targetY - others[i].ypos) * friction;
32        xspeed -= (ax);
33        yspeed -= (ay);
34        others[i].xspeed += (ax);
35        others[i].yspeed += (ay);
36      }
37    }
38  }
39 }
```

In line 2, we define an integer called `id`, which will hold the ID number of the current element so that it can be compared to the other elements for collision. Then in line 7 we define an array called `others[]` to hold information about the other elements in the scene. So, next we use the constructor to hold the ID number and to pass the array of the other element (see line 9 to 12). We will use those two pieces of information in the `collide()` method shown in lines 24 to 38 in the preceding code. In the `collide()` method, we first loop through all elements in the scene (except the current one) and determine the distance between the current element and all others. If any element is within a collision distance (i.e., less than two times the radius), then we compute the angle of direction in which both elements are approaching one another before they collide. This is done by using the `atan2()` function that takes the y and x difference between the two elements' coordinates and returns the angle between a line passing from the point and the origin and the x-axis. We then use this angle to determine the next position of the elements after the collision. This position we call `ax` and `ay`, which we use to reverse the direction of the element and its colliding other element (see lines 32 to 35). So, the main code will become:

```
1 int nelements = 4;
2 MyElement [] e = new MyElement[nelements];
3
4 void setup(){
5   for(int i=0; i<nelements; i++){
6     e[i] = new MyElement(i, e);
7     e[i].xspeed = random(1);
8     e[i].yspeed = random(1);
9   }
10 }
11 void draw(){
12   background(200);
13   for(int i=0; i<nelements; i++){
14     e[i].collide();
15     e[i].move();
16   }
17 }
18
19  void mouseDragged(){
20  for(int i=0; i<nelements; i++)
21    if(dist(mouseX,mouseY,e[i].xpos,e[i].ypos)<20){
22    e[i].xspeed = mouseX-pmouseX;
23    e[i].yspeed = mouseY-pmouseY;
24  }
```

First, we define four elements and allocate memory for them (see line 2). Next, in the `setup()` section, we go through all four elements and construct them (line 6) and then set them at random speeds. In the `draw()` section, we use the `collide()` and `move()` methods to detect a collision and then move the element into its next position. In the `mouseDragged()` section, we provide the means to interfere with the moving elements by being able to "push" an element that is close to the mouse (i.e., within 20 pixels). The result of this process is shown in Figure 6-13.

**Figure 6-13:** Collision of elements in a scene

## 6.8 Elastic Motion

In the context of this book, elastic motion will be considered a behavior that simulates elasticity, that is, reversible deformation under stress. We will use the physical properties of elastic objects to move an object in the screen. The mouse will be used to force the object off its original position and the elastic motion will bring the body back to its original position. Consider the following code:

```
1 float M = 0.8;     // Mass
2 float K = 0.2;     // Spring constant
3 float D = 0.92;    // Damping
4 float R = 100;     // Rest position
5 float ypos;        // Position
6 float v = 0.0;     // Velocity
7 float a = 0;       // Acceleration
8 float f = 0;       // Force
9 boolean released = false;
10
11 void setup() {
12    size(200, 200);
13    ypos = height/2;
14 }
15
16 void draw() {
17    background(200);
18    if(released)move();
19    ellipse(width/2, ypos , 50,50);
20 }
21
22 void move(){
23    f = -K * (ypos - R); // f=-ky
24    a = f / M;             // Set the acceleration, f=ma == a=f/m
25    v = D * (v + a);       // Set the velocity
26    ypos += v;             // Updated position
```

```
27   if(abs(v) < 0.01) {
28     v = 0.0;
29     released = false;
30   }
31 }
32 void mouseMoved() {
33   if(dist(mouseX,mouseY,width/2,ypos)<50)
34     stroke(255,0,0);
35   else
36     stroke(0);
37 }
38 void mouseDragged() {
39   released = false;
40   ypos = mouseY;
41 }
42 void mouseReleased(){
43   released = true;
44 }
```

The first eight lines of code define the parameters of elasticity, that is, mass, a spring constant, damping, and the resting position, and then we define the simulation parameters, that is, the vertical position, velocity, acceleration, and force. The boolean variable, called `released`, will be used to determine whether the mouse was released in order to start the elastic motion. In the `setup()` section, we define the initial position to be at the center of the screen. In the `draw()` section, we move a circle when the mouse is released. The `move()` method is a simulation of elastic motion, so we use the following formulas: $f = -k\text{Ð}y$, where $f$ is the force applied to the object-spring, $k$ is the spring's constant and $y$ is the position of the spring. The next equation is $a = f/m$, which return the acceleration of an object as the ratio of force over mass. Finally, we use the equation $v = D (v + a)$, which computes the velocity $v$ as a function of the damping factor times the addition of velocity and acceleration. This velocity value $v$ is added to the current position of the object in line 26 to determine its new position. Lines 27 to 30 are added to provide a stability balance to the object, forcing it to stop when the velocity is below 0.01.

In the `mouseMoved()` section, we provide a simple way to identify the object to be moved by changing its color to red when the mouse approaches it. In the `mouseDragged()` section, we move the object at the same location as the mouse's horizontal location. Finally, in the `mouseReleased()` section, we set the variable released to true in order to start the elastic motion, which is performed in the `draw()` section of the code. The result of this process can be seen to the left in Figure 6-14 later in this chapter.

In the next part of this section, we will generalize the elastic motion for multiple object in any direction in space. To do that we will use the existing code (above) and group the information associated with a spring into a class called `MySpring`. The code for this new class is shown here:

```
1 class MySpring{
2  float M = 0.8;     // Mass
3  float K = 0.2;     // Spring constant
4  float D = 0.92;    // Damping
5  float Rx = 100;    // Rest position
6  float Ry = 100;    // Rest position
7  float xpos;        // Position x
8  float ypos;        // Position y
9  float vx = 0.0;    // Velocity x
10  float vy = 0.0;    // Velocity y
11  float a = 0;       // Acceleration
12  float f = 0;       // Force
13  boolean released = false;
14
15  void move(){
16    f = -K * (xpos - Rx);  // f=-ky
17    a = f / M;             // Set the acceleration, f=ma == a=f/m
18    vx = D * (vx + a);     // Set the velocity
19    xpos += vx;            // Updated x position
20    f = -K * (ypos - Ry);  // f=-ky
21    a = f / M;             // Set the acceleration, f=ma == a=f/m
22    vy = D * (vy + a);     // Set the velocity
23    ypos += vy;            // Updated y position
24    if(abs(vx)<0.01 && abs(vy)  < 0.01) {
25      vx = 0.0;
26      vy = 0.0;
27      released = false;
28    }
29  }
30 }
```

The class `MySprng` contains information about a spring. This information is the same as in the previous code, except that we use double parameters for x and y direction. So, we have two resting positions, two spring positions, and two velocity values for both x and y direction. The rest of the code should be obvious, since it is a repetition of the code shown earlier, except with an addition of the second dimension.

The main code controls the location/configuration of the springs and the mouse movements. The source code is shown here:

```
1  int nsprings = 4;
2  MySpring [] s = new MySpring[nsprings];
3  void setup() {
4    size(200, 200);
5    for(int i=0; i<nsprings; i++){
```

```
6        s[i] = new MySpring();
7        s[i].xpos = random(width);
8        s[i].ypos = random(height);
9        s[i].Rx = s[i].xpos;
10       s[i].Ry = s[i].ypos;
11   }
12 }
13
14 void draw() {
15   background(200);
16   for(int i=0; i<nsprings; i++){
17      if(s[i].released)s[i].move();
18      ellipse(s[i].xpos, s[i].ypos , 10,10);
19   }
20   for(int i=0; i<nsprings-1; i++)
21   line(s[i].xpos, s[i].ypos ,s[i+1].xpos, s[i+1].ypos);
22 }
23
24 void mouseDragged() {
25   for(int i=0; i<nsprings; i++)
26      if(dist(mouseX,mouseY,s[i].xpos,s[i].ypos)<10){
27      s[i].released = false;
28      s[i].xpos = mouseX;
29      s[i].ypos = mouseY;
30   }
31 }
32 void mouseReleased(){
33   for(int i=0; i<nsprings; i++)
34      s[i].released = true;
35 }
```

In the main code, we define an array of four springs, called s[]. We allocate memory for the array in line 2 and then we populate each array member with new MySpring objects (see line 6. Once we create the new objects, we initiate their variables by setting them as random locations on the screen. In the draw() section, we simply move all the object-springs when the mouse is released (line 17). The rest of the code is the same as the previous example, except that we apply the processes to all the array members.

The result is shown in Figure 6-14.

 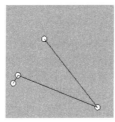

**Figure 6-14:** Springs in elastic motion

## Summary

This chapter introduced basic concepts of animation in Processing. It showed how to produce simple motion by redrawing the screen with one object or image or multiple objects or images. Then it showed certain constraining factors that affect the motion of objects either by moving only orthogonally or by snapping to a grid. Next, it showed physics-based motion with friction, collision, and elasticity. You also learned how to use double buffering to increase redrawing speed and avoid screen flickering.

## Exercises

**NOTE** Answers to the exercises are provided in Appendix B.

1. Write the code that will draw a spring that opens or closes, depending on the position of the mouse. See Pattern 1-1:

Pattern 1.1

2. Use multiple transformation to produce the following static patterns:

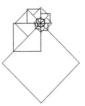

Pattern 2.1

Pattern 2.2

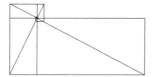

Pattern 2.3

3.  Use multiple transformation to produce the following patterns using the mouse's position:

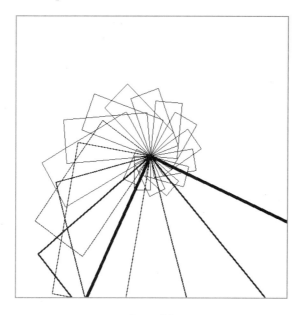

Pattern 3.1

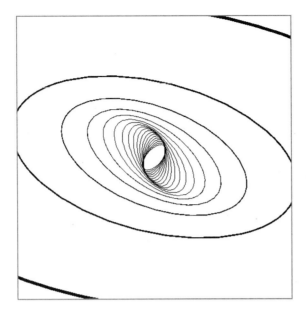

Pattern 3.2

Pattern 3.3

# Notes

1. The image (maple_leaf.gif) is originally a rectangular image, except that we have used transparency to carve out its profile. The way to do this is: take an image of a leaf to Photoshop. Select the area you need to make transparent. Then select from the Menu Help ➪ Export Transparent Image, and follow the steps.

# CHAPTER 7

# Advanced Graphics Algorithms

An algorithm is a computational procedure for addressing a problem in a finite number of steps. In the world of design, and in particular, architecture, the problems designers are called upon to solve are not necessarily solvable in the traditional sense of finding a path between A and B. Apart from specific quantitative localized sub-problems that occur within some standardized patterns of construction, the general formal, aesthetic, or planning considerations are barely addressable as discrete solvable problems. Consequently, it may be more appropriate to use the term *problem addressing* rather than *problem solving* in order to characterize the solution strategy.

Contrary to common belief, algorithms are not always based on a solution strategy conceived entirely in the mind of a human programmer. Many algorithms are simulations of the way that natural processes work and as such they must not be regarded as human inventions but rather as human discoveries. Unlike inventions, discoveries are not conceived, owned, or controlled by the human mind, yet as abstract processes they can be codified to be executed by a computer system. In this case, the human programmer serves the purpose of codifying a process, that is, a translator of a process external to the human mind to be compiled into machine language, which is also external to the human mind.

In this chapter, we will present a series of algorithms that although not directly conceived, constructed, or applied for design purposes, can be used indirectly to address design issues. A Voronoi tessellation, stochastic search, hybridization, fractals, cellular automata, and evolutionary algorithms are just a few of the algorithms that can be used to address design issues.

# 7.1 Voronoi Tessellation

A Voronoi tessellation is the partitioning of a plane into sets of points, each set based on their points' position from a set of marked points. All points closest to the mark are considered sets of a Voronoi tessellation. For instance, if two pixels are marked in a computer screen, they will produce two areas that will divide all pixels into those that are closest to either one of the two points. These two areas will be bordered by a straight line, dividing the pixels of the screen into these two areas. This line, of course, is perpendicular to the line connecting the two marked points. (See Figure 7-1.)

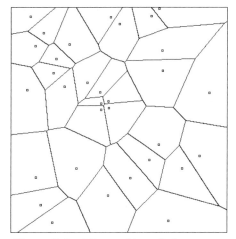

**Figure 7-1:** A Voronoi tessellation

The problem of the Voronoi tessellation can be addressed in at least in two ways: either by finding the lines and their intersections that divide the plane into areas or by coloring each pixel of the plane based on its proximity to a mark. In other words, the problem can be solved either as an analytical geometrical problem or as a finite element problem. In this section, we will use the second method:

```
1  float [] px = new float[0];      // hold the mouse pressed marks
2  float [] py = new float[0];
3  float [] distance = new float[0];  //holds the pixel's distance to the
     marked point
4  int [] idx = new int[0];   //used for sorting the pixels
```

```
5   PImage MyImage;
6   void setup(){
7     size (400,400);
8     MyImage = createImage (width, height, RGB);  //create an image
9     image(MyImage,0,0);
10  }
11  void draw(){
12    stroke(0);
13    for(int i=0; i<px.length; i++)
14      rect(px[i],py[i],3,3);  //draw the mark as a tiny rectangle
15  }
16
17  void mousePressed(){     //if the use presses the mouse
18    px = append(px,mouseX);  //add that clicked point
19    py = append(py,mouseY);
20    distance = append(distance,0);  //allocate memory for the distance
21    idx = append(idx,0);                    // and the id
22    for(int x=0; x<width; x++)        //for all pixels
23      for(int y=0; y<height; y++){
24        for(int i=0; i<px.length; i++)    //for all already defined marks
25          distance[i] = dist(x,y,px[i],py[i]);  //find the distance from all
    points
26        for(int i=0; i<idx.length; i++)
27          idx[i]=i;
28        for(int i=1; i<distance.length; i++)  //sort all distances together with
    ids
29          for(int j=0; j<distance.length-1; j++)
30            if(distance[i]>distance[j]){
31              float t = distance[i];        //swap in ascending order
32              distance[i] = distance[j];
33              distance[j] = t;
34              int tr = idx[i];
35              idx[i]=idx[j];
36              idx[j] = tr;
37            }
38          for(int i=0; i<idx.length; i++)             //color the area with random
    colors
39            set(x,y,color((idx[i]*126)%255,(idx[i]*133)%255,(idx[i]*144)%255));
40      }
41  }
```

In the first four lines of the preceding code, we define four arrays to hold information about the marks' position, as well as the distance, and the index number of each Voronoi area. Then we define an image called MyImage that will be used to show the colored Voronoi areas; that is, we will paint each area with a random color using the image as a canvas. This image is created in line 8. In the draw() section, we draw the image and then draw all the marks.

However, in the `mousePressed()` section, we acquire the marks by saving the mouse's location. This is done in lines 18 and 19. Lines 20 and 21 expand the arrays `distance[]` and `idx[]` by one element set to 0. Next, we loop through all pixels in the image and through all already marked points and calculate the distance between the new mouseX and mouseY point with all other marks. Also, we set the `index[]` array in ascending order. Then we sort the `distance[]` array in the order of their distance from the new mark (sorting also at the same time the index numbers). So, at the end we have the `distance[]` and `idx[]` arrays sorted, which we use to color each area with a random color (lines 38–39). The mapping process can be seen in Figure 7-2, and the result of this process can be seen in Figure 7-3.

| dist | id |     | dist | id |
|------|----|-----|------|----|
| 25   | 1  |     | 3    | 2  |
| 3    | 2  |     | 12   | 3  |
| 12   | 3  |     | 20   | 5  |
| 21   | 4  | →   | 21   | 4  |
| 20   | 5  |     | 25   | 1  |
| 56   | 6  |     | 33   | 7  |
| 33   | 7  |     | 56   | 6  |

**Figure 7-2:** The distribution of distances in correlation with the identity number of a color is being redistributed based on the distance.

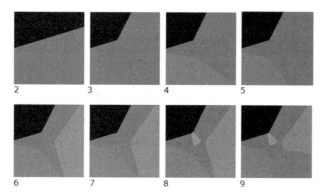

**Figure 7-3:** The Voronoi tessellation for 2 to 9 points

Notice that the preceding code will paint areas with a different color in order to differentiate them. If we extract the edges of each area, a visually clearer effect can be created. The following code will extract the edges of each area by simply going through every pixel on the image and checking the difference of color between adjacent pixels. If they are different, we paint them black (i.e., the edge); otherwise, we paint the pixel white (i.e., interior). The following code should be added at the end of line 40:

```
40  for(int x=1; x<width-1; x++)
41    for(int y=1; y<height-1; y++) //check the difference between adjacent
      pixels
42      if(abs(red(get(x,y))-red(get(x+1,y)))>0 ||
43        abs(red(get(x,y))-red(get(x,y+1)))>0   )
44          set(x,y,color(0));   //black
45      else
46          set(x,y,color(255)); //white
```

In the preceding code, we extract the edges of the colored regions and eliminate the colors. So, we start by going through all the pixels in the screen and checking the difference in color between each pixel and the ones next to it (the neighbor immediately below or the one on its right). If the difference is greater than 0, that is, there is a color difference, then we set that pixel to black. If the difference is 0, that is, they are the same color, we set the pixel to white. The result is shown in Figure 7-4.

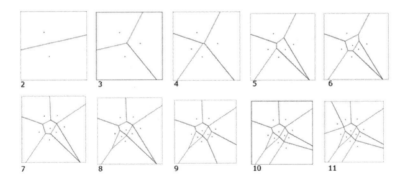

**Figure 7-4:** The Voronoi tessellation for 2 to 11 points

While the problem of a Voronoi tessellation is the main focus here, the methodology used to solve the problem is worth mentioning. In the field of computer graphics, geometrical problems are dealt with by using numerical methods. These methods involve usually analytical geometry as the main method of mapping the set of numbers to the set of computer elements (i.e., registers, memory locations, pixels, etc.). However, because of physical limitations, computer elements are finite in size, yet the analytical mapping assumes infinite resolution. While the advantage of analytical methods lies in their precision, efficiency, and universality, discrete methods offer a more simple, specific, and realistic approach to the same problem. In this case, the code used to address the Voronoi tessellation problem is simple, as it explicitly describes the solution to the Voronoi classification problem, and thus it is closer to the realistic material representation. Further, such methods can easily combine multiple parameters for each discrete element, resulting in far more complex effects. This complexity is a typical characteristic of materials and material behavior. Analytical methods, while precise and efficient, offer only an idealized version of a non-ideal world.

## 7.2 Stochastic Search

A *stochastic search* is defined here as a random search in space until a given condition is met. For instance, the placement of toys in a playpen so that each toy does not overlap any other and they all fit within the limits of the playpen can be addressed with a stochastic search. This algorithm can be represented as follows:

```
while(no more toys are left to place){
        choose randomly a position  (rx, ry) within the playpen
        compare it with all previous toy locations
        is there an overlap?
        if no then place the toy at (rx, ry)
    }
```

This algorithm can be used to place objects within a site so that that there is no overlap (or some other criterion is satisfied). In the following code, a series of 10 × 10 rectangles are placed within an area of the screen (300 × 300 here):

```
1 float [] xp = new float[0];  //used to store the allocated elements
2 float [] yp = new float[0];
3 int numObjects = 0;  //used to count the number of allocated elements
4 void setup(){
5   size(300,300);
6 }
7 void draw(){
8   background(255);
9   for(int i=0; i<xp.length; i++)  //draw anything that has been allocated
10     rect(xp[i],yp[i],10,10);
11 }
12 void keyPressed(){
13   int k = 0;
```

```
14   while(true){  //until you find a successful location (i.e. without an
     overlap)
15     boolean overlap = false;  //use it to mark overlaps
16     float xrand = random(10,width-10);  //produce a random possible location
17     float yrand = random(10,height-10);
18     for(int j=0; j<xp.length; j++){  //go through all the remaining elements
19       float distance = dist(xrand,yrand,xp[j],yp[j]);  //find distance
20       if(distance < 10) overlap = true;  //if too short then it will overlap
21     }
22     if(overlap==false){  //if no overlap then this is a successful location
23       xp = append(xp,xrand);  //add it to memory
24       yp = append(yp,yrand);
25       break;
26     }
27     k++;
28     if(k>10000){   // will exit if after 10,000 attempts no space is found
29       println(xp.length + " impass");  //warn the user
30       break;
31     }
32   }
33   println(numObjects++);
34 }
```

First, we define two arrays, xp and yp, that will hold the positions of the newly placed objects. We also need a variable called numObjects, which will hold to the number of objects. In the setup() section, we define the size of the window (300 × 300) and in the draw() section we draw rectangles (representing the objects to be allocated) at the locations defined by the coordinates xp[] and yp[]. These coordinates are calculated in the keyPressed() section so that each time a key is pressed an object is allocated. This section is composed basically of two loops: one for suggesting a random position and one for checking for the validity of the potential position (i.e., whether it overlaps the other objects already placed in the scene). We start with a "while" loop (line 14) that repeatedly creates random locations that are input into the variables xrand and yrand. We also define a boolean variable called overlap that we set to false. Next, we loop through all the already existing objects in the scene, and that is done by looping from 0 to the length of the existing objects (x.length or y.length). Then we calculate the distance between the suggested locations xrand and yrand from each already defined object. If it is less than a tolerance value (in this case 10), we consider this to be an overlap and set the variable overlap to true. If not, we create a new random location and try again. If we have no overlaps, we assign the xrand value as a valid new location and exit the loop (line 25). However, it is possible that there is no more space, so there will always be an overlap (in which case we will run into an infinite loop). So, we use lines 28 to

31 as a way of forcing an exit from the loop if 10,000 attempts have been made and there is always an overlap. At each successful allocation of a new object we add one to the number of objects (line 33). The result of this algorithm is shown in Figure 7-5.

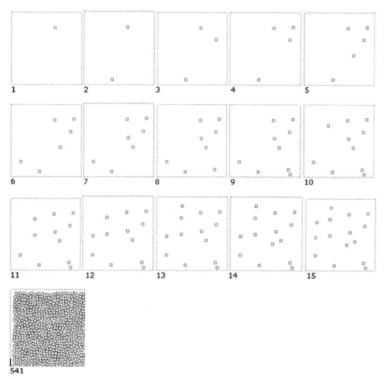

**Figure 7-5:** Stochastic search allocating 1 to 15 and then 541 squares

An alternative approach to the problem of stochastic allocation is to search for space availability that is adjacent to the last successful allocation. In other words, after allocating an object, then look around it for available space to allocate the next one. This can be interpreted as an attempt to fill the local region before searching further out. The effect of such a search mechanism is the creation of snake-like blobs of objects that move along the empty space populating it with new objects. The code is shown here:

```
1 float [] xp = new float[0];
2 float [] yp = new float[0];
```

```
3 int numObjects = 0;
4 void setup(){
5   size(300,300);
6   xp = append(xp,random(10,width-10));
7   yp = append(yp,random(10,height-10));
8 }
9 void draw(){
10   background(255);
11   for(int i=0; i<xp.length; i++)
12     rect(xp[i],yp[i],10,10);
13 }
14 void keyPressed(){
15   int k = 0;
16   while(true){
17     boolean overlap = false;
18     float xrand = random(xp[xp.length-1]-20,xp[xp.length-1]+20);
19     float yrand = random(yp[yp.length-1]-20,yp[yp.length-1]+20);
20     for(int j=0; j<xp.length; j++){
21       float distance = dist(xrand,yrand,xp[j],yp[j]);
22       if(distance < 10 || xrand>width-20 || xrand<20 ||
23                        yrand >height-20 || yrand<20 ) overlap = true;
24     }
25     if(overlap==false){
26       xp = append(xp,xrand);
27       yp = append(yp,yrand);
28       break;
29     }
30     k++;
31     if(k>10000){
32       println(xp.length + " impass");
33       break;
34     }
35   }
36   println(numObjects++);
37 }
```

This code is similar to that shown previously, except for three parts (shown in bold font): First, we start with a random initial location (lines 6 and 7). Second, we calculate a random new location, and we give it a range within which it can generate possible coordinates. This range is within 40 points of the previous (last) position. Finally, we change the condition for overlap by assuming that if the distance is greater than the minimum tolerance (i.e., 10), or the new location is out of the greater region (i.e., the screen), then the overlap is true. The result of this algorithm is shown in Figure 7-6.

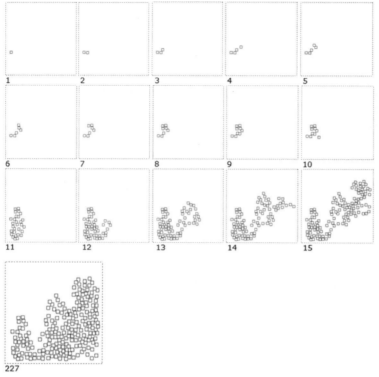

**Figure 7-6:** Stochastic search allocating 1 to 15 and then 227 squares

# 7.3 Fractals

A *fractal* is a geometric object generated by a repeating pattern, in a typically recursive or iterative process. Some of the best examples can be divided into parts, each of which is similar to the original object. Fractals are said to possess infinite detail, and some of them have a self-similar structure that occurs at different levels of magnification. The term fractal was coined in 1975 by Benoît Mandelbrot, from the Latin *fractus* or "fractured."

In a fractal, there are at least two shapes: a base and a generator. In each iteration, the generator replaces each segment of the base shape. Theoretically, this process can continue infinitely. The algorithm to create fractals consists of a basic procedure that fits a shape between two points. The process of fitting involves scaling, rotation, and translation of the generator to fit between two points of a segment of the base. The following code shows the procedure:

```
1 float [] px = new float[0];  //temp array
2 float [] py = new float[0];
3 float [] gx = {-10,10,20,30,40};   //generator data
4 float [] gy = {0, 0,-10, 0, 0};
5 float [] bx = {0,100,200,300,400};  //base data
```

```
6 float [] by = {200, 200,100,200, 200};
7
8 void setup(){
9   size(400,400);
10 }
11
12 void draw(){
13   background(200);
14   for(int i=1; i<bx.length; i++)
15     if(bx[i]!=999 && bx[i-1]!=999)  //skip
16       line(bx[i-1],by[i-1],bx[i],by[i]);
17 }
18
19 void mousePressed(){
20   px = expand (px,0); //empty px
21   py = expand (py,0);
22   for(int j=0; j<bx.length-1; j++){  //for all base lines
23     if(bx[j]!=999 && bx[j+1]!=999)  //skip if marked
24       for(int i=0; i<gx.length; i++){  //for all generator lines
25         float db = dist(bx[j],by[j],bx[j+1],by[j+1]);  //get dist of each
    base segment
26         float dg = dist(0,0,gx[gx.length-1],gy[gy.length-1]); //get the
    distance of the generator
27         float x = gx[i] * db/dg;  //divide to get the scale factor
28         float y = gy[i] * db/dg;
29         float angle = atan2(by[j+1]-by[j],bx[j+1]-bx[j]); //angle between
    the origin and each point
30         float tempx = x * cos(angle) - y * sin(angle); //rotate
31         y = y * cos(angle) + x * sin(angle);
32         x = tempx;
33         x += bx[j];   //translate
34         y += by[j];
35         px = append(px,x);  //add the newly transformed point
36         py = append(py,y);
37       }
38     px = append(px,999);  //mark the end of a polyline sequence with 999
39     py = append(py,999);
40   }
41   //copy p to the base array
42   bx = expand (bx,0);
43   by = expand (by,0);
44   for(int i=0; i<px.length; i++){
45     bx = append(bx,px[i]);
46     by = append(by,py[i]);
47   }
48 }
```

In the first six lines of code we define the coordinates of the generator shape (gx[] and gy[]), the base shape (bx[] and by[]) as well as a temporary array to hold the points of the resulting fractal shape (px[] and py[]). In the draw() section, we just draw the lines that describe the base as it is being replaced with the generator. The number 999 is simply a mark to indicate the end of a polyline and the beginning of a new polyline. It is assumed that there will not be no more than 999 replacement polylines to construct.

In the `mousePressed()` section, we perform the replacement operation. First, we set the resulting fractal shape array to 0. We do this every time we produce a new fractal shape. The Processing command used is `contract()`, which essentially shrinks the array to 0, that is, it empties it. Then we go for all the base array points (stored in the `bx[]` and `by[]` arrays), skipping the end points (marked with the 999 number), and then loop for all the generator points and adjust them through the following three transformations:

1. Calculate the distance between two sequential base points and the distance between the first and last point of the generator array, then divide the distances to get the scaling factor (which we multiply by each generator point).

2. Find the angle between the base and the generator, using the `acos()` function that returns the angle between two vectors (i.e., two lines whose first points are at the origin 0,0), then rotate the base by that angle (line 30).

3. Translate the base back to its location within their original location.

Finally, we add the newly transformed base points to the temporary array `px[]` and `py[]`, adding a mark (999) at the end of each polyline to separate them later on when we draw them. When we are done with all the parts of the base, we empty `bx[]` and `by[]` and populate them with the `px[]` and `py[]` arrays. The result of this process is shown in Figure 7-7.

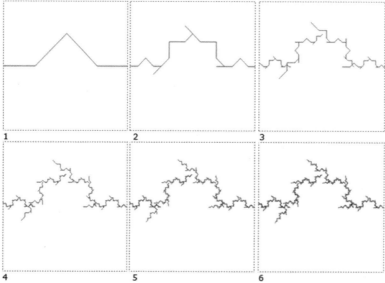

**Figure 7-7:** Fractal process of 1 to 6 replacements of Polyline

# 7.4 Interpolation/Extrapolation

*Hybridization* (a.k.a. *morphing*) is a procedure in which an object changes its form gradually in order to obtain another form. Morphing is a gradual transition that results in a marked change in the form's appearance, character, condition, or function. The operation of morphing consists basically of the selection of two objects and the assignment of a number of in-between transitional steps. The first object then transforms into the second in steps. The essence of such a transformation is not so much in the destination form but rather in the intermediate phases this type of transformation passes through, as well as, in the extrapolations, which go beyond the final form. It is the transitional continuity of a form that progresses through a series of evolutionary stages.

Morphing can be seen as either an image or a geometrical transformation. Geometrical morphing preserves the structural integrity of the objects involved, that is, an object changes into another object as a single entity. A cube, for instance, may be gradually transformed into a pyramid. From the viewer's point of view, there are always two objects: *the original (or source)*, to which transformation is applied, and the *destination object (or target)*, which is the object one will get at the final step of the transformation. However, theoretically, there is only one object, which is transformed from one state (original) into another (destination). This object combines characteristics of both parent objects, which are involved in the transformation, and is called a *hybrid object*. This object is actually composed of the topology of the one object and the geometry of the other. It is an object in disguise. Although it is topologically identical to one parent, it resembles the geometry of the other parent.

*Interpolation* is a method for estimating values that lie between two known values.[1] The hybrid object derives its structure from its parents through formal interpolations. While it is easy to derive hybrid children from isomorphic parents, a challenge arises for heteromorphic parents. In an isomorphic transformation, a one-to-one correspondence applies between the elements of the two parent sets, such that the result of an operation on elements of one set corresponds to the result of the analogous operation on their images in the other set. In the case of heteromorphism, the lack of homogeneity between the parents leads necessarily to a selective process of omission and inclusion of elements between the two sets. The guiding principle in this mapping process is the preservation of the topological and geometrical properties of the hybrid object. For instance, in the case of a square mapped to a triangle, the addition of a fourth point to the triangle preserves the topology of the square, and yet its disguised location preserves the geometrical appearance of the triangle.

In the following example, a square is mapped to a triangle: the hybrid child is a four-sided polygon in which two of the vertices overlap and these vertices are ordered to form a triangle. The problem here is to map two counters so that, when the one is counting points from one object to another, counter $kc$ should skip points from the other object. For example, if the counter $k1$ increments as 01234 the counter $k2$ should increment as 00123 (or 01123 or 01223 or 01233). To obtain such behavior, we use the formula $kc = k/(p1/p2)$ or $kc = k/(p2/p1)$.

```
1  float [] x1 = {200,100,100,200,200};  //parent1
2  float [] y1 = {200,200,300,300,200};
3  float [] x2 = {350,300,400,350};      //parent2
4  float [] y2 = {200,300,300,200};
5  float [] xc, yc;    //child
6  float ratio=0.5;  //percentage of interpolation
7  int k1, k2, maxpoints; //number of points for the arrays
8  void setup(){
9    size(500,400);
10   smooth();   //for visual effect
11   maxpoints = max(x1.length, x2.length);    //the max number of
either array
12   xc = new float[maxpoints];  //create a child with points as the
     largest parent
13   yc = new float[maxpoints];
14 }
15 void draw(){
16   background(255);
17   stroke(0);
18   for(int i=1; i<xc.length; i++)  //draw the child's lines
19     line(xc[i],yc[i],xc[i-1],yc[i-1]);
20   for(int i=0; i<xc.length; i++)  //draw the child's vertices
21     rect(xc[i]-1,yc[i]-1,3,3);
22   stroke(255,0,0);
23   for(int i=1; i<x1.length; i++)  //draw parent 1
24     line(x1[i],y1[i],x1[i-1],y1[i-1]);
25   for(int i=1; i<x2.length; i++)   //draw parent 2
26     line(x2[i],y2[i],x2[i-1],y2[i-1]);
27 }
28
29 void mouseDragged(){
30   for(int k=0; k<maxpoints; k++){
31     if(x1.length>=x2.length){  //if p1 is greater than p2
32       k1 = k;  //counter 1 remains as is
33       k2 = int(k/((x1.length*1.)/(x2.length*1.)));
34     }   //counter 2 must be adjusted
35     else{ //if p2 is greater than p1
36       k1 = int(k/((x2.length*1.)/(x1.length*1.)));
37       k2 = k;
38     }
39     xc[k] = x1[k1] + (mouseX*1./width*1.) * (x2[k2] - x1[k1]);
40     yc[k] = y1[k1] + (mouseX*1./width*1.) * (y2[k2] - y1[k1]);
41   }
42 }
```

In the first five lines of the code, we declare six arrays to hold the coordinates of two parents and the child. We define a ratio of interpolation as 0.5 (that is half the distance of the path). Then we define three variables to hold the number of points of the parents and the child. In the `setup()` section, we increase the array `xc[]` and `yc[]` that will hold the child's points to the length of the largest (in number of points) parent. This is done because we know that the child will hold the number of the largest parent but the coordinate locations of the smallest parent.

In the `draw()` section, we simply draw the child's lines (stored in arrays `xc[]` and `yc[]`) and also the vertices as little rectangles (for visual purposes). Then we draw the two parents.

In the `mouseDragged()` section, we loop through all points of the child and distinguish two possibilities:

1. If parent 1 is greater than parent 2 (i.e., has more points than parent 2), then the counter *k1* remains as is, but the counter *k2* (which will collect points for the smaller parent) is modified according to the formula described earlier.

2. If parent 2 is greater than parent 1 (i.e., has more points than parent 1), then the counter *k2* remains as is, but the counter *k1* (which will collect points for the smaller parent) is modified according to the formula described earlier.

The result of this algorithm is shown in Figure 7-8 and 7-9.

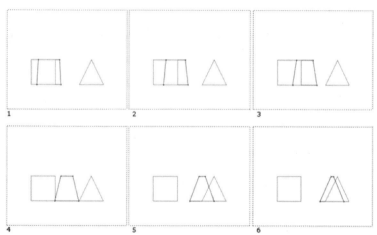

**Figure 7-8:** Interpolation of a square into a triangle in six steps

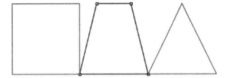

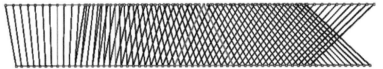

**Figure 7-9:** Interpolation of a square to a triangle, halfway (above), and multiple steps of interpolation and extrapolation of a square into a triangle and beyond (below)

## 7.5 Cellular Automata

A cellular automaton (plural: cellular automata) is a discrete model that consists of a finite, regular grid of cells, each in one of a finite number of states. Time is also discrete, and the state of a cell at a time slice is a function of the state of a finite number of cells called the neighborhood at the previous time slice. Every cell exhibits a local behavior based on the rules applied, which in turn are based on values in their neighborhood. Each time the rules are applied to the whole grid, a new generation is produced. See Figure 7-10.

While cellular automata (a.k.a. CA) were developed originally to describe organic self-replicating systems, their structure and behavior were also useful in addressing architectural, landscape, and urban design problems. From vernacular settlements and social interaction to material behavior and air circulation, CA may provide interesting interpretations of urban and architectural phenomena. The basic idea behind CA is not to describe a complex system with complex equations but to let the complexity emerge by interaction of simple individuals following simple rules. Typical features of CA include: absence of external control (autonomy), symmetry breaking (loss of freedom/heterogeneity), global order (emergence from local interactions), self-maintenance (repair/reproduction metabolisms), adaptation (functionality/tracking of external variations), complexity (multiple concurrent values or objectives), and hierarchies (multiple nested self-organized levels).

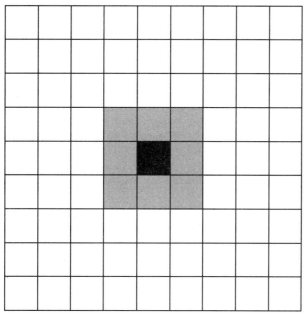

**Figure 7-10:** An 8-neighborhood for the black square
in the center

The following algorithm was developed as a kernel to implement cellular
automata for architectural purposes. It produces sets of lines and paths that,
when seen from a distance, form a maze:

```
1 PImage MyImage;  //define an image
2 int [][] memory; //use it as a copy of the image's data
3 void setup(){
4   size(400,400);
5   MyImage = createImage(width, height, RGB);
6   for(int x=0; x<width; x++)
7     for(int y=0; y<height; y++){
8       if(random(1)>0.5)    //create a random bitmap
9         set(x,y,color(0,0,0));
10       else
11          set(x,y,color(255,255,255));
12      }
13   memory = new int[width][height];
14 }
```

```
15 void draw(){
16
17 }
18
19 int gen = 0;   //marks the number of generations
20 void keyPressed(){
21   for(int x=5; x<width-5; x++)    //go through all pixels
22     for(int y=5; y<height-5; y++){
23       int k=0;
24       for(int i=-1; i<=1; i++)   //go through all 8-neighbors
25         for(int j=-1; j<=1; j++){
26           if(i==0 && j==0)continue;   //skip if the same one
27             color c = get(x+i,y+j);  //if the neighbor is black
28           if(red(c)==0.)k++;   //add it to the counter
29         }
30       if(k==3)    //if all black neighbors are exactly 3
31         memory[x][y]=0;   //become black
32       else if(k>=5)  //if all black neighbors are greater or equal to 5
33         memory[x][y]=255;    //become white
34     }
35   for(int x=0; x<width; x++)
36     for(int y=0; y<height; y++)
37       set(x,y,color(memory[x][y]));   //copy memory[] to image
38   println(gen++);
39 }
```

We first define an image called My Image, where we will draw the cellular automata (CA). Then we define an array called memory to hold temporary information about each CA. In the setup() section, we first create the image and then randomly color each pixel either black or white (lines 6–12). In the keyPressed() section, we loop through all pixels of the image MyImage, and for each pixel we loop in its 8-neighborhood (lines 24–26) and count the number of black pixels (using the counter $k$). Then we apply the following rules: if the number of black neighbors is exactly 3, then we set the memory[][] array (which functions as a copy of the image) to 0 (i.e., black); otherwise, if the number of black neighbors is greater or equal to 5, then we set the memory[] [] array to 255 (i.e., white). When done, we copy the memory[][] elements to the image and draw it. We repeat the process for every mousePressed, which corresponds to the generations. The result of this process is shown in Figures 7-11 and 7-12.

**Figure 7-11:** Cellular automata progression on 1 till 50 generations

**Figure 7-12:** Thirty generations later on a 400 × 400 pixelmap

## 7.6 Evolutionary Algorithm

An evolutionary (a.k.a genetic) algorithm is a search technique for optimizing or solving a problem. Its mechanism is based on evolutionary biology, using terms and processes such as genomes, chromosomes, crossover, mutation, or selection. The evolution starts from a population of completely random individuals and happens in generations. In each generation, the fitness of the whole population is evaluated, multiple individuals are stochastically selected from the current population (based on their fitness), and modified (mutated or recombined) to form a new population, which becomes current in the next iteration of the algorithm. For example, let's say that a secret number is to be guessed: 001010. First, we try out some initial guesses (just generated randomly). These guesses are known as genomes.

a. 110100

b. 111101

c. 011011

d. 101100

We then evaluate how good the guesses are (this is called their *fitness score*). The scores for each of the guesses are given below and represent the number of digits that are exactly correct.

a. 110100 score 1

b. 111101 score 1

c. 011011 score 4

d. 101100 score 3

We then select the best and combine them with other good solutions. This is known as *reproduction*. We shall combine solutions c and d. We may split the solutions (cross them over) any way we like. Below we use four digits of one solution and two of another. This creates the four new solutions shown here:

Crossover: take first 2 digits of c + last 4 of d: e 011100

Crossover: take first 2 digits of d + last 4 of c: f 101011

Crossover: take first 4 c + last 2 d: g 011000

Crossover: take first 4 d + last 2 c: h 101111

Now we get the fitness of each of the new solutions. Their scores follow.

Remember this is just the number of digits in exactly the right place.

  e.  011100 score 3

  f.  101011 score 4

  g.  011000 score 4

  h.  101111 score 3

We then select the best of these new solutions for reproduction. We shall choose g + f.

This time, we cross them over by taking five digits of one number and one of the other.

  Crossover 1st f + last 5 g: i 111000

  Crossover 1st g + last 5 f: j 001011

  Crossover first 3 f + last 3 g: k 101000

  Crossover first 3 g + last 3 f: l 011011

  Random change of one of k's digits: m 001010

Now we determine the fitness for each of these new solutions. These scores follow and are based on the number of digits that are exactly right. Note that we must get all six digits right. We are, therefore, hoping for a score of 6. Luckily solution "m" gets a score of 6 and is the correct answer; it matches our secret number. We have managed to find the answer in 13 guesses. This is better than complete random guesses (the average chance of success of which is about 64).

  i.  111000 score 3

  j.  001011 score 5

  k.  101000 score 4

  l.  011011 score 4

  m.  001010 score 6 = solution in 13 guesses

What we have done is to start off with some guesses of a hidden number (a string of six 1s and 0s), selected the fittest (closest to the number), and crossed them over (mixed them with each other) to produce (reproduce) some new solutions. We kept doing this until we got an ideal solution (all six digits correct).

While genetic algorithms appear to solve a predefined problem (i.e., guess the specific string 001010), they can also be used to address a problem whose solution is not known in advance but can be described through attributes or other indirect characteristics. In that sense, the operation of matching can be applied to an attribute instead of to a fixed pattern. For instance, if symmetry was the sought-out principle to match instead of 001010 (a fixed pattern), then a series of other patterns may have occurred, such as 100001, 011110, 101101, 010010, or the like. In the following code, an evolutionary algorithm is presented that seeks to satisfy the condition of symmetry on a 200 × 200 bitmap.

```
1  int       GA_POPSIZE=    300;    // GA population size
2  int       GA_MAXITER=    200;    // maximum iterations
3  float     GA_ELITRATE=   0.10;   // elitism rate
4  float     GA_MUTATION=   0.25;   // mutation rate
5  String [] population  = new String[GA_POPSIZE]; // array to hold
      possible solutions
6  int [] population_fitness = new int[GA_POPSIZE]; // array to hold the
      fitness value
7  String [] buffer           = new String[GA_POPSIZE]; // a copy of
      population
8  int    [] buffer_fitness   = new int[GA_POPSIZE];    // a copy of
      fitness values
9  int  esize = (int)( GA_POPSIZE *  GA_ELITRATE);   //elitism size
10 String  character = "";      // a dummy String used to create words
11 int w = 30;           //side of the bitmap (30x30)
12 int  tsize = w*w;   // the size (length) of the target String
13 int iter = 0;
14
15 void setup(){
16   size(200,200);
17   // initialize the population: creates a number of randomom Strings
18   for(int i=0;  i< GA_POPSIZE;  i++){
19     character = "";
20     population_fitness[i] = 0;
21     for(int j=0;  j< tsize;  j++)      // for tsize characters
22       character += str(int(random(2)));  //create a random String
23     population[i] = character;
24   }
25 }
26
27 void draw(){
28   background(255);
29   int i=0;
30   for(int x=0; x<w*5; x+=5)
31     for(int y=0; y<w*5; y+=5){
32       if(population[0].charAt(i)=='1'){
33         fill(0);
34         rect(25+y,25+x,5,5);
35       }
36       i++;
37     }
38 }
```

In the first 13 lines of the code, we declare the variables of the problem: the population size, maximum number of iterations, the elitism ratio, mutation rate, and so forth (all are defined in the comments section of the code). In the `setup()` section, we create a string called `character` that is composed of a random set of 0s and 1s. We use this string to draw the bits of the bitmap in the `draw()` section. Notice that the screen is 200 × 200. So, we draw a 5 × 5 rectangle every 5 pixels. The reason for this is simply to make the effect visible by magnifying the bits.

```
39 void keyPressed(){
40 // calculate fitness
41 for(int i=0; i<GA_POPSIZE; i++){
42     int k=0;
43     int pop_length = population[i].length();
44     for(int idx=0; idx<pop_length/2; idx++)
45       if(population[i].charAt((idx/15)*30+(idx%15))==
                population[i].charAt((idx/15)*30+(30-idx%15-1)))
46         k++;
47     population_fitness[i] = (w*w/2) - k;
48   }
49   // sort them (simple bubble sort)
50   for(int i=1;  i< GA_POPSIZE;  i++)
51     for(int j=0;  j< GA_POPSIZE-1;  j++)
52       if( population_fitness[i] <  population_fitness[j]){
53         //swap values
54         int  temp =  population_fitness[ i];
55         population_fitness[i] =  population_fitness[j];
56         population_fitness[j] =  temp;
57         String  stemp =  population[i];
58         population[i] =  population[j];
59         population[j] =  stemp;
60 }
61   // print the best one
62   println( (iter++) + " Best fitness: " +  population_fitness[0] );
63   // mate take half of the population and cross it with the other half
64 int  spos,  i1,  i2;
65   for (int i=0;  i< GA_POPSIZE;  i++) {
66     i1  = (int)(random(1.) *  esize);  //random position within the elite
       population
67     i2  = (int)(random(1.) *  esize);  //random position within the elite
       population
68     spos = (int)(random(1.) *  tsize);  //random position of character
       within a String
69     buffer[i] = population[i1].substring(0, spos ) +
70                 population[i2].substring(spos, tsize);  //crossover
71
```

```
72     // mutate: take a tring and alter one of its characters
73     if(random(1.) < GA_MUTATION) {  //if chance is 1:mutation rate
74       int ipos = (int)(random(1.) * tsize); //select a random character
75       character = "";
76       for(int j=0; j< tsize; j++)
77         if( j== ipos)
78           character += str(int(random(2))); //replace a random character in
       the String
79         else
80           character += buffer[i].charAt(j);
81     }
82     buffer[i] = character;
83   }//for
84
85     // swap buffers
86   for (int i=0; i< GA_POPSIZE; i++) {
87     population[i] = buffer[i];
88     population_fitness[i] = buffer_fitness[i];
89   }
90 } // key pressed
```

In the `keyPressed()` section, we calculate the evolution of one generation for every mouse button pressed. This evolution consists generally of four steps: calculating the fitness of each population, sorting them by fitness, mating each population, and then mutating it. The code for each step is described here:

1. To calculate the fitness, we go through all members of a population and we check symmetrically whether the members are the same, that is, we start checking the first member with the last, then the second with the one before the last, then the third with the one two places before the last, and so forth. This is done in line 45. For every match we increase the counter $k$. When done with the population, we store the counter $k$ in the `population_fitness[]` array (actually we store its difference from the perfect number of matches, i.e., $w*w/2$).

2. Sorting the populations by fitness requires a simple bubble-sorting technique: we loop through all populations twice, and if one fitness is greater than the other, then we swap both the population id and the population's fitness (lines 49 to 60). We then print the best fitness on the screen to inform the user.

3. Mating the population requires taking two-at-a-time randomly selected populations (which in this case are strings) and copying the first $x$ characters from the one string to the other string. So, we define $i1$ and $i2$, which will be random numbers from the total of populations, and `spos`, which is a random position in a string. Once we get these three random numbers, we use them to go through the first `spos` numbers of characters from string at position $i1$ and the remaining characters from string at position $i2$ and compose a new string in the `buffer[]` array (this array will copied back to the population one).

4. If a mutation is required (because a random possibility is less than the mutation ratio GA_MUTATION), then we create a random number within the number of characters of the string population and replace the character at that position with another randomly chosen character (in this case either a 0 or a 1). This is done in line 78.

Finally, we swap the values in the buffer with those of the population and wait for the user to click on the mouse so that the process will be repeated.

The result of this algorithm is shown in Figure 7-13.

**Figure 7-13:** Steps in the evolutionary algorithm. After 177 generations of 200 iterations each, the symmetry condition is satisfied.

## Summary

In this chapter, we have been introduced to a series of algorithms that although not directly related to design can have significant influence in a design problem. One of the main differences between such algorithms versus design-specific algorithms is in their methodology. Most design algorithms are driven by a user in a top-down fashion, where decisions are propagated from the designer's idea toward the physical implementation. The algorithms introduced here are very different because they do not start from a conscious idea but rather from a random pattern and then, through the application of rules, this pattern emerges through a bottom-up process into a coherent pattern that may be used as a possible solution.

# Exercises

**NOTE** Answers to the exercises are provided in Appendix B.

1.  Write the code that will generate the following fractal pattern:

Step 1

Step 2

2.  Create a fractal that will produce the following pattern:

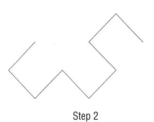

Step 1

Step 2

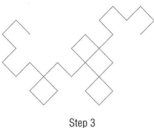

Step 3

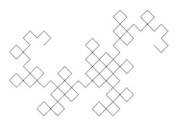

Step 4

3.  Using the stochastic search algorithm introduced in section 7.2, distribute seven sets of squares that contain 7, 2, 4, 6, 6, 5, and five squares in each set within a 5 × 7 grid. For example, one solution may be:

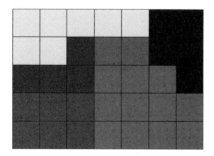

Possible solution for 7 sets of squares
arranged on a 5x7 grid.

## Notes

1. The word *interesting* is derived from the Latin word *interesse*, which means "to be between, make a difference, concern, from inter- + esse (= to be). (See Merriam-Webster 11th Collegiate Dictionary) Interestingly, the in between is literally … interesting!

# 3-D Space

Perspective systems are designed to construct pictures that, when viewed, produce in the trained viewer the experience of depicted objects that match perceivable objects. Space perception theorists have written about how our capacities to see are constrained by the perspective system that we use, that is, by our way of depicting what we see. Pictorial spaces are constructed through geometrical models. Each model is expressed as a geometrical transformation applied to Cartesian shapes of the physical environment. These transformations show how shapes are projected in pictorial space. For instance, the mapping of a cube residing in Cartesian space is projected to the surface of the viewing plane through straight lines representing light rays.

In architectural design, the methods of projection also serve a subliminal purpose. While axonometric views are considered exact, precise, accurate, and measurable, perspective views are empirical, observable, factual, and expressive. Perspective projection is about the viewer's identity, existence, location, and orientation, while orthographic projection is about the depicted object's identity and characteristics, not the viewer's. Isometric and oblique views are exaggerated and, often, extreme methods of orthographic projection, whose purpose is to express, focus, and attract attention to certain parts or angles of the depicted form. Another model of depiction is that of abstraction: black-and-white line drawings convey a clear, sharp, and sterile impression of the depicted form, whereas blueprints are understood as working drawings. In contrast, rendered drawings convey materiality, completeness, substance, and effect.

The problem with rendered views is that form is not always conceived as made out of matter. In fact, form is rather an abstract entity that possesses certain geometric characteristics. For instance, dots on a piece of paper may imply a shape not because they are made out of ink but because of their geometric relationships. The attachment of material qualities constrains the behavior of form and restricts the designer's imagination. In contrast, the lack of materiality liberates the form from its constraints and introduces behaviors closer to intuition rather than perception.

This chapter shows how to project rays of light on a flat surface and how to rotate the projected shape in such a way as to produce the behavior of a 3D object rotating in space.

# 8.1 The Third Dimension

By observing the world around us, we do notice that all objects exist in a three-dimensional space. Yet the eye through which we see and conceive the world is an organ whose functionality is based on an almost two-dimensional surface. This implies that there must be a connection between two and three dimensions for us to be able to see. The connection is that our understanding of a three-dimensional world is based not on its 3D nature per se but on the *behavior* of 3D projections on the surface of our eye (or the screen).

Consider the following example: the object shown in Figures 8-1 and 8-2 can be claimed to be either of a two-dimensional surface or a three-dimensional face of a solid. Nevertheless, if we rotate the object, then we can perceive its true nature. But rotating still involves a two-dimensional representation, that is, the projection on the surface of the eye. So, the determination of the three-dimensional nature of an object is based on the relationships of the shapes on the projection surface.

In Figures 8-1 and 8-2, you can see that when an object is rotated, it conveys more information about its 3D nature. In fact, the more movements we allow it to have, the more understanding one would have of the form and its position in space. Unfortunately, we always have to work with projections because both the computer screen and our eyes are flat projection surfaces. So, we need to find a technique of displaying the projection of 3D objects in such a way that the viewer will recognize them. To accomplish that, we need to first define the objects and then project them. Until we project them on the screen, we will not know their dimensional nature. The following sections show how to define 3D objects and how to project them using the existing 2D graphics methods discussed so far.

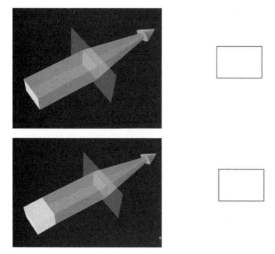

**Figure 8-1:** An object is projected on the screen. The resulting projection (right) can be confusing or misleading about the shape, type, or volume of the 3D object (in this case a square panel as opposed to a cube).

**Figure 8.-2:**  After a rotation in space the object is projected on the screen. The resuprojection (right) convinces the viewer about the shape, type, and volume of the 3D object.

## 8.2 Defining 3D Objects

Chapter 3 dealt with points, segments, and shapes, using two coordinates to describe their geometry. These two coordinates we called x and y, and we declared them to be of type float. The rationale for using floats instead of integers is that the measurements can have a fractional value, that is, 3 feet and 2 inches, or 5.25 meters, yet their display on a pixel-based screen will automatically have them converted into integer values. In fact, graphic objects in Processing, such as point(), rect(), ellipse(), line(), and the like, automatically cast the real (or float) numbers into integers in order for them to be drawn on the screen, because a computer screen uses pixels that are defined as whole numbers ( i.e., we cannot say 2.2 pixels long; it is 2 pixels instead).

In the case of the class MyPoint, we used the following definition:

```
class MyPoint {
float x, y;  // data members

  // Constructor
  MyPoint(float xinput, float yinput){
    x = xinput;
    y = yinput;
  }
}
```

Now we will add one more float (called z) as the third member. This action will automatically allow us to assign values to a third dimension, which can also be referred to as height or depth. The class will become:

```
class MyPoint {
  float x, y, z;
}
```

and the constructor of the MyPoint class will be:

```
MyPoint(float xinput, float yinput, float zinput){
  x = xinput;
  y = yinput;
  z = zinput;
}
```

Now we can adjust the standard transformation methods we introduced in Chapter 3 (i.e., move, scale, and rotate). Move and scale can be adjusted simply by adding the third dimension as a copy of the previous two dimensions:

```
void move(float xoff, float yoff, float zoff){
  x = x + xoff;
  y = y + yoff;
  z = z + zoff;
}

void scale(float xs, float ys, float zs){
  x = x * xs;
  y = y * ys;
  z = z * zs;
}
```

Rotation involves three adjustments instead of one. The reason is that rotation occurs in three ways in three-dimensional space (i.e., around three axes). So we need to convert the 2D rotation method (that involved only x and y) into three methods for x-y, y-z, and z-x. As a reminder, the 2D rotation procedure (from Chapter 3) is displayed here:

```
void rotate (float angle  ){  //2D rotation
  float tempx = x * cos(angle) - y * sin(angle);
  float tempy = y * cos(angle) + x * sin(angle);
  x = tempx;
  y = tempy;
}
```

In fact, this particular rotation is one around the z-axis (since only x and y are affected), so we will keep it as is. The other two rotations will use a combination of x, y, and z in such a way that rotation around the x-axis involves the y and z dimensions, and rotation around the y-axis involves the x and z dimensions. In the following code, we demonstrate the use of all possible combinations of x, y, and z to create all three rotations. The result is:

```
// Rotation around the z-axis
void rotatez(float angle  ){
  float tempx = x * cos(angle) - y * sin(angle);
  float tempy = y * cos(angle) + x * sin(angle);
  x = tempx;
  y = tempy;
}


//Rotation around the x-axis
void rotatex(float angle  ){
  float tempy = y * cos(angle) - z * sin(angle);
  float tempz = z * cos(angle) + y * sin(angle);
  y = tempy;
  z = tempz;
}


//Rotation around the y-axis
void rotatey(float angle  ){
  float tempx = x * cos(angle) - z * sin(angle);
  float tempz = z * cos(angle) + x * sin(angle);
  x = tempx;
  z = tempz;
}
```

The explanation of the formulas used above is shown in the following paragraph. Suppose that we want to rotate a point A (x, y) to position B (x', y') around a center O (0,0) by an angle b, as shown in Figure 8-3.

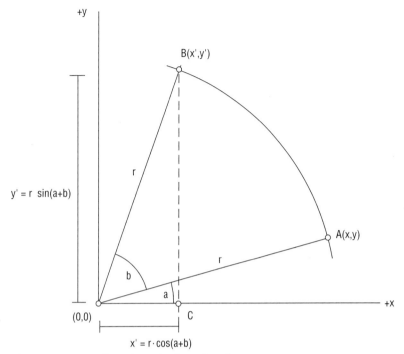

**Figure 8-3:** Rotation of a point from location A to B.

Consider the triangle OBC: the sine of its a + b angle is y' /r, and its cosine is x' /r. So that means:

```
x' = r*cos(a+b)   and
y' = r*sin(a+b).
```

Thus, both expressions can be extended into:

```
x' = r*cos(a+b) = r*cos(a)*cos(b) - r*sin(a)*sin(b)
y' = r*sin(a+b) = r*sin(a)*cos(b) + r*cos(a)*sin(b)
```

But since `x = r * cos(a)` and `y = r* sin(a)`, the preceding expression becomes:

```
x' = r*cos(a)*cos(b) - r*sin(a)*sin(b) = x*cos(b) - y*sin(b)
y' = r*sin(a)*cos(b) + r*cos(a)*sin(b) = y*cos(b) + x*sin(b)
```

So, it follows that for a rotation angle b:

```
x' = x*cos(angle_b) - y*sin(angle_b);
y' = y*cos(angle_b) + x*sin(angle_b);
```

If we apply the same logic in the other directions, we end up with the two other procedures: rotatex() and rotatey() shown earlier. The combinatorial logic of transformations is part of an area of mathematics called *linear algebra*. It is possible to construct "techniques" for creating all possible combinations of an operation given a set of parameters, such as (in this case) the rotational transformations. These "techniques" are referred to as *matrices*, and they represent a visual way for making sure that all possibilities are expressed. For example, the following matrix:

$$\begin{bmatrix} x' \\ y' \\ z' \\ 1 \end{bmatrix} = \begin{bmatrix} sx & 0 & 0 & 0 \\ 0 & sy & 0 & 0 \\ 0 & 0 & sz & 0 \\ 0 & 0 & 0 & 1 \end{bmatrix} * \begin{bmatrix} x \\ y \\ z \\ 1 \end{bmatrix}$$

can be transformed into the following set of equations which represent the scaling transformation (around the origin point 0,0,0):

```
x' = sx * x  + 0  * y  + 0  * z  + 0 * 1  =  sx * x
y' = 0  * x  + sy * y  + 0  * z  + 0 * 1  =  sy * y
z' = 0  * x  + 0  * y  + sz * z  + 0 * 1  =  sz * z
1  = 0  * x  + 0  * y  + 0  * z  + 1 * 1  =   1 * 1
```

# 8.3 Projecting on the Screen

After establishing the structure of a 3D point, we need to create an object out of these points (e.g., a cube) and then project them on the screen to see the object. First, we define the points of a cube using an array:

```
MyPoint[] points;
void setup(){
  points = new MyPoint[8];

  points[0] = new MyPoint(-20.,  -20.,  -20.);
  points[1] = new MyPoint( 20.,  -20.,  -20.);
  points[2] = new MyPoint( 20.,   20.,  -20.);
  points[3] = new MyPoint(-20.,   20.,  -20.);
  points[4] = new MyPoint(-20.,  -20.,   20.);
  points[5] = new MyPoint( 20.,  -20.,   20.);
  points[6] = new MyPoint( 20.,   20.,   20.);
  points[7] = new MyPoint(-20.,   20.,   20.);
}
```

Second, we need to draw these points using the `point()` method as we did in the Chapter 3. The problem is that we need two integer numbers, xp and yp, and we have (from the `MyPoint` structure) three float variables x, y, and z. This situation is illustrated in Figure 8-4.

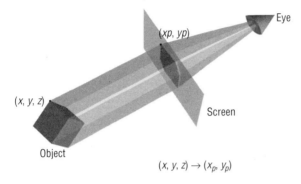

$$(x, y, z) \rightarrow (x_p, y_p)$$

**Figure 8-4:** Projection of a 3D point on a 2D plane

The answer can be quite simple: let's use only the x and y values and omit the z value. So, the `draw()` method would look as follows:

```
void draw(){
  background(255);
  strokeWeight(4);
  for(int i=0; i<8; i++)
    point( 50+ points[i].x, 50+ points[i].y);
}
```

To rotate the points in an interactive manner, we simply need to use the mouse-dragging event and connect the mouse's x and y location to the points' x and y rotations. The following code illustrates this connection:

```
void mouseDragged(){

int xoff = mouseX - pmouseX;
int yoff = mouseY - pmouseY;

for(int i=0; i<points.length; i++){
  points[i].rotatey(radians(xoff));
  points[i].rotatex(radians(yoff));
  }
}
```

In the preceding code, we use the `mouseDragged` section to rotate the cubical point arrangement as the mouse is dragged. First, we get the difference (`xoff` and `yoff`) between the current position of the mouse (i.e., `mouseX` and `mouseY`) and its immediate previous position (i.e., `pmouseX` and `pmouseY`). We then use that difference to rotate the points by calling the `rotatey()` and `rotatex()` methods of the `MyPoint` class. The output is a rotating cubical arrangement of points, an instance of which is shown in Figure 8-5.

**Figure 8-5:** Eight points rotating in a cubical formation

To better visualize the cube, we can use lines that connect each point to all the other ones. This can be done by altering the `draw()` method as follows:

```
void draw(){
  background(255);
  for(int j=0; j<8; j++)
    for(int i=0; i<8; i++)
      line(50+points[i].x, 50+ points[i].y,
      50+points[j].x, 50+points[j].y  );
}
```

For each point, we draw a line to all the other points. The result is shown in Figure 8-6.

**Figure 8-6:** Lines connecting opposite vertices in a cube formation

## 8.4 Perspective Projection

We have seen how to derive the projection points xp and yp through the x, y, and z coordinates by selecting only the x and y coordinates and omitting the z. This method is also referred to as *orthographic projection*. Such a projection involves the collapse of a point (x,y,z) to a point perpendicularly to the screen (that is, along the z-axis). In other words, by omitting the z coordinate, we are implicitly assuming that it is 0, assuming that the screen is coinciding with the xy plane, as shown in Figure 8-7.

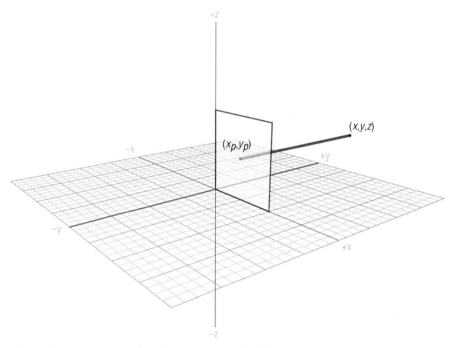

**Figure 8-7:** Projection of a 3D point onto a 2D plane

Please note that the z coordinate does not play any role in the projection method. This means that no matter how far away the object gets from the screen, or how far away the viewer gets from the object, its projection will always remain the same. In contrast, in perspective projection, the z-dimension (depth) does play a role in the projection method. According to the perspective formula that follows, x and y are related to z so that, as the object moves along the z axis, its projection changes.

```
float eye = 128.;
float t = 1.0/(1.0+((float) z / eye ));
```

```
xP = (int)( x * t);
yP = (int)( y * t);
```

The variable "eye" represents the distance of the viewer from the plane of projection. The smaller the number, the closer one gets to the screen resulting in a "wide angle" projection. We can implement these projections in the existing MyPoint classes in the following way: define a method where we pass the MyPoint coordinates, and it returns a modified MyPoint x and y projection coordinate. This is demonstrated in the following code:

```
int xP(float eye){
   float t = 1.0/(1.0+((float) z / eye ));
   int px = int( x * t);
   return(px);
}

int yP(float eye){
   float t = 1.0/(1.0+((float) z / eye ));
   int py = int( y * t);
   return(py);
}
```

The perspective projection ratio is equal to 1/(1+z/eye) where, as mentioned, eye is the distance of the viewer to the projecting plane. Both methods(above) can be called from the main code within the draw() method in the following way:

```
for(int j=0; j<8; j++)
   for(int i=0; i<8; i++){
      line(50+points[i].xP(128.), 50+points[i].yP(128.),
            50+points[j].xP(128.), 50+points[j].yP(128.)   );
   }
```

The output for a perspective projection using the same MyPoint and the xP() and yP() methods is shown in Figure 8-8.

**Figure 8-8:** A perspective projection

## 8.5 Three-Dimensional Graphics in Processing

While the information so far aims at showing how the theory of projection can be applied to objects, Processing has a series of built-in commands that handle 3D projections. These commands are convenient for the user because one does not need to deal with the details of how transformations apply in 3D, yet it is important for the student to know at least theoretically how these operations work, at least at the mathematical level. The next sections introduce the ways in which Processing deals with 3D space and try to connect it with an object's class in 3D space.

As you have seen, a two-dimensional representation is established by setting a window view to a plane upon which an object of interest is drawn. For example, in the code that follows the command `size()` establishes a view to a plane (the grey area in Figure 8-9) upon which a rectangle is drawn as the object of interest using the `rect()` command:

```
size(100,100);
rect(25,25,50,50);
```

**Figure 8-9:** A 2D rectangle

Moving from two dimensions to three dimensions requires two points of reference: a viewer and an object. The following code shows a cube in a three-dimensional environment clipped within a viewing window. In this case, the `size()` command creates a clipped window view into a 3D world (grey area in Figure 8-10) which is accomplished by using a library called P3D (i.e., the third parameter of `size()`). The `camera()` command defines the viewer's position by taking nine parameters: the xyz location of the viewer's eye, the xyz location of the point towards viewing, and a vector representing the direction of the axis perpendicular to the ground. The `box()` command constructs a cube positioned at the center of the camera's view.

```
size(200,200,P3D);
camera(100,100,-100,0,0,0,0,0,1);
box(50);
```

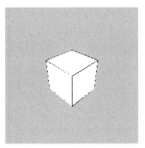

**Figure 8-10:** A 3D cube

The camera offers a fixed point of view. In this case, it is stationed at location 100,100,-100. In order to rotate the camera and offer an interactive view of the scene, we can replace the x an y parameters of the camera's position with the mouse's x and y position. In addition, we need to redraw the screen, using the `draw()` loop, while continuously repainting the background:

```
void setup(){
  size(100,100,P3D);
}
void draw(){
  background(200);
  camera(mouseX,mouseY,-100,0,0,0,0,0,1);
  box(50);
}
```

The result is shown in Figure 8-11.

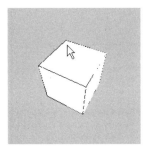

**Figure 8-11:** A 3D cube that
can be rotated in space

To transform the location, rotation, and size of an object we can use the `translate()`, `rotateX()`, `rotate()`, `rotateZ()`, and `scale()` commands. Note that these should be enclosed between the `pushMatrix()` and `popMatrix()`

commands. A matrix is a mathematical table by which each xyz coordinate of each point in a 3D scene is operated upon. In essence, the original matrix, the one we start with before a transformation is applied, is modified after each transformation. In order to avoid a propagating effect, whereby each transformation is affecting the next one, we need to reset the matrix to the original form, using the pushMatrix() / popMatrix() sequence. For example, a series of transformations on two box() objects may look as follows:

```
size(100,100, P3D);
camera(-100,100,-100,0,0,0,0,0,1);
  for(int x=0; x<3; x++){
    pushMatrix();
    translate(x*60, 0, 0);
    box(40);
    popMatrix();
}
```

The result will be three cubes of a length of 40 units positioned every 60 units apart, as shown in Figure 8-12.

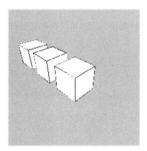

**Figure 8-12:** Three cubes aligned

The problem with the Processing/P3D representation mentioned above is that, while objects do appear in the scene, they are not identifiable. For instance, suppose that one object is to be selected after it is created. This is not possible with the current code. There is no reference or memory of any drawn object in the scene. They are simply displayed on the screen. In order to establish an identity for each object in the scene, we need to create classes of 3D objects that will contain the information about their unique name, position, attributes, and transformations. Thus, we will construct a class called MyObject that will illustrate a partial solution to this problem.

```
1    class MyObject{
2        float dim = 40;              //size of the object
3        float x,y,z;                 //position coordinates
4        boolean picked = false;      //picked status
5        color c_face = color(255);   //color of object
```

```
6
7        //determine whether an object is picked
8        void pick(float xp, float yp){
9          //is the distance enough to pick?
10         if(dist(xp,yp,screenX(x,y,z),screenY(x,y,z))<dim)
11           picked = true;
12         else
13           picked = false;
14       }
15
16       void draw3(){
17         if(picked==true)
18           fill(255,0,0);          //paint red to indicate picked
19         else
20           fill(c_face);           //normal color
21         box(dim);
22       }
23     }
24
25     MyObject b = new MyObject(); //create an object
26     void setup(){
27       size(500,500, P3D);          //setup the screen
28       camera(-100,100,-100,0,0,0,0,0,1); //get a viewpoint
29     }
30     void draw(){
31         b.draw3();                //draw the object
32     }
33     void mousePressed(){
34         b.pick(mouseX,mouseY);    //see if the mouse can pick
35     }
```

The class defined as MyObject contains as its members its size (i.e., the length of the side of a cube), the coordinates of its location, the status of whether it is picked or not, and the color of its faces. The first method assigns the state of whether an object has been picked. It takes two numbers as parameters (i.e., the mouse's coordinates after being projected on the screen) and calculates the distance between those and the projection of the objects location on the screen. These projections are calculated though the Processing methods screenX() and screenY(), which calculate the pixel location of an xyz point in a scene after it is projected on the screen. If the distance is within the object's size (i.e., dim), then it is assigned as picked; otherwise, it is not. Next, we create a method called draw3, which will draw the object (which happens to be a box in this case) and paint it according to the pick status.

Meanwhile, in the main code, we define an object b and then set up the screen with a viewing position. Next, we draw the object b using the expression b.draw3(), which will call the draw3 method within the b object's class (see lines 16–23). Finally, we use the expression b.pick() to call the pick method within the object's class and pass the mouse's coordinates at the moment when the user presses the mouse.

In the Figure 8-13 an object is selected (left) and deselected (right) by either clicking on the object (or within 40 pixels close to the center of the object) or clicking anywhere else to deselect it.

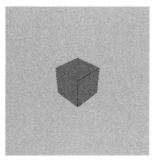 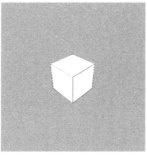

**Figure 8-13:** A red (left) and a white (right) cube

In the next code a more complete version of the selection/transformation structure is provided. Here, an object is defined as a class called `MyObject`, and it contains the size, coordinates of location, angles of rotation, scaling factors, picked status, and colors of the faces and edges. The first three methods assign the values of the desired transformation to the members of the class. For instance, `rotate3()` receives as parameters three angles, which are passed to the corresponding x, y, and z rotational angles of the class. These will be used later in the `draw3()` method. Next, we define a method that will determine whether an object is picked or not (see previous code example). The `draw3()` method paints and transforms the object in the scene: first it selects the color to paint the object depending on whether it is picked or not. Then it pushes the transformation matrix into a stack that will then push up at the end of the transformation. Within this sequence all transformations are applied to the object (i.e., `translate()`, `rotateX()`, `rotateY()`, `rotateZ()`, and `scale()`). Finally, the object is drawn (in this case, a cube) in the scene.

```
1    class MyObject{
2        float dim = 30;         //size of object
3        float x,y,z;            //location member
4        float ax,ay,az;         //rotational values
5        float sx=1, sy=1,sz=1;  //scaling factors
6        boolean picked = false; //picked status
7        color c_face = color(255,255,255); //color of face
8        color c_edge = color(0);           //color of edge
9
10       //translation
11       void move3(float xin, float yin, float zin){
```

```
12        x = xin;
13        y = yin;
14        z = zin;
15      }
16      //three rotations
17      void rotate3(float axin, float ayin, float azin){
18        ax = axin;
19        ay = ayin;
20        az = azin;
21      }
22      //scaling
23      void scale3(float sxin, float syin, float szin){
24        sx = sxin;
25        sy = syin;
26        sz = szin;
27      }
28      //determine whether an object is selected
29      void pick(float xp, float yp){
30        if(dist(xp,yp,screenX(x,y,z),screenY(x,y,z))<10)
31          picked = true;
32        else
33          picked = false;
34      }
35      //draw the object
36      void draw3(){
37        stroke(c_edge);
38        if(picked==true) //if picked
39          fill(255,0,0); // then red
40        else
41          fill(c_face);  // else its own color
42        pushMatrix();
43        translate(x,y,z);
44        rotateX(ax);
45        rotateY(ay);
46        rotateZ(az);
47        scale(sx,sy,sz);
48        box(dim);
49        popMatrix();
50      }
51    }
```

In the main code, we define an array called b of type MyObject and a variable called zoom to store the zoom in and out values. In the setup section, we define an array of 100 objects and we create (in a loop) the objects one by one.

In the draw() section, we paint a background color to refresh the screen and we position a camera looking at the 55th object (i.e., close to the center of the configuration). The camera's position is determined by the mouse's location through the differential variables xd and yd, which will be discussed in the next paragraph. The z location of the camera is adjusted through the zoom factor, which is controlled through the mouse's wheel (discussed two paragraphs below). Then we loop in a 10 × 10 nested loop, upon which we translate each newly created object (line 69). We also use a counter called k to assign the objects to the array in an ascending order.

In line 22, we define two variables, xd and yd, that are used to store the difference between the current location of the mouse (i.e., mouseX) and its previous position when the mouse was first pressed (i.e., pmouseX). These differential values are used to move the camera in the x and y directions.

Next, in line 31 we use the pick() command of each object to determine whether an object is picked given the mouse coordinates.

The last method is a graphic user interface method that enables to get the rotational positions of the mouse's wheel. These values are added accumulatively to the zoom variable and then used to move the camera in the z direction.

```
1    MyObject [] b;                //define an array of objects
2    int zoom;                     //zoom in/out factor
3    void setup(){
4      size(400,400,P3D);
5      b = new MyObject[100];       //populate the array
6      for(int i=0; i<b.length; i++)
7        b[i] = new MyObject();     //construct objects
8    }
9
10   void draw(){
11     background(200);             //redraw the background
12     camera(xd,yd,getWheel(),  b[55].x,b[55].y,b[55].z,  0,0,1);
13     int k=0;                     //object counter
14     for(int x=0; x<10; x++)      //10x10 grid
15       for(int y=0; y<10; y++){
16         b[k].draw3();            //draw the object
17         b[k].move3(x*60,y*60,0); //move on a grid configuration
18         k++;                     //increment the counter
19       }
20   }
21
22   float xd,yd; // difference between current and previous mouse
23   void mouseDragged(){
24     xd += mouseX-pmouseX;        //get the difference
25     yd += mouseY-pmouseY;
26     camera(xd,yd,100+(zoom*5),  b[55].x,b[55].y,b[55].z,  0,0,1);
27   }
28
29   void mousePressed(){
30     for(int i=0; i<b.length; i++)
31       b[i].pick(mouseX,mouseY);  //pick an object
32   }
33
```

```
34    int getWheel(){
35      addMouseWheelListener(new MouseWheelListener() {
36        public void mouseWheelMoved(MouseWheelEvent e){
37          zoom+=e.getWheelRotation();}});
38      return(zoom);
39    }
```

The result of this code is shown in Figure 8-14.

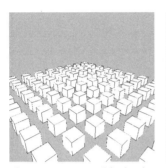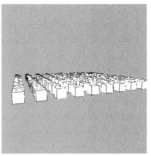

**Figure 8-14:** A grid of cubes where any one of them can be selected

# 8.6 3D Point Formations

Using the Processing graphics command `point(x,y,z)` in conjunction to a 3D world and a camera viewpoint, we can construct any point formation. Since the `point()` methods takes three coordinates and the camera orients the viewer to a specific viewpoint, the task is simply to arrange patterns of numbers that will illustrate point formations.

## 8.6.1 Cubical Formations

One of the simple formations of points is a linear one. A set of points is generated in one direction and the points are placed at equal intervals. The following code demonstrates such an arrangement:

```
1    size(500,500, P3D);              //setup the screen
2    camera(-20,20,-20,0,0,0,0,0,1); //get a viewpoint
3    for(int x=-10; x<10; x++)        //loop in one direction
4        point(x,0,0);
```

Similarly, a two-dimensional arrangement may be in the form of a grid, where points are generated upon a two-dimensional plane and arranged at equal intervals. The following code demonstrates such an arrangement:

```
1    size(500,500, P3D);                  //setup the screen
2    camera(-20,20,-20,0,0,0,0,0,1); //get a viewpoint
3    for(int x=-10; x<10; x++)         //loop in two directions
4      for(int y=-10; y<10; y++)
5        point(x,y,0);
```

Finally, a three-dimensional arrangement may be in the form of a cubical formation, where points are generated along three directions and arranged at equal intervals. The following code demonstrates such an arrangement, also shown in Figure 8-15.

```
1    size(500,500, P3D);                  //setup the screen
2    camera(-20,20,-20,0,0,0,0,0,1); //get a viewpoint
3    for(int x=-10; x<10; x++)         //loop in three directions
4      for(int y=-10; y<10; y++)
5        for(int z=-10; z<10; z++)
6          point(x,y,z);
```

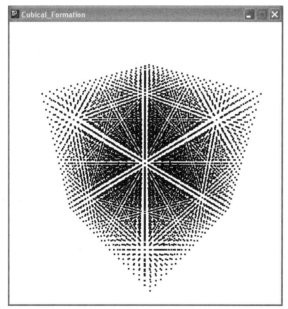

**Figure 8-15:** A cubical formation of points created by looping in three directions

## 8.6.2 Spherical Formations

As Chapter 2 discussed, the parametric equations of a circle are:

```
x=r*cos(theta), y=r*sin(theta)
```

`theta` is the parameter that changes, whereas `r` is the radius of the circle. The parametric equations of a circle in a three-dimensional world should be exactly the same, including a z coordinate that will be 0 if the circle is placed on the x-y plane. Consider the following:

```
x = v cos(u)
y = v sin(u)      u = [0, 2*Pi) ,
z = 0
```

This describes a circle of radius `v` in the xy plane. Suppose that we vary `v` from `0` to some constant radius `r`. We would obtain a series of concentric circles in the xy plane. These circles correspond to what would happen if we sliced a hypothetical sphere with radius `r` perpendicular to the z-axis. For some `v`, we see that such a sphere has a z coordinate equal to sqrt($r^2 - v^2$). It follows that these equations

```
x = v cos(u)
y = v sin(u)      u = [0, 2*Pi)
z = sqrt(r2-v2)   v = [0, r]
```

are the parametric equations of a hemisphere above and including the xy plane. To get the whole sphere, we could mirror it in the xy plane and let the square root take on both positive and negative values, but this is not very elegant. Rather, consider replacing `v` with $r \cos(v)$. As this new `v` goes from 0 to p/2, $r*\sin(v)$ goes from 0 to `r`. So, let `v` go from –p/2 to p/2, and $z = \sqrt{(r^2 - v^2)\cos^2(v)} = r*\cos(v)$. Hence

```
x = r sin(v) cos(u)
y = r sin(v) sin(u)      u = [0, 2*Pi)
z = r cos(v)             v = [0, Pi]
```

are the parametric equations of the whole sphere of radius *r* in 3D. The algorithm for a parametric sphere in 3D is shown in the following source code and in Figure 8-16.

```
1    size(500,500, P3D);                    //setup the screen
2    camera(-15,15,-15,0,0,0,0,0,1); //get a viewpoint
3      for(int i=0; i<360; i+=10)
4        for(int j=0; j<360; j+=10){
5          float x = 10 * sin(radians(i)) * cos(radians(j));
6          float y = 10 * sin(radians(i)) * sin(radians(j));
```

```
7          float z = 10 * cos(radians(i));
8          point(x,y,z);
9        }
```

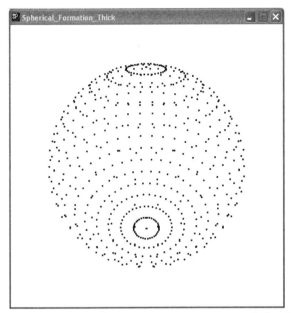

**Figure 8-16:** A spherical formation using sampled points

While a point is the simplest way of visualizing the position of three coordinate numbers in 3D space, in some cases, this information is not enough. Instead, we can connect consecutive points to form segment that will appear overall as geodesic lines. This technique is shown in the following code:

```
1    size(500,500, P3D);                //setup the screen
2    camera(-15,15,-15,0,0,0,0,0,1); //get a viewpoint
3    background(255);
4    for(int i=0; i<360; i+=10)
5      for(int j=0; j<360; j+=10){
6        float x =  10 * sin(radians(i)) * cos(radians(j));
7        float y =  10 * sin(radians(i)) * sin(radians(j));
8        float z =  10 * cos(radians(i));
9        float xn =  10 * sin(radians(i+10)) * cos(radians(j));
10       float yn =  10 * sin(radians(i+10)) * sin(radians(j));
11       float zn =  10 * cos(radians(i+10));
12       float xu =  10 * sin(radians(i)) * cos(radians(j+10));
13       float yu =  10 * sin(radians(i)) * sin(radians(j+10));
14       float zu =  10 * cos(radians(i));
15       line(x,y,z, xn,yn,zn);
16       line(x,y,z, xu,yu,zu);
17     }
```

The result is shown in Figure 8-17.

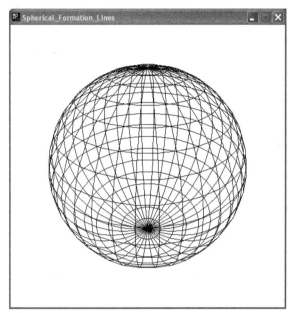

**Figure 8-17:** A spherical formation using line segments connecting sampled points

## 8.6.3 Superquadrics

As we saw in the last section, the parametric equation of a sphere is:

```
x = r cos(v) cos(u)
y = r cos(v) sin(u)      u = [-Pi, Pi)
z = r sin(v)             v = [-Pi/2, Pi/2]
```

This representation can be seen as part of a more generalized set of representations, where the sphere is just one instance. These representations are described through the following parametric equations:

```
x = rx cosn(v) cose(u)
y = ry cosn(v) sine(u)    u = [-Pi, Pi)
z = rz sinn(v)            v = [-Pi/2, Pi/2]
```

The set of objects that are produced through such representations are called superquadrics. The interesting part of these objects is their ability to transform between different primitive forms, that is, from a cube to a cylinder and from a sphere to a rhomboid. For example, in the preceding equations, if rx = ry = rz = 10 and n=1 and e=1, then we have a sphere of radius 10 (see the first set of equations above). In the following code, we show the algorithm for creating superquadrics:

```
int samples = 20;
float a1 = 10., a2 = 10., a3 = 10.;
float u1 = 0., u2 = 20., v1 = 0., v2 = 20.;
float dU = (u2 - u1) / samples;
float dV = (v2 - v1) / samples;
float n = 1., e = 1.;
void setup(){
  size(500,500, P3D);          //setup the screen
  camera(-20,20,-20,0,0,0,0,0,1); //get a viewpoint
  float u = u1;
  for(int i=0; i<samples; i++){
    float v = v1;
    for(int j=0; j<samples; j++){
      float x = a1 * sqCos (u, n) * sqCos (v, e);
      float y = a2 * sqCos (u, n) * sqSin (v, e);
      float z = a3 * sqSin (u, n);
      point(x,y,z);
      v += dV;
    }
    u += dU;
  }
}

float sign ( float x ) {
  if ( x < 0 )return -1;
  if ( x > 0 )return 1;
  return 0;
}
float sqSin( float v, float n ) {
  return sign(sin(v)) * pow(abs(sin(v)),n);
}
float sqCos( float v, float n ) {
  return sign(cos(v)) * pow(abs(cos(v)),n);
}
```

which is a cube because we start with n = e = 0. The chart shown in Figure 8-18 illustrates how a superquadric transforms for different values of n and e.

The behavior of a superquadric for negative or large values of n and e can be quite interesting, as shown in Figure 8-19.

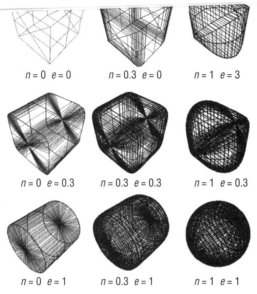

$n = 0 \ e = 0$  $n = 0.3 \ e = 0$  $n = 1 \ e = 3$

$n = 0 \ e = 0.3$  $n = 0.3 \ e = 0.3$  $n = 1 \ e = 0.3$

$n = 0 \ e = 1$  $n = 0.3 \ e = 1$  $n = 1 \ e = 1$

**Figure 8-18:** The behavior of a superquadric for different values of $e$ and $n$

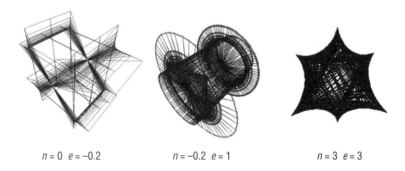

$n = 0 \ e = -0.2$  $n = -0.2 \ e = 1$  $n = 3 \ e = 3$

**Figure 8-19:** The behavior of a superquadric for extreme values of $e$ and $n$

## Summary

In this chapter, you have been introduced to the concept of 3D space. At this point, you should be able to define a point and project it using an orthographic or perspective method. Also, you saw how to use Processing graphic commands to place points, lines, and boxes in 3D space and how to select them. We also introduced the concept of parameterization, and we showed how to create a sphere and a superquadric. The purpose was to show the use of parametric equations in 3D space.

## Exercises

**NOTE** Answers to the exercises are provided in Appendix B.

1. Using the analytical equation of a sphere, that is, $x^2 + y^2 + z^2 = r^2$, construct a sphere that has a radius of 10.

2. A superhyperboloid is defined by the following parametric equations:

```
x = rx sec^n(v) cos^e(u)
y = ry sec^n(v) sin^e(u)          u = [0, 2*Pi)
z = rz tan^n(v)                   v = [-Pi/2, Pi/2]
```

   Modify the existing superquadric code to handle superhyperboloids. Explore the different values of $e$ and $n$.

3. Write the code that will produce the following pattern of 36 1 × 1 × 1 cubes in a circular arrangement of a radius of 10 units:

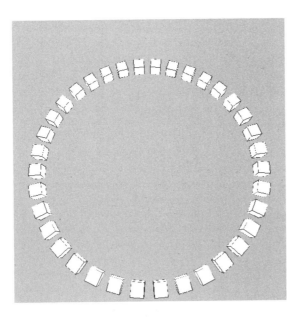

```
for(int phi=0; phi<360; phi+=10){
    float x =
    float y =
}
```

4. Write the code that will produce a spiral staircase as shown here:

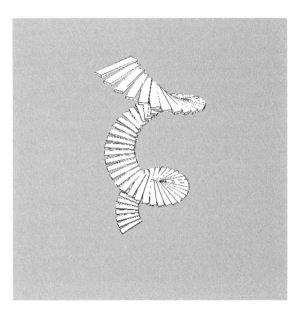

5. Create a spiral curve, using the `curveVertex()` command (try to use as few lines of code as possible):

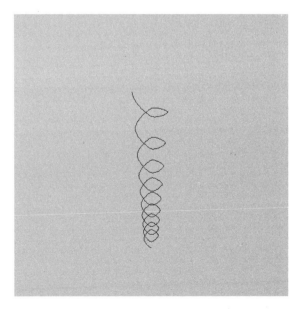

6.  In a perspective projection, we use the following equations to extract the x and y coordinates on the screen:

$$x_p = x \cdot t, \quad y_p = y \cdot t \qquad \text{where} \qquad t = \frac{1}{1 + z/d}$$

Modify and implement the following equations to project on the screen:

$$x_p = x \cdot \sin(t) + y \cdot \cos(t) \qquad y_p = y \cdot \sin(t) + x \cdot \cos(t)$$

# 9

# Solid Geometry

So far, you have dealt only with points or sets of points in a 3D space. You have seen how to project points on a 2D plane of sight and also how to arrange discrete points in the formation of cubes, spheres, and superquadrics. This chapter shows you how to construct more complex objects such as faces, solids, and groups of solids. You will also look into the identity and memory of these objects, that is, selecting and transforming their position.

The next sections define objects as collections of faces and faces as collections of points. This structural arrangement enables you to store information in a hierarchical way and to get access to subelements of objects by, for example, selecting a face or moving a vertex or a face within an object.

## 9.1 Class MyPoint

First, create a class called MyPoint. It will be used to store three numbers that correspond to the coordinates of a point:

```
1    class MyPoint{
2        float x,y,z;  //a 3D coordinate
3
```

```
4       MyPoint(float xin, float yin, float zin){
5         x = xin;
6         y = yin;
7         z = zin;
8       }
9     }
```

Next, create a second class called `MyFace` to store information about a face:

```
1     class MyFace{
2       MyPoint[] points = new MyPoint[0];   //array of points
3
4       MyFace(MyPoint[] inp){    //construct a face out of points
5         points = new MyPoint[inp.length];
6         for(int i=0; i<points.length; i++)
7             points[i] = new MyPoint(inp[i].x, inp[i].y, inp[i].z);
8       }
9
10      //add a point to a face one at a time
11      void addPoint(float addX, float addY, float addZ){
12        points = (MyPoint[])append(points, new MyPoint(addX,addY,addZ));
13      }
14
15      void plot(){
16        if(points.length==4)        //if we have four point faces
17          beginShape(QUADS);   //use the QUADS setup
18        else
19          beginShape(POLYGON); //else POLYGONS
20        for(int i=0; i<points.length; i++)
21          vertex(points[i].x,points[i].y,points[i].z);
22        endShape(CLOSE);        //close the face
23      }
24    }
```

The class is defined through an array of points called p that is initialized as an empty array. This way points can be added to the face one at a time. The method addPoint() takes three floats as input parameters and adds them to the p[] array. This is done in line 6 using Processing's append() command. Here, it is adjusted (i.e., *cast*) to append arrays of MyPoint elements.

Next, you draw the face as a series of connected vertices that form a polygon. The distinction here between QUADS and POLYGON is made because in Processing four-sided objects that are planar (i.e., a plane can pass through all points) can be drawn as solid planes in all directions in space whereas polygons (i.e., polylines that contain more than four points) are drawn as solid planes only in the direction of the horizontal plane. So, if later you want to extrude a multiple-point curve from the ground up, you will draw the two horizontal faces (top and bottom) using the POLYGON configuration but use the QUADS for the size faces since all of them will be four-sided and orthogonal by definition.

```
1   class MyObject{
2    MyFace[] f = new MyFace[6];   //below are the orientations of a cube
3    int[] xc =
      {-1,-1,1,1, 1,1,-1,-1, 1,-1,-1,1, 1,1,1,1, -1,1,1,-1, -1,-1,-1,-1};
4    int[] yc =
      {-1,1,1,-1, -1,1,1,-1, -1,-1,-1,-1, 1,-1,-1,1, 1,1,1,1, -1,1,1,-1};
5    int[] zc =
      {1,1,1,1, -1,-1,-1,-1, -1,-1,1,1, -1,-1,1,1, -1,-1,1,1, -1,-1,1,1};

6
7     MyObject(float s){
8        for(int i=0; i<f.length; i++){
9          f[i] = new MyFace();              //make a face
10         for(int j=i*4; j<i*4+4; j++)   //retrieve 4-ades every
11            f[i].addPoint(xc[j]*s,yc[j]*s,zc[j]*s); //collect
12       }
13     }
14
15    void draw3(){
16       for(int i=0; i<f.length; i++)
17         f[i].draw3();
18     }
19   }
```

Here, the class MyObject is defined as:

```
1    MyObject b = new MyObject(40);          //create an object
2    void setup(){
3      size(500,500, P3D);                    //setup the screen
4      camera(-100,100,-100,0,0,0,0,0,1); //get a viewpoint
5    }
6    void draw(){
7      background(255);
8      pointLight(255, 255, 255, -200,300,-400);
9      b.draw3(); //draw the object
10   }
```

## 9.1.1 Class MyFace

In the previous section, you defined a new class called MyFace to hold information about a closed polygon in a plane. Now you will connect the faces to form
a solid object and then organize them into groups of solids.

The source code of a face is:

```
1   class MyFace  {
2     int npoints = 0;      //the number of points
3     MyPoint [] points;  //array of points
4
```

```
5    MyFace(MyPoint[] inPoints){
6      points = new MyPoint[inPoints.length];
7      npoints = inPoints.length;
8      for(int i=0; i<inPoints.length; i++)
9        points[i] = new
10       MyPoint(inPoints[i].x, inPoints[i].y, inPoints[i].z);
11   }
12}
```

An alternative constructor would be to create a blank face and then add points to it:

```
1  MyFace (){
2      points = new MyPoint[0];
3  }
4
5  void addPoint(float addX, float addY, float addZ){
6      npoints++;
7    points=(MyPoint[])append(points, new MyPoint(addX,addY,addZ));
8  }
```

The class MyFace needs an array of points, so the constructor gets an input array, which is used to fill out the points[] member array. After constructing a face, you need to transform it into 3D. But since it is composed of MyPoints and you already defined all the transformation methods for them, you can use the point's methods instead. In that way, when you want to move, scale, and rotate, you simply use the MyPoint class methods:

```
void move(float xoff, float yoff, float zoff){
  for(int i=0; i<npoints; i++)
    points[i].move(xoff, yoff, zoff);
}

void rotatex (float angle, MyPoint ref) {
  for(int i=0; i<npoints; i++)
    points[i].rotatex(angle, ref);
}

void rotatey (float angle, MyPoint ref) {
  for(int i=0; i<npoints; i++)
    points[i].rotatey(angle, ref);
}
void rotatez (float angle, MyPoint ref) {
  for(int i=0; i<npoints; i++)
    points[i].rotatez(angle, ref);
}

void scale(float xs, float ys, float zs, MyPoint ref){
  for(int i=0; i<npoints; i++)
    points[i].scale(xs, ys, zs, ref);
}
```

to draw the array of MyPoints in the formation of a polygon. Here is the code:

```
void draw(){
    beginShape(QUADS);
    for(int i = 0; i < npoints; i++){
      vertex(points[i].x,points[i].y, points[i].z);
    }
    endShape(CLOSE);
}
```

This completes the MyFace class. You now need to call it from the main program. This means that you need to construct a face from points and then draw/transform it. So the main code must be modified as follows:

```
1    MyFace face;
2    void setup(){
3      size(200, 200, P3D);
4      noFill();
5      camera(70.0, 35.0, 120.0, 0.0, 0.0, 0.0, 0.0, 1.0, 0.0);
6      face = new MyFace();
7      face.addPoint( 50,  50, 0);
8      face.addPoint(-50,  50, 0);
9      face.addPoint(-50, -50, 0);
10     face.addPoint( 50, -50, 0);
11   }
12   int xf, yf;
13   void draw(){
14     background(255);
15     face.rotatex((mouseX - xf) * PI/180.,origin);
16     face.rotatey((mouseY - yf) * PI/180.,origin);
17     face.draw();
18     xf = mouseX;
19     yf = mouseY;
20   }
```

The result is shown in Figure 9-1.

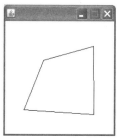

**Figure 9-1:** A planar polygon in 3D space

## 9.1.2 Sets of Faces

With the same rationale you can construct more than one face and draw them together. The source code below modifies the previous MyFace class to accommodate two faces that you put into an array called face[]. First, you create a face out of the points array and then you create another face with the same array and move it 100 units in the z direction.

```
MyFace[] faces;

void setup(){
  size(200, 200, P3D);
  noFill();
  camera(70.0, 35.0, 120.0, 0.0, 0.0, 0.0, 0.0, 1.0, 0.0);
  faces = new MyFace[2];
  faces[0] = new MyFace();
  faces[0].addPoint( 50,  50, 0);
  faces[0].addPoint(-50,  50, 0);
  faces[0].addPoint(-50, -50, 0);
  faces[0].addPoint( 50, -50, 0);
  faces[1] = new MyFace();
  faces[1].addPoint( 50,  50, 0);
  faces[1].addPoint(-50,  50, 0);
  faces[1].addPoint(-50, -50, 0);
  faces[1].addPoint( 50, -50, 0);
  faces[1].move(0., 0., 20.);
}
void draw(){
  background(255);
  faces[0].draw();
  faces[1].draw();
}
```

The result is shown in Figure 9-2.

**Figure 9-2:** Two parallel planar polygons in 3D space

The previous example makes it apparent that you can create as many faces as you want by populating the face[] array with more faces. However, since certain arrangements of faces form known solid objects, such as a cube, a pyramid, or a sphere, you can construct a new class, called MySolid, in which you create an arrangement of faces that will form known solids. Begin with a formation process for solids called *extrusion*. In extrusion, you construct solids out of a base polygon and a *height of extrusion*, as shown in Figure 9-3.

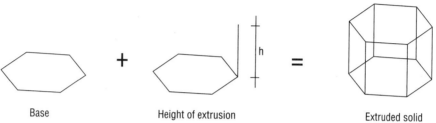

Base                Height of extrusion              Extruded solid

**Figure 9-3:** Extrusion of a polygon into a solid

To create a class that represents a solid object, the constructor should accept a set of points that forms the base and a number representing the height of extrusion. The following code shows how an extruded solid can be created (one of the many ways):

```
class MySolid  {

  MyFace[] faces;
  int  nfaces;
  color c;

  //*****************************
  MySolid(MyPoint[] inPoints, float height){

    nfaces = 0;
    faces = new MyFace[inPoints.length + 2];

    //bottom
    faces[0] = new MyFace(inPoints);
    nfaces++;

    //top
    faces[ nfaces] = new MyFace(inPoints);
    faces[ nfaces].move(0., 0., height);
    nfaces++;
```

```
        side[1] = new MyPoint(faces[0].points[i+1].x,
                   faces[0].points[i+1].y, faces[0].points[i+1].z );
        side[2] = new MyPoint(faces[1].points[i+1].x,
                   faces[1].points[i+1].y, faces[1].points[i+1].z  );
        side[3] = new MyPoint(faces[1].points[i].x, faces[1].points[i].y,
                   faces[1].points[i].z  );
        faces[ nfaces] = new MyFace(side);
        nfaces++;
    }

    // last side face
    int last = inPoints.length-1;
    side[0] = new MyPoint(faces[0].points[last].x,
               faces[0].points[last].y, faces[0].points[last].z );
    side[1] = new MyPoint(faces[0].points[0].x, faces[0].points[0].y,
               faces[0].points[0].z );
    side[2] = new MyPoint(faces[1].points[0].x, faces[1].points[0].y,
               faces[1].points[0].z  );
    side[3] = new MyPoint(faces[1].points[last].x,
               faces[1].points[last].y, faces[1].points[last].z  );
    faces[ nfaces] = new MyFace(side);
    nfaces++;
    // reverse the order of the bottom face
    MyPoint[] revPoints;
    revPoints = new MyPoint[inPoints.length];
    for(int i=0; i<inPoints.length; i++){
      revPoints[i] = new MyPoint(inPoints[inPoints.length-1-i].x,
      inPoints[inPoints.length-1-i].y,
      inPoints[inPoints.length-1-i].z);
    }
    faces[0] = new MyFace(revPoints);

  }
}
```

Let's take a closer look at the constructor. The class MySolid has two data members:

```
MyFace[] faces;
int numFaces;
```

Those members are: a set of points (that form the base) and the number of faces (numFaces). The constructor takes two arguments, a set of input points (inPoints) and the height of extrusion. The first thing to do is allocate memory for the faces. That is easy, because you know in advance how many faces you

```
faces = new MyFace[inPoints.length + 2];
```

Next, you create the bottom face, which is formed by whatever points are in the input base:

```
faces[0] = new MyFace(inPoints);
```

Then you do the same thing for the top, except you move it by height units in the z direction:

```
faces[1] = new MyFace(inPoints);
faces[1].setMove(0., 0., height);
```

You also increment the numFaces as you add more faces:

```
numFaces++;
```

Finally, you need to construct the side faces. Thus, you loop for the number of incoming point minus one, and for each loop you collect:

1. The current point of the bottom face
2. The next point of the bottom face
3. The next point of the top face
4. The current point of the top face

Put these four points in a MyPoint[] array called side[], which you use to construct the side face.

```
MyPoint[] side;
side = new MyPoint[4];
for(int i=0; i<inPoints.length-1; i++){
    side[0] = new MyPoint(faces[0].points[i].x, faces[0].points[i].y,
            faces[0].points[i].z );
    side[1] = new MyPoint(faces[0].points[i+1].x, faces[0].points[i+1].y,
            faces[0].points[i+1].z );
    side[2] = new MyPoint(faces[1].points[i+1].x, faces[1].points[i+1].y,
            faces[1].points[i+1].z );
    side[3] = new MyPoint(faces[1].points[i].x, faces[1].points[i].y,
            faces[1].points[i].z );
    faces[numFaces] = new MyFace(side);
    numFaces++;
}
```

Figure 9-4 illustrates the position of the points and faces for a hexagon:

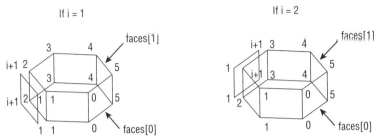

**Figure 9-4:** Sequence of point in an extruded solid

These loops take care of the `inPoints.length-1` sides, that is, $n-1$, where $n$ is the number of points. You cannot construct the last face because $i + 1$ will take you out of the boundaries of the array when $i =$ `inPoints.length`. So, you construct the first $n - 1$ side-face and, then, construct the last side face, which is:

```
int last = inPoints.length-1;
side[0] = new MyPoint(faces[0].points[last].x,faces[0].
points[last].y,
          faces[0].points[last].z );
side[1] = new MyPoint(faces[0].points[0].x, faces[0].points[0].y,
          faces[0].points[0].z );
side[2] = new MyPoint(faces[1].points[0].x, faces[1].points[0].y,
          faces[1].points[0].z   );
side[3] = new MyPoint(faces[1].points[last].x,faces[1].
points[last].y,
          faces[1].points[last].z   );
faces[numFaces] = new MyFace(side);
numFaces++;
```

```
void draw(Graphics g){

    for(int i=0; i<numFaces; i++)
        faces[i].draw(g);

}
```

The standard transformations can be invoked using their inheriting methods `move()`, `scale()`, and `rotate()`:

```
void setRotatex ( float angle) {
    for(int i=0; i<numFaces; i++)
        faces[i].setRotatex(angle);

}
```

```
        }

        void setRotatez ( float angle) {
            for(int i=0; i<numFaces; i++)
                faces[i].setRotatez(angle);
         }

        void setScale( float xs,   float ys,   float zs){
            for(int i=0; i<numFaces; i++)
                faces[i].setScale(xs, ys, zs);
        }

        void setMove( float xoff,   float yoff,   float zoff){
            for(int i=0; i<numFaces; i++)
                faces[i].setMove(xoff, yoff, zoff);
        }
```

In the main code, you create an array of points that functions as the profile polyline to be extruded. This array (i.e., points[]) is passed to the constructor new MySolid(points, 20.) together with a float that indicates the height to be extruded (i.e., 20.). The solid object can be drawn using the draw() method that is also passing down to the face's method draw().

```
MyPoint [] points;
MySolid solid;
void setup(){
  size(200, 200, P3D);
  noFill();
  camera(70.0, 35.0, 120.0, 0.0, 0.0, 0.0, 0.0, 1.0, 0.0);
  points = new MyPoint[4];
  points[0] = new MyPoint( 50,   50, 0);
  points[1] = new MyPoint(-50,   50, 0);
  points[2] = new MyPoint(-50, -50, 0);
  points[3] = new MyPoint( 50, -50, 0);
  solid = new MySolid(points, 20.);
}
int xf, yf;
void draw(){
  background(255);
  solid.rotatex((mouseX - xf) * PI/180.,origin);
solid.rotatey((mouseY - yf) * PI/180.,origin);
solid.draw();
xf = mouseX;
yf = mouseY;
  }
```

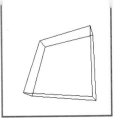

**Figure 9-5:** Six planar polygon
in the formation of a cube (wireframe)

You may notice that the faces do not appear in the right order. In fact, when `paint()` draws the faces, it fills a polygon in the index order 0, 1, 2, 3, 4, 5, and so forth. But `faces[0]` is the bottom, `faces[1]` is the top and the rest are side faces. This order from the furthest away to the closest is not the order they should be painted. The solution to this problem is to either paint them in the right order or find a way to omit the faces that are hidden, that is, the faces in the back. This is discussed in the following section.

## 9.1.4 Face Visibility

Imagine a cube in 3D: the cube is composed of six faces, and each face is constructed in a clockwise fashion. However, the projection of each face is not all clockwise. It seems that the faces that are in the back of the object are counter-clockwise. These faces are shown in light grey in Figure 9-6.

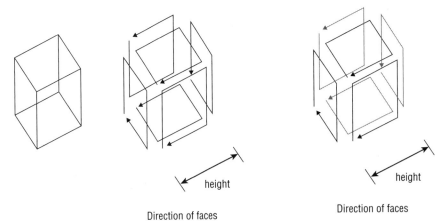

**Figure 9-6:** Direction of polygon creation in an extruded solid

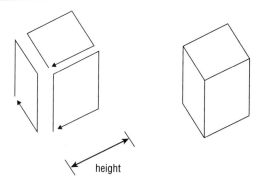

height

Direction of faces

**Figure 9-7:** Direction of faces can determine a polygon (face) visibility

The algorithm to determine whether a 2D polygon is clockwise or counter-clockwise is based on a simple algorithm that uses the cross product of vectors. The method belongs to the MyFace class and is shown here (cross products of vectors are covered in Chapter 10):

```
boolean isVisible()  {
    float x1, y1, x2, y2, norm=0;
    int ahead1, ahead2;

    for (int i=0; i<npoints; i++) {
      ahead1 = i+1;
      ahead2 = i+2;
      if(i == (npoints-2)) ahead2 = 0;
      if(i == (npoints-1)) {
         ahead2=1;
         ahead1=0;
      }
      //make vector 1
      x1 = points[ahead1].xscreen() - points[i].xscreen();
      y1 = points[ahead1].yscreen() - points[i].yscreen();
      //make vector 2
      x2 = points[ahead1].xscreen() - points[ahead2].xscreen();
      y2 = points[ahead1].yscreen() - points[ahead2].yscreen();
      //cross product
      norm += (x1*y2 - y1*x2);
    }
    if(norm > 0.0) return false;  //if clockwise
    else  return true;            //else ccw
}
```

sequence (see Figure 9-8). Please n...
product will be discussed in section 9.2.1.

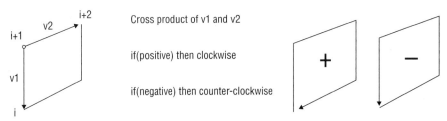

**Figure 9-8:** If the cross-product is positive, the sequence of points is clockwise, and vice-versa.

However, the points that you use are not the actual xyz points of MyPoint. Instead, you get their projections on the screen. To do that you constructed two methods that are added to the MyPoint class that return the screen projection:

```
float xscreen(){
    float sx = screenX(x, y, z);
    return sx;
}
float yscreen(){
    return screenY(x, y, z);
}
```

This hidden-line method is then used in the draw() method in the mySolid class in the following way:

```
void draw(){
    for(int i=0; i< nfaces; i++)
        if(faces[i].isVisible())faces[i].draw();
}
```

However, in the solid object you created, you did not reverse the order of the bottom face. You constructed all the faces in a clockwise direction, except the bottom face, as shown in Figure 9-9.

To correct this problem, you do the following in the end of the MySolid constructor:

```
// reverse the order of the bottom face
MyPoint[] revPoints;
revPoints = new MyPoint[inPoints.length];
for(int i=0; i<inPoints.length; i++){
    revPoints[i] = new MyPoint(inPoints[inPoints.length-1-i].x,
                                inPoints[inPoints.length-1-i].y,
                                inPoints[inPoints.length-1-i].z);
}
faces[0] = new MyFace(revPoints);
```

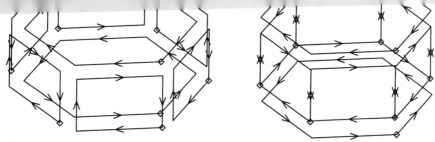

**Figure 9-9:** Direction of point on all faces of an extruded solid

The result is shown in Figure 9-10.

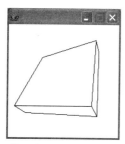

**Figure 9-10:** An extruded solid (cube)
with back-face elimination

# 9.2 Shading

Often reality is considered as the ultimate objective for the representation of architectural scenes.[1] While the computer-graphical search for a representation of reality that is indistinguishable is, in essence, a search for completeness, its value as a means of architectural communication is debatable. Reality is about actuality, perfection, completeness, and objectivity. Nonetheless, the notions of incompleteness, imperfection, and subjectivity have a complementary value that often surpasses that of an explicit presentation. Tacit, suggestive, connotative, implicit, subtle, and evocative are qualities that invite the viewer to participate in the visual composition. Sketching, drawing, and painting are means of visual expression aimed not at representing reality as it is but rather at implying, suggesting, and inviting the viewer to explore and participate in how reality may be.

Consistency is a phenomenon that ties together seemingly disparate entities. Traditionally, projection systems were constructed to simulate reality either

The distortion may not be recognized by reference to previous experience, but it is consistent within the new rules. More than ever now, through the use of applied physics and computation, design space can become a dynamic simulation environment for the exploration of visual behaviors far beyond experience or prediction.

This section presents techniques for depicting solid objects in a realistic manner, incorporating shades and colors. Sets of objects will be sorted to convey the impression of depth.

Shading is the process of determining the color of a face based on the direction of light. Observe the faces of the cube shown in Figure 9-11.

You can see that, as a projection on the screen, we have three polygons (1, 2, and 3). By using the `fill()` and `stroke()` routines we can color the pixels of each polygon with a different shade of red (although the color is not visible in this book). The direction of the incoming light will determine the amount of red to be used to fill the polygon. So, you need two things:

- A table of shades of red to pick from.

- A way of determining the direction of the surface of each polygon (in world space) in order to find the angle with the light direction (the lighter colored arrow). The larger the angle between the surface and the light, the more increased the shade is.

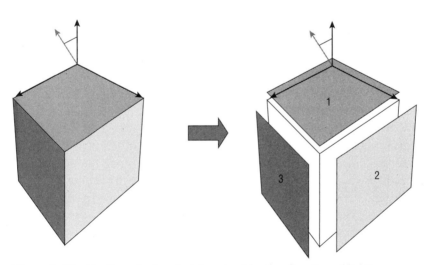

**Figure 9-11:** Shading of a face is determined by the direction of lighting

code the addition of `lights()` will render all surfaces that are created using the `beginShape(QUADS)` method when drawing the faces:

```
background(255);
lights();
solid.draw();
```

However, in the next few sections you see how to create shades on solid faces in order to cover the theory behind these rendering operations. You will be using vectors that will allow you to detect light angles in 3D space and show how to produce a series of shades. The first step is to learn about vectors and their attributes.

## 9.2.1 Vectors

*Vectors* are three-dimensional entities that show direction in space. Think of yourself as being at point (0,0,0) and looking at direction x, y, z. Practically, as shown in Figure 9-12, a vector is a set of three numbers that tell us where to look, assuming that we are standing at the origin (0,0,0).

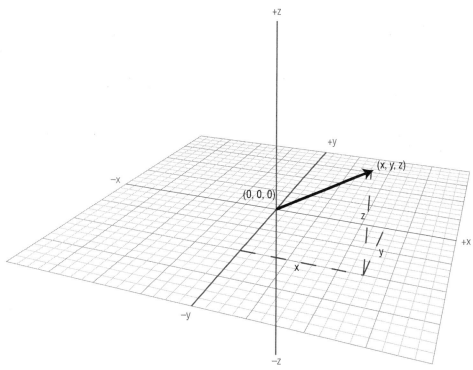

**Figure 9-12:** A vector

```
      y = yin;
      z = zin;
}
```

Notice that we use the u, v, w letters instead of x, y, z because a vector is different from a point even though it is defined in the same way. A vector shows a direction being looked at from the origin. A point shows a location.

Given two points in space you can create a vector by positioning it back to the (0,0,0) reference point:

```
MyVector buildVector( MyPoint vert2, MyPoint vert1){
    x = vert2.x-vert1.x;
    y = vert2.y-vert1.y;
    z = vert2.z-vert1.z;
    return this;
}
```

## 9.2.2 Normalization

A normalized vector is a vector where each of its components is divided by its length, that is, a vector that has unit length. The length of a vector is the square root of the addition of the squares of its components.

```
sqrt(x*x + y*y + z*z);
```

Normalization serves a purpose. As mentioned earlier, vectors show direction. Their length should be insignificant, since their purpose is to show a direction. For example, if you are told to look one foot ahead, then a foot right, and then another foot up it is the same as being told to look three feet ahead, three feet right, and three feet up. We are still looking in the same direction. In the following example, after normalization, the two normalized vectors are the same length (see Figure 9-13).

When you normalize, you actually equalize the length of the two vectors. The normalization operation is:

```
void norm(){
    float t = sqrt(x*x+y*y+z*z);
    x = x/t;
    y = y/t;
    z = z/t;
}
```

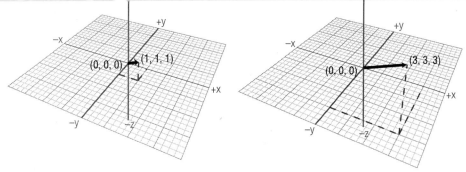

**Figure 9-13:** Vector normalization

## 9.2.3 Cross Product

The *cross product* of two vectors is an operation that results in a vector perpendicular to the two vectors (see Figure 9-14):

```
void cross(MyVector a){
   MyVector temp = new MyVector();
   temp.x = a.y * z   - a.z * y;
   temp.y =   x * a.z - z * a.x;
   temp.z = a.x * y   - a.y * x;
   x = temp.x;
   y = temp.y;
   z = temp.z;
}
```

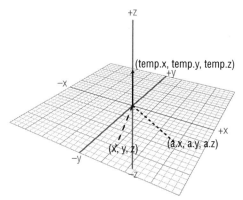

**Figure 9-14:** Cross product of two vectors

### 9.2.4 Dot Product

The dot product gives us the cosine of the angle between two vectors (in radians), as shown in Figure 9-15.

```
float dot(MyVector v1){
    return v1.x*x+v1.y*y+v1.z*z;
}
```

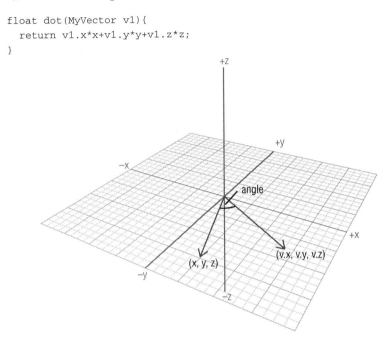

**Figure 9-15:** Dot product of two vectors

### 9.2.5 MyVector Class

The following class MyVector defines a vector and its related operations:

```
1   class MyVector{
2   float x,y,z;
3
4   MyVector(){
5       x=y=z=0.;
6   }
```

```
■0    z = zin;
11 }
12  MyVector buildVector( MyPoint vert2, MyPoint vert1){
13     x = vert2.x-vert1.x;
14     y = vert2.y-vert1.y;
15     z = vert2.z-vert1.z;
16     return this;
1)  )
18  float dot(MyVector v1){
19     return v1.x*x+v1.y*y+v1.z*z;
20  }
21  void cross(MyVector a){
22     MyVector temp = new MyVector(0.,0.,0.);
23     temp.x = a.y * z   - a.z * y;
24     temp.y =   x * a.z - z * a.x;
25     temp.z = a.x * y   - a.y * x;
26     x = temp.x;
27     y = temp.y;
28     z = temp.z;
29  }
30  void norm(){
31     float t =  sqrt(x*x+y*y+z*z);
32     x = x/t;
33     y = y/t;
34     z = z/t;
35  }
36}
```

For the purposes of this book:

- Two vectors determine a plane in space. The cross product is a vector perpendicular to that plane.

- The cross product is a vector that shows the direction of a plane. The light is a vector that shows the direction of the incoming light. The dot product gives us the angle between the two vectors and, as a consequence, the amount of light that falls on that plane.

## 9.2.6 Color Tables

In Processing, a color is defined with three numbers:

```
color myColor = color(int red, int green, int blue);
```

```
color white    = color(255,255,255)
color red      = color(255,0,0)        //is red
color green    = color(0,255,0)        //is green
color blue     = color(0,0,255)        //is blue
```

## 9.2.7 Array of Shades

To paint the faces of a solid you need a palette of colors, or shades of a color.
To get that you need an algorithm that will create an array of colors that are
alterations of one basic color (i.e., red). The algorithm is:

```
color[] shadeTable;    //define a table array
void setShades(color c) {
  float r, g, b;
  r = red(c);   //extract the color
  g = green(c);
  b = blue(c);
  r /= 255.;   //get a unit
  g /= 255.;
  b /= 255.;
  shadeTable = new color[256];   //allocate memory
  for( int i = 0; i < 255; i++ )
    shadeTable[i] = color((int)(r*i),(int)(g*i),(int)(b*i));
                            //draw the shade
}
```

This algorithm will take a basic color and create 256 shades of that color and
then fill the shadeTable[] array of colors. To draw them, you simply use the
following code:

```
void setup(){
  size(100,255);
  setShades(color(255,0,0));
  for( int i = 0; i < 255; i++ ){
    fill(shadeTable[i]);
    noStroke();
    rect(0,i,100,1);
  }
}
```

Notice that each basic color is associated with 256 other colors called *shades*
(see Figure 9-16). So, when you define 10 colors to use to paint objects in a scene,
you actually allocate 10 × 256 = 2,560 colors. This used to be a problem because

**Figure 9-16:** A range of shades

## 9.2.8 Shade Calculation

At this point, you know how to create an array of color shades and how to represent the direction of planes in 3D using vectors. Now you need to determine which shade to choose from the `colorShade[]` array:

Figure 9-17 shows a red surface (although the color is not evident in this book); you will determine the shade of red depending on the direction of the light.

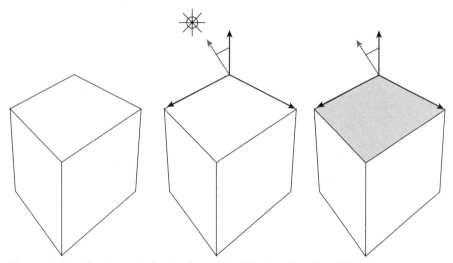

**Figure 9-17:** Shading of a face is determined by the direction of lighting

First, declare a light vector:

```
MyVector vlight = new MyVector(-1, 1, 2);
```

Since you have three points in a face, you can build two vectors out of points [0],[1] and [1],[2]. Then take the cross product, normalize it, and find the dot product with the light vector (see Figure 9-18).

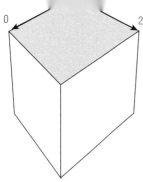

**Figure 9-18:** Building two vector on two edges to determine the angle of the face with the light.

The code for calculating the shade and returning an integer between 0 and 255 (which is the index of the shade array) is as follows:

```
MyVector vlight = new MyVector(1.,1.,1.);
int getShade(){
    int shade;
    MyVector v1 = new MyVector();
    MyVector v2 = new MyVector();
    vlight.norm();
//first side of triangle
    v1.buildVector( points[1], points[0] ).norm();
//second side of triangle
v2.buildVector( points[1], points[2] ).norm();
v1.cross(v2);                                    //get normal to triangle
    shade = int( 100.+(155.*v1.dot(vlight))); //find angle with sun
    if (shade <= 0) shade = 0;
    return shade;
}
```

First, you build two vectors v1 and v2, one from points [0] and [1] and the other from points [1] and [2]. You then calculate the cross product to define the perpendicular vector v1, then normalize v11 to give it a unit length. Next, you calculate the dot product v1 with the light vector vlight. The dot product will be a number between -1 and 1 since it is a cosine. You multiply that number by 255 in order to scale it between -255 and 255. If it is negative, that means that the vlight vector is under the surface and is not visible. If it is positive, you return an integer number between 0 and 255, which is the array index for the shadeTable[].

This will ensure that if the angle is 90, the shade table will still be at least 100. The variable shade will oscillate now between 100 and 255. That will create a more realistic shading effect.

Next, in the `MyFace` class you need to create a method `setColor()` that will set the color for each face:

```
void setColor(color cin){
  c = cin;
  setShades(c);
  c = shadeTable[getShade()];
}
```

which, of course, will assign a color in the `draw()` method of the `MyFace` class, using the `fill(c)` method.

The `setColor()` method can be also added to the `MySolid` class and then be called from the main code, using the line: `solid.setColor(color(255.,0.,0.));`

The output is shown in Figure 9-19.

**Figure 9-19:** A shaded cube

In this way, it is possible to paint each face in a different color, maintaining of course the shades. So, you can make a five sided object and color it in random colors, as shown in Figure 9-20.

```
void setup(){
  size(500, 500, P3D);
  camera(70.0, 35.0, 120.0, 0.0, 0.0, 0.0, 0.0, 1.0, 0.0);
  int nsides = 6;
  points = new MyPoint[nsides];
  for(int i=0; i<nsides; i++)
  points[i] = new MyPoint((40.*sin((360./nsides)*i*PI/180.)),
                          (40.*cos((360./nsides)*i*PI/180.)),0.);
  solid = new MySolid(points, 20.);
```

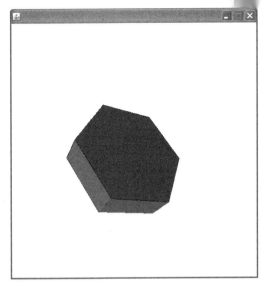

**Figure 9-20:** A randomly colored solid

## 9.2.9 Class MyGroup

So far, you have created a hierarchical structure of points, faces, and solids. The rationale was that solids contain faces, and faces contain points or, reversibly, points compose faces, and faces compose solids. With the same rationale, we can say that solids compose groups and groups contain solids. This simple hierarchy looks like Figure 9-21.

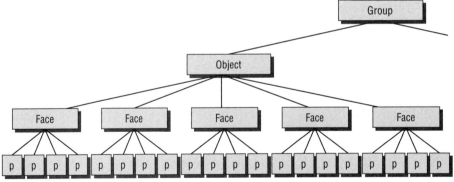

**Figure 9-21:** The hierarchical structure of a 3D group of solids

```
class MyGroup  {
  MySolid [] solids;
  int nsolids;

  MyGroup (){
    solids = new MySolid[0];
  }
  void addSolids(MyPoint[] points, float hite){
    nsolids++;
    solids = (MySolid[])append(solids, new MySolid(points,hite));
  }
  void draw(){
    for(int i=0; i<nsolids; i++)
      solids[i].draw();
  }
 void rotatex (float angle, MyPoint ref) {
    for(int i=0; i<nsolids; i++)
      solids[i].rotatex(angle, ref);
  }
  void rotatey (float angle, MyPoint ref) {
    for(int i=0; i<nsolids; i++)
      solids[i].rotatey(angle, ref);
  }
  void rotatez (float angle, MyPoint ref) {
    for(int i=0; i<nsolids; i++)
      solids[i].rotatez(angle, ref);
  }
  void scale(float xs, float ys, float zs, MyPoint ref) {
    for(int i=0; i<nsolids; i++)
      solids[i].scale(xs, ys, zs, ref);
  }
  void move(float xoff, float yoff, float zoff){
    for(int i=0; i<nsolids; i++)
      solids[i].move(xoff, yoff, zoff);
  }
}
```

The constructor of a solid uses a constructor similar to the MyFace one. Here, you create an empty array to be a member of the MyGroup class and then add solids, using the addSolids() method. All other methods are self-explanatory, as they inherit their functionality from the MySolid class.

```
   MyGroup group;
MyPoint origin = new MyPoint(0.,0.,0.);
void setup(){
   size(500, 500, P3D);
   camera(70.0, 35.0, 120.0, 0.0, 0.0, 0.0, 0.0, 1.0, 0.0);
   int nsides = 6;
   points = new MyPoint[nsides];
   for(int i=0; i<nsides; i++)
   points[i] = new MyPoint((10.*sin((360./nsides)*i*PI/180.)),
                           (10.*cos((360./nsides)*i*PI/180.)),0.);
   group = new MyGroup();
   for(int i=0; i<10; i++){
     group.addSolids(points, 20.);
     group.solids[i].setColor(color(255,255,255));
     group.solids[i].scale(.3,.3,.3, origin);
     group.solids[i].move(0.,0.,i*30);
   }
}

int xf, yf;
void draw(){
   background(255);
   group.rotatex((mouseX - xf) * PI/180.,origin);
   group.rotatey((mouseY - yf) * PI/180.,origin);
   group.draw();
   xf = mouseX;
   yf = mouseY;
}
```

In the `setup()` method, you first create a `MyGroup`, using the constructor:

```
group = new MyGroup();
```

This method constructs an empty `MyGroup` object called group. You then add solids to the group by using the `addSolids()` method. You loop 10 times, using the counter to add, set the color, scale, and move in space by an increment of 30 units. Finally, to manipulate and draw the group, you use the `draw()`, `rotatex`, and `rotatey` methods of the `MyGroup` class. The output is shown in Figure 9-22.

**Figure 9-22:** A group of solids (not sorted)

Following the same logic, we can create grids of solids placed in three dimensions. The code is:

```
group = new MyGroup();
int k=0;
for(int z=-nsides; z<nsides; z++)
  for(int y=-nsides; y<nsides; y++)
    for(int x=-nsides; x<nsides; x++){
      group.addSolids(points, 10.);
      group.solids[k].setColor(color(255,255,255));
      group.solids[k].scale(.5,.5,.5, origin);
      group.solids[k].move(x*20.,y*20.,z*20.);
      k++;
    }
```

This results in what you see in Figure 9-23.

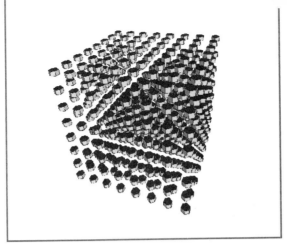

**Figure 9-23:** A group of (12 × 12 × 12 = 1,728) solids (not sorted)

## 9.2.10 Sorting Solids (Painter's Algorithm)

Notice in Figure 9-23 that some objects appear to be in front of others in the wrong direction. That happens because the solids are drawn in the order in which they were created, not in the order of their depth. So, for example, the third solid that was created will always be painted when $i$ is equal to 2, regardless of the orientation of the objects along the line of sight. The correct way to draw the solids would be to sort them in distance from our eye and then paint them from the furthest to the closest (that is, in reverse order). In that way, the closest object will be painted last, covering the ones further behind. This algorithm is also called "the painter's algorithm." In the following example, you sort the solids and then paint them in reverse order. Such a sorting algorithm looks as follows:

```
void sort(){
    float[] zc;
    zc = new float[nsolids];
    int knt;
    float centerz;

    // Calculate the centroids of each solid
    for(int i=0; i<nsolids; i++){
      centerz = 0;
      knt = 0;
```

```
        knt++;
      }
    }
    zc[i] = centerz/knt;
  }

  // Sorting the objects
  for(int i=0; i<nsolids; i++)
    for(int j=0; j<nsolids; j++)
      if(zc[i] > zc[j]){
        MySolid tobj = solids[i];
        solids[i] = solids[j];
        solids[j] = tobj;
        float temp = zc[i];
        zc[i] = zc[j];
        zc[j] = temp;
      }
}
```

Sorting is done in two steps:

1. Calculate the centroids of each solid.

2. Sort them according to the centroids.

To calculate the centroids, loop through all points or all faces of all solids and get the average of the points, which you then store in the array `zc[]`. To sort the solids, you use two counters `i` and `j` that loop through all solids and compare the `zc[i]` with the `zc[j]` values. If the one is greater than the other, swap them and the solids those counters are pointing at.

When you're done, sort the faces and paint in reverse order, as shown in the following `paint()` method:

```
void draw(){
  sort();
  for(int i=0; i<nsolids; i++)
    solids[i].draw();

}
```

The result is shown in Figure 9-24.

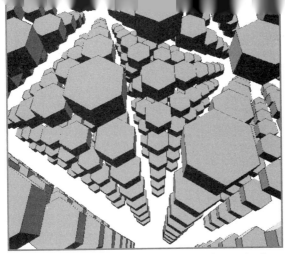

**Figure 9-24:** A grid of solids sorted in the eye's view direction

## 9.3 3D User Interaction

Interaction is the notion of two or more things acting on each other. While interaction between equal members of a class, that is, human to human, has traditionally been a rich area of study, a challenge arises when one of the interacting members is a machine and not a living organism. And, in particular, computer interaction is different from that with other machines in that computers incorporate a degree of responsiveness that is normally associated with a living organism. A response is a reaction to a specific stimulus. Responsiveness is associated with vital, animated, and soulful organisms. What distinguishes a living animal from a dead, stuffed, or artificial one is not its form or its movements but rather its response to external stimuli.

In interactive environments, there is a tendency to revert to a former state. While the minimal definition of any response involves at least two consecutive moments of time as a measure of comparison, the definition of form itself does not involve time. As a result, "interactive form" is not a contradiction but rather an extension to the notion of form as a motionless boundary. It is about the idea that a response is not only conceived directly through physical change but also indirectly through visual interpretation. This section shows how, through a series or internal representation, you can add interactivity to

## 9.3.1 Picking Objects in the Scene

Picking an object in a scene is basically a matter of clicking on the screen and getting back the serial number of that object. If the object you are looking for is a solid, then `pick` should apply to solids, if it is a face, then to faces, and so on. You first learn how to pick solids in a scene. The `pick` method should apply to the `MyGroup` class, since you have to search a group to find the picked solid. You start with the x and y coordinates of the screen, acquired when the mouse is clicked. The "pick" algorithm should return an integer, which is the serial number of the picked object. Therefore, the `pick` method should be in the `mouseClicked()` method and should look (approximately) like this:

```
for(int i=0; i<group.nsolids; i++)
    if(group.solids[i].pick(mouseX,mouseY))
        println("You picked solid number =" + i);
}
```

This code directs that `MyGroup` should have a method called `pick`. `MyGroup.pick()` will transfer its jurisdiction to the `solids[i].pick()` one level below:

```
boolean pick(int xmouse, int ymouse){
    for(int i=0; i< nsolids; i++)
        if(solids[i].pick(xmouse,ymouse))
            return true;
    return false;
}
```

The statement:

```
if(solids[i].pick(xmouse, ymouse))   return true;
```

indicates that if an object was found, there is no need to continue. This could be changed to allow multiple objects to be picked (i.e., those along the line of sight where the mouse is clicked).

At this point, `MyGroup` transfers its jurisdiction one level below, asking the `MyObject` class to find whether an object was selected within its domain. Here, the method is similar to `pick()` in `MyGroup`. In turn, `MySolid` transfers its jurisdiction one level below, asking `MyFace` to find whether a face was selected.

```
boolean pick(int xmouse, int ymouse){
    for(int i=0; i< nfaces; i++)
        if(faces[i].pick(xmouse,ymouse))
            return true;
    return false;
}
```

```
        isSelected = what;
    }
```

where `isSelected` is a boolean variable of the `MyFace` class. At the `MyFace` level, the pick method is as follows:

```
    boolean pick(int xmouse, int ymouse){
        if(!isVisible())return false;//no need to select what is not visible
        Polygon poly = new Polygon();   //make a polygon
        for(int i=0; i<npoints; i++){
            float px = screenX(points[i].x,points[i].y,points[i].z);
                                    //get the points on the screen
            float py = screenY(points[i].x,points[i].y,points[i].z);
            poly.addPoint(int(px),int(py));
        }
        if(poly.contains(xmouse, ymouse)){
                        //use the contains() operation of the Polygon
            setSelected(true);
            return true;   //if one is found no need to continue
        }
        return false;
    }
```

The face is projected on the screen through the `screenX()` and `screenY()` operation, and now the problem is simply to find whether a 2D point (`xmouse`, `ymouse`) is within a 2D polygon area. This can be done manually or you can use the `contains()` method of the Java object `Polygon`. If `poly.contains()` is true, a face was indeed selected; otherwise, it's not. Next, you draw the face (or whatever is selected) using the `draw()` method within the `MyFace` class:

```
    void draw(){
        fill(c);      //c is the object's color
        stroke(0);    //black is default
        if(isSelected)stroke(255,0,0);
                        //make the stoke red to indicate selection
        beginShape(POLYGON);
        for(int i = 0; i < npoints; i++){
            vertex(points[i].x,points[i].y, points[i].z);
        }
        endShape(CLOSE);
    }
```

only if ..e entity is selected. For example, for the `MyGroup` class:

```
class MyGroup {
   MySolid[] solids;
   int numSolids;
   boolean isSelected = false;
     ....
```

So, the variable `isSelected` indicates whether a face, solid, or group is selected. In the main code you can use it to select a face, solid, or group by indicating at which hierarchical level to use the `pick()` method. For example, below, a solid is picked and (commented out) is the way to pick only a face:

```
void mouseClicked(){
  group.setSelected(false);
  for(int i=0; i<group.nsolids; i++)
     if(group.solids[i].pick(mouseX,mouseY)){
        group.solids[i].setSelected(true);
     //for(int ii=0; ii<group.solids[i].nfaces; ii++)
       //if(group.solids[i].faces[ii].pick(mouseX,mouseY))
          return;
     }
```

The output is shown in Figure 9-25.

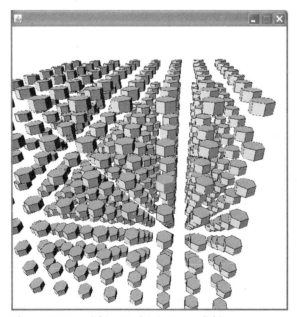

**Figure 9-25:** Picking (selecting) a solid in a scene

## 9.3.2 Simulating Menu Bars

In this example, you simulate a menu bar using choice buttons. The reason is that real menu bars need detached windows to exist, and you would like to use the existing applet window. So, choice buttons are "glued" to a frame window that can be moved anywhere in the scene. Here is the code for a simple menu bar:

```
class MyControl extends Frame{
    String transform_type = "Move";
    String level_type = "Solid";
    Choice transform;
    Choice level;

    MyControl() {

        transform = new Choice();
        transform.addItem("Move");
        transform.addItem("Rotate");
        transform.addItem("Scale");
        transform.setLocation(0, 30);
        transform.setSize(150, 20);

        level = new Choice();
        level.addItem("Group");
        level.addItem("Solid");
        level.addItem("Face");
        level.setLocation(150, 30);
        level.setSize(150, 20);

        setSize(300, 60);
        setLocation(20, 20);
        setLayout(null);
        add(transform);
        add(level);
        show();

        transform.addItemListener(new ItemListener() {
          public void itemStateChanged(ItemEvent e) {
            transform_type =
            transform.getItem(transform.getSelectedIndex());
          }});
```

```
                ....getItem(level.getSelectedIndex());
        }});
    }
}
```

A frame is created first. This is a window parented by the Processing screen. Then two choice interfaces are defined and attached to the frame, as shown in Figure 9-26. A set of `Choice` interfaces called `transform` and `level` are defined. The listeners keep track of which choice item is selected.

**Figure 9-26:** The choice interfaces attached to the frame

Once a choice is selected, it can be invoked by using the `control.level_type.equals()` expression. That will inform the system which transformation to apply to which hierarchical level:

```
void mouseClicked(){
  group.setSelected(false);
  if(control.level_type.equals("Group")){
    if(group.pick(mouseX,mouseY))
      group.setSelected(true);
  }
  else
    if(control.level_type.equals("Solid")){
      for(int i=0; i<group.nsolids; i++)
        if(group.solids[i].pick(mouseX,mouseY)){
          group.solids[i].setSelected(true);
          return;
        }
    }
    else {
      for(int i=0; i<group.nsolids; i++)
        for(int ii=0; ii<group.solids[i].nfaces; ii++){
          if(group.solids[i].faces[ii].pick(mouseX,mouseY))
            return;
        }
    }
}
```

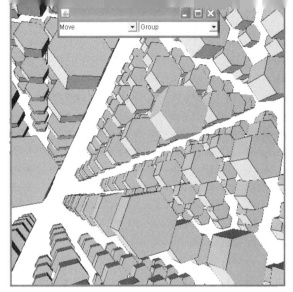

**Figure 9-27:** A simple GUI

## Summary

In this chapter, you saw how to create a hierarchical structure to represent solids using points and faces. You also learned how to eliminate the back faces if they are not visible. Then you were shown how to create shades on those faces, create groups of solids, and sort them in reverse depth order.

The purpose of this chapter was to show how objects (groups, solids, or faces) can be selected in 3D. This adds interactivity to the scene, allowing the user to select and manipulate entities. In addition, a few GUI objects were shown to allow the user to explore combinations of options. Next, you learn how to import and export files in various file formats.

## Exercises

1. Create a user interface where the user can specify the type of polygons (triangle, square, pentagon, etc.) and the type of the grid (1-, 2-, or 3-directional).

3. Create a converging extrusion of a polygon, as shown in the following figure:

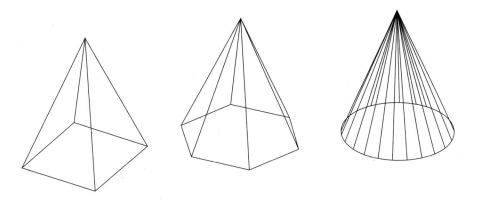

## Notes

1. One of the long goals of computer graphics has been the reproduction of realistic scenes. See, for instance, Tole P., F. Pellacini, B. Walter, and D. Greenberg, "Interactive global illumination in dynamic scenes," in John F. Hughes (editor) *SIGGRAPH 2002 Conference Proceedings*, ACM SIGGRAPH, July 2002, pp. 537–546.

# 10

# File Read/Write

Memory is the mental faculty of retaining and recalling past experience; it is the act of remembering or recollecting. Lack of memory results in a permanent state of "present time" because no comparison can be made between "before" and "after." The dominant mode for discussing the notion of time has been that of a linear progression, where events happen in a sequential fashion. The notions of "before" and "after" imply direction and polarity between two points of reference. Time is often depicted as a line that starts in negative infinity and ends in the positive infinity. The problem with this model is that it assumes that every moment in time is of identical importance and that the same exact event in time never occurs twice. This is quite contrary to the personal experience of time, where some moments are more important than others and events do seem to repeat themselves quite often, as well as the exaggeration of certain moments and the reduction of others.

In human memory, there is significant difference between retrieval and insertion. While retrieval is a voluntary act, the insertion of memories is not. Because of its involuntary nature, memory insertion is performed almost automatically, whereas denial to insert a memory is not an option. Furthermore, the processes of memory may be influenced by cultural criteria. The same event may be understood and, therefore, remembered differently by two members of different cultures. In addition, the recollection of the same event can be articulated in a whole different way as a result of "filtering" through cultural values. This chapter shows how to "insert" and "retrieve" memories, using digital media,

## 10.1 File Formats

A file is a collection of data that can be stored and recalled at any time. In computer graphics, the file's collection of data can represent a set of graphic objects. In our case, we would need to create a file where we can store all the information associated with points, faces, solids, and groups in order to work with them later. That information would be stored as text (letters, numbers and symbols), indicating geometrical objects, their relationships, and quantities associated with them. For example, the word "vertex" may represent a point followed by three numbers indicating its x, y, and z coordinates. Such an entity can be stored using a hierarchical structure that, instead of storing just the vertices alone, will also store all the groups, solids, faces, and edges as well as their x, y, and z coordinates. The format to store/retrieve data is referred to as the file format. In our case, our file format, which we will call *native*, is a simple hierarchical structure that leads to a list of x, y, and z coordinates. In other file formats, such as DXF (Drawing eXchange Format), there is a different and more complex way of saving/retrieving data. We will show how to write/read data in a native format and how to write/read using some of the specifications of the DXF and VRML formats, as well as how to transfer data over the Internet.

## 10.2 Basic Write/Read in Processing

In Processing, to create a file we first need to create a `PrintWriter`, which is an *output stream*. This creates a file with the name that we want by using the `createWriter()` constructor. Once a file is created, we can use that file to write out the data by using its `print()` or `println()` methods. For example, the following code demonstrates the creation of a file called hello.txt

```
1    PrintWriter output;
2    output = createWriter("hello.txt");// Create a new file
3    output.println("Hello there");  //write to the file
4    output.flush(); // Writes the remaining data to the file
5    output.close(); // Closes the file
```

The preceding code will create an output file that can then be opened in any text editor (i.e., Notepad, WordPad, TextPad, etc.). The file should be located in

```
output = createWriter("c:/data/textFile.txt");
```

will put the new file in the c drive inside a folder called data. Please note that the slashes (/) are forward, as opposed to DOS where they are back-slashes. When opened, the output file will look like Figure 10-1.

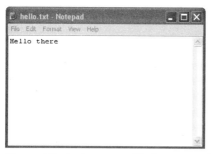

**Figure 10-1:** An output file in Notepad

An output file can be created using a dialog box by utilizing the following command (in place of line 2 in the preceding code):

```
output = createWriter(outputFile().getName());
```

The opposite process of reading the contents of a file can be done by going through the reverse set of actions. That is, after we open the file, we loop through every line in the output file to extract the data. The following code shows a fast way of extracting the text of a file:

```
1    String lines[] = loadStrings("textFile.txt");
2    for (int i=0; i < lines.length; i++) {
3        println(lines[i]);
4    }
```

The first line loads the file that we want to read and returns an array that includes all the lines of the file as strings. We then use that array to loop through all lines and print out the content of each line. The result should be as shown in Figure 10-2.

**Figure 10-2:** Reading a simple file

multiple lines to a file (the coordinates of each line to extract the coordinate values:

```
1     PrintWriter output;
2     void setup() {
3        output = createWriter("positions.txt");
4        size(300,300);
5     }
6     void draw() {
7     }
8     void mouseDragged(){
9        point(mouseX, mouseY);
10       output.println(mouseX + "," + mouseY + "\r");
11    }
12    void keyPressed() {
13       output.flush();
14       output.close(); // Closes the file
15    }
```

In the first five lines of code, we create a file and open a 300 × 300 window to draw in it. In lines 8 to 11 we draw the position of the mouse as points on the screen as we drag the mouse. In line 10, we write the coordinates (derived from mouseX and mouseY variables), using a comma to separate them and then adding a return character, which is indicated by a \r (we could have used the \n, but some versions of Notepad do not recognize that). Next, we use the key-Pressed() section to write out the file and close it. The output of this process follows; on the left you see a pattern drawn by dragging the mouse, and on the right you see the corresponding coordinates for that pattern in the newly created file called "positions.txt."

Now, in the following code, we will read the output file from the previous code and extract the coordinates as integer numbers, which we will then use to redraw the previous pattern:

```
1     size(300,300);
2     String lines[] = loadStrings("positions.txt");
3     for (int i=0; i < lines.length; i++) {
4        String [] words = split(lines[i],", ");
5        point(int(words[0]),int(words[1]));
6     }
```

In the first line, you create a 300 × 300 window that you will use to mark the pattern stored in the file. You then open the file using the loadStrings() command that creates an array called lines[]. You then loop through all the lines (using the command lines.length to invoke its size) and then split every line

separator is a comma and an empty space). After the split, the resulting words will be only two that are the x and y coordinates. Those you use to draw a point on the screen using the `point()` command and converting the strings `word[0]` and `word[1]` into integers (see line 5).

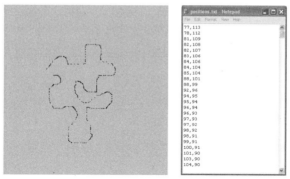

**Figure 10-3:** Outputting a pattern and its coordinates

## 10.2.1 Exporting PDF and DXF File Formats Using Processing Libraries

Processing is equipped with libraries that can export as a `.pdf` or a `.dxf` file anything drawn on the screen. In the following code, a simple way of exporting a drawing as a `.pdf` file is shown. (Please note that this can only produce the standard geometrical shapes provided by Processing.)

```
1    import processing.pdf.*;
2
3    void setup() {
4      size(300, 300);
5      beginRecord(PDF, "positions.pdf");
6    }
7    void draw() {
8    }
9    void mouseDragged() {
10     fill(random(255));
11     rect(mouseX, mouseY,10,10);
12   }
13   void keyPressed() {
14     endRecord();
15     exit();
16   }
```

which means "everything"). In line 5, you use the beginRecord() command that takes as parameters the format you wish to save as (i.e., PDF) and the file name to be exported (i.e., positions.pdf). This recording will end only when you call the endRecord() command (see line 14). This, of course, is located under the keyPressed() section in order to invoke the end by pressing any key. Otherwise, any drawing action within the draw() or mouseDragged() section will be recorded. The result is shown in Figure 10-4.

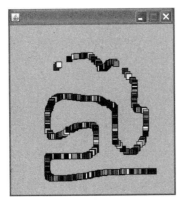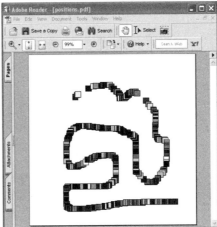

**Figure 10-4:** A pattern created in Processing and the corresponding PDF file opened in Acrobat

Similarly, the following code shows a simple way of exporting anything drawn on the screen as a .dxf file. (The DXF file format is described later in this chapter.)

```
1    import processing.dxf.*;
2
3    void setup() {
4      size(300, 300, P3D);
5      beginRaw(DXF,"positions.dxf");
6    }
7    void draw() {
8    }
9    void mouseDragged() {
10     rect(mouseX, mouseY,10,10);
11   }
```

The result is shown in Figure 10-5.

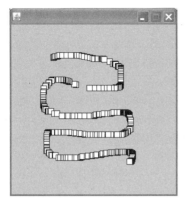
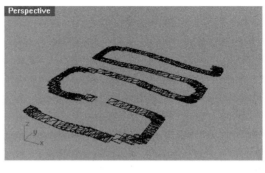

**Figure 10-5:** A pattern created in Processing and the corresponding DXF file opened in Rhino

## 10.2.2 Native File Write

As was discussed earlier, in order to create a file, you need to create a `PrintWriter`, which is an output stream. Then you use that file to write out the data, using its `print()` or `println()` methods. So, after you create the file, you loop through the data structure of our 3D classes as described in the previous chapter and write out the data in the order in which you loop:

```
ivoid saveNative(String filename){
    PrintWriter out = createWriter(filename);
    out.println("native format");
    out.println(nsolids);
    for(int i=0; i< nsolids; i++){
        out.println(solids[i].nfaces);
        for(int ii=0; ii<solids[i].nfaces; ii++){
          out.println(solids[i].faces[ii].npoints);
            for(int iii=0; iii<solids[i].faces[ii].npoints; iii++){
                out.print(solids[i].faces[ii].points[iii].x + " " );
                out.print(solids[i].faces[ii].points[iii].y + " " );
                out.print(solids[i].faces[ii].points[iii].z + " " );
                out.print("\n");
            }
        }
    }
}
```

The first `write` statement is the simple string `native format` (it can be any-thing, of course), which you will use later as an identifier for reading the file format. Then, as you loop, you write the number of solids, faces, and points, using the `print()`, and finally the x, y, and z coordinates. When finished, you flush and close the file.

## 10.2.3 Native File Read

To read a native file format, you need to follow steps similar to those of the writing process in the reverse order. Specifically, you use the `loadStrings()` command. This will load all lines of text in the array called `lines[]`. Next, you read each line and then extract the numbers that indicate information about the data structure, that is, the number of solids, faces, or points, and then the actual coordinates. In other words, you read all the text that you created using the `saveNative()` method discussed earlier. So, you loop through the `lines[]` array to extract the data one line at a time. Yet, the process is not as straightforward as in the case of writing because here you need to read the data and construct the data structures at the same time. The following is the code:

```
1    void openNative(String filename){
2
3        String lines[] = loadStrings(filename);
4        if(lines.length==0)return;
5        int k=0;
6        if(!lines[k++].equals("native format")){
7            println("File format not native");
8            return;
9        }
10       // loop to read the data
11       nsolids = int(lines[k++]);
12     solids = new MySolid[nsolids];
13       for(int i=0; i< nsolids; i++){
14          int nfaces = int(lines[k++]);
15          MyFace [] f = new MyFace[nfaces];
16          for(int ii=0; ii<nfaces; ii++){
17             int npoints = int(lines[k++]);
18             MyPoint [] p = new MyPoint[npoints];
19             for(int iii=0; iii<npoints; iii++){
20                String coords[] = split(lines[k++], ",");
21                p[iii] = new
                   MyPoint(float(coords[0]),float(coords[1]),float(coords[2]));
```

```
25              solids[i] = new MySolid(f);
26          }
27
28      }
```

First, you open the file and read the data as lines of strings. Then you check to see whether this is a valid native format, by reading the first line and comparing it with the string `native format` for identification purposes. If it is not equal, you print an error message and return without doing anything. If it is a valid file, then you proceed to loop and read data all the way down to the x, y, and z coordinates. Specifically, you read the number of elements, and when you gather enough information, you construct `MyPoint`, `MyFace`, `MySolid`, and `MyGroup` objects. During the process you convert the strings to integers, using the `int()` method, or to floats, using the `float()` method. In addition, each coordinate was written as a triad of float numbers, so you need to split the string and then read each one individually (line 20).

Every time a set of elements is read you use a constructor to create them, like this:

```
f[ii] = new MyFace(p);   and   solids[i] = new MySolid(f);
```

Now, these constructors do not exist, so you need to include them as alternative constructors in the following classes. `MyFace` needs the following constructor:

```
MyFace(MyPoint[] inPoints){
    npoints = inPoints.length;
    points = new MyPoint[npoints];
    for(int i=0; i<inPoints.length; i++)
        points[i] = new MyPoint(inPoints[i].x,inPoints[i].y,inPoints[i].z);
}
```

At the `MySolid` class, you include the following constructor:

```
MySolid(MyFace[] inFaces){
    nfaces = inFaces.length;
    faces = new MyFace[nfaces];
    for(int i=0; i<nfaces; i++)
        faces[i] = new MyFace(inFaces[i].points);
}
```

And in the `MyGroup` class, you include the following constructor:

```
MyGroup(MySolid[] inSolids){
    nsolids = inSolids.length;
    solids = new MySolid[nsolids];
```

From the main code, you can read a file (in this case `out.txt`, using the following code:

```
MyPoint [] points;
MyGroup group;
MyPoint origin = new MyPoint(0.,0.,0.);
void setup(){
  size(500, 500, P3D);
  camera(70.0, 35.0, 100.0, 0.0, 0.0, 0.0, 0.0, 1.0, 0.0);
  group = new MyGroup();
  group.openNative("out.txt");
}
```

## 10.2.4 The DXF File Format

DXF (Drawing eXchange Format) is an international convention on how 2D and 3D graphics files should be written. It was invented by AutoDesk, the company that developed the drafting program AutoCAD. DXF allows the exchange of drawings between AutoCAD and other drafting programs. DXF files are text files (also called ASCII files) that can be opened in any text editor to view or edit. They have the `.dxf` extension to be identified. If you open a DXF file, you will notice a series of code names and numbers. The code names represent the entities involved in saving, such as 3DFACE, and the numbers representing actual data, such as, colors or coordinates. A code is a reserved word that declares the name of an entity, but it can also be a number between 0–999 that refers to an entity (according to the DXF specifications); for example, 8 means layer, 10 means x coordinate, 62 means color, 999 means comments. Every code name or number is always followed by the actual data. For example, if after the number 10 follows the number 5.2245, that means that 5.2245 is the x coordinate. For more information on DXF codes, read the DXF reference at www.autodesk.com/dxf. Figure 10-6 shows a simplified version of a DXF file that describes the geometry of a square.

A simple DXF file represents geometry with faces and vertices. A face will start with the code name 3DFACE. In between there will be many coordinates that need to be drawn in groups of three (i.e., triangulate). Each face is then made out of three coordinates each of which is preceded by the codes 10, 20, and 30 for the first vertex x, y, and z coordinates, then by the codes 11, 21, and 31 for the second vertex coordinates, followed by the codes 12, 22, and 32 for the third vertex coordinates, and finally by the codes 13, 23, and 33 for the last vertex coordinates. The whole file will start with the name SECTION, which refers

entities. Finally, the whole DXF file will end with EOF, which stands for "end of file."

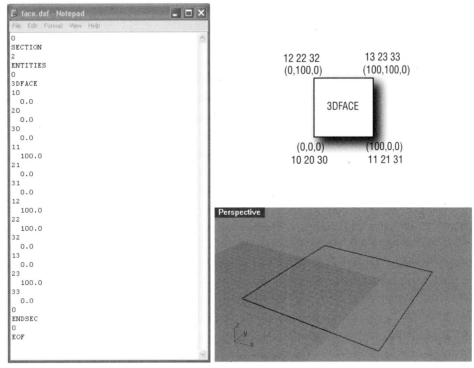

**Figure 10-6:** File (left) schematic (upper right), and 3D view (lower right) of a DXF file

## 10.2.5 Writing DXF Files

To write a `.dxf` file you need to write all the preceding information in sequence in a file. First, you need to open a file as a stream to write characters sequentially to the file. Then you loop and use the `println()` method to write the triangulated-point information as 3DFACE-vertex sequences in the form of ASCII text:

```
1    void writeDXF(String filename) {
2
3        PrintWriter out = createWriter(filename);
4
5        out.println("0\nSECTION");
6        out.println("2\nENTITIES");
```

```
11          for(int iii=0; iii<solids[i].faces[ii].npoints-2, iii++){
12              out.println("  0 ");
13              out.println("3DFACE");   //triangulation of face
14              out.println(" 10\n"+solids[i].faces[ii].points[0].x);
15              out.println(" 20\n"+solids[i].faces[ii].points[0].y);
16              out.println(" 30\n"+solids[i].faces[ii].points[0].z);
17              out.println(" 11\n"+solids[i].faces[ii].points[iii+1].x);
18              out.println(" 21\n"+solids[i].faces[ii].points[iii+1].y);
19              out.println(" 31\n"+solids[i].faces[ii].points[iii+1].z);
20              out.println(" 12\n"+solids[i].faces[ii].points[iii+2].x);
21              out.println(" 22\n"+solids[i].faces[ii].points[iii+2].y);
22              out.println(" 32\n"+solids[i].faces[ii].points[iii+2].z);
23              out.println(" 13\n"+solids[i].faces[ii].points[iii+2].x);
24              out.println(" 23\n"+solids[i].faces[ii].points[iii+2].y);
25              out.println(" 33\n"+solids[i].faces[ii].points[iii+2].z);
26          }
27      out.println("  0 \nENDSEC");
28      out.println("  0\nEOF");
29      // Finish
30      out.flush();
31      out.close();
32   }
```

In line 5 and 6, you write the code names of a section and an entity. Then you loop for all the objects and faces in the data structure as indicated in lines 7 and 9. Next, you go through all the coordinates and select them in groups of three. This is accomplished by starting with the first point of every face and then selecting sequentially the points that correspond to the counter + 1 and the counter + 2, as shown in Figure 10-7. Please note that because 3DFACE specifications require four points, we duplicate the last point.

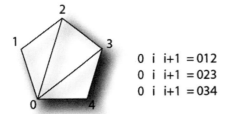

```
0 i i+1 = 012
0 i i+1 = 023
0 i i+1 = 034
```

**Figure 10-7:** A triangulated pentagon (left) and collection of points based on a counter (right).

... a ... ... ... ... ... ... ... ... ... ... than writing because you do not know in advance how many points-shapes-solids you will encounter in order to pre-allocate the appropriate memory for the arrays. This problem is similar to that of a butterfly hunter discussed in Chapter 1 section 1.4.1: The hunter does not know how many jars to have in advance because it is unknown how many butterflies will be caught. So the hunter starts with a number of jars, and if she runs out of jars, she gets more. The case is similar here with points. You do know in advanced how many points or faces the file contains. Processing and Java recognize the difficulty of predicting this and, therefore, provide a solution: allocating memory one element at a time. An array can be expanded in order to add or remove elements on the fly. You use commands append() and expand() whenever you want to add an element or clear out the array. For example:

```
MyFace [] f = new MyFace[0];

f = (MyFace[])append(f,new MyFace(p));

f = (MyPoint[])expand(f,0);
```

The first line of the preceding code defines an array, called f, of MyFace elements and initializes it to 0. In the next line of code, you allocate memory for just one MyFace element, using the append command. Specifically, you create a new MyFace element in the second part of the append command and then you cast the whole array into a MyFace[] type. In the last line of code, you clear the array by expanding it to contain 0 elements. In the following code, you will use these commands to read data from a DXF file:

```
1 void openDXF_3DFACE(String filename){
2
3     String lines[] = loadStrings(filename);
4     if(lines.length==0)return;
5     int k=0;
6     MyFace [] f = new MyFace[0];
7     MyPoint [] p = new MyPoint[0];
8     float tx=0.,ty=0.;
9     boolean face_found = false;
10
11    for(int ii=0; ii<lines.length; ii++){
12      String code = trim(lines[ii]);
13     if(code.equals("AcDbFace"))face_found=true;
14      if(face_found && (code.equals("10")||code.equals("11")||
           code.equals("12")||code.equals("13")))
15      tx = float(lines[ii+1]);
16      if(face_found && (code.equals("20")||code.equals("21")||
           code.equals("22")||code.equals("23")))
```

```
19      p = (MyPoint[])append(p, new MyPoint(tx,ty,float(lines[ii+1])));
20      if(p.length==4){
21         face_found=false;
22         f = (MyFace[])append(f,new MyFace(p));
23         solids = (MySolid[])append(solids,new MySolid(f));
24         nsolids++;
25         p = (MyPoint[])expand(p,0);
26         f = (MyFace[])expand(f,0);
27      }
28   }
29   }
```

Figure 10-8 illustrates reading a DFX file.

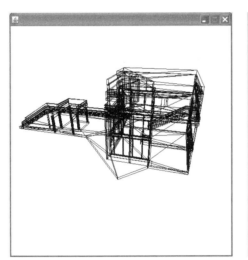

**Figure 10-8:** Reading a DXF file as 3D faces and rendered as wireframe (left) and as shaded (right)

First, you define a method called openDXF_3DFACE and pass the name of the file to read from. Using the loadStrings() command, you load all the lines of the file as text in an array called lines[]. Then, you define two arrays, f and p, of MyFace and MyPoint, respectively, to hold the point coordinates and the face connections. These two arrays are initialized to 0. Next, you define two float variables to hold the x and y coordinates of a point and a boolean variable face_found to denote the beginning and end of information about a face.

In lines 11 till 29, you loop through all the lines of the file looking for keywords: if the word AcDbFace is encountered, you set the face_found flag to value in the variable `tx` (after casting it to a float). Similarly, if the number 20, 21, or 22 is found, you read the next line and assign its value in the variable `ty` (after casting it to a float). Finally, if the number 30, 31, or 32 is found, you read the next line and assign it together with the previous two `tx` and `ty` variables to construct a point (see line 19). This process will be repeated by collecting coordinates and then constructing new points. Once four points are read, there is enough information to construct a face (see line 22). You then create a solid out of the face, increase the counter `nsolids` (line 24), and clear out the `p[]` and `f[]` arrays. This process will be repeated until all lines are read. Please note that the 3DFACE DXF representation does not distinguish between faces and objects, so each face is also an object. Different keywords of DXF files provide more elaborate information that distinguishes a face from an object. For example, the keywords "VERTEX," "POLYLINE," and "ENTITY" distinguish between points, faces, and solids. For more information on DXF file formats, please see www.autodesk.com.

## 10.2.7 The VRML File Format

Another file format that has been used extensively in CAD systems is VRML. In this section you will be introduced briefly to this file format because it has, like DXF, become a common file format for the exchange of solid objects with CAD applications. The initials VRML stand for Virtual Reality Markup (or Modeling) Language and was developed in the mid-1990s as a means to represent three-dimensional objects using a web browser. The idea was to incorporate graphics libraries (such as openGL or direct3D) that would take advantage of the hardware graphics cards that the mid-1990s computers used. The idea was that a web browser (such as Netscape or IE) would run a plug-in that would process solid objects in a 3D-navigated environment in real-time motion. This technology was initiated in the first version of VRML in 1993 and completed in the second version in 1997. Later on, VRML was extended by another standard called X3D. The file extension of a VRML file is .wrl, and most browsers recognize it and run the corresponding plug-in within a browser. Such plug-ins (such as cosmo, or cortona) together with information on the history, specifications, and techniques can be found on the wed 3D consortium at www.web3d.org.

A VRML file is an ASCII text file. The syntax of the text represents the geometry of a 3D object but also abides by the rules of a language. Simple geometrical objects can be defined through vertices and faces. Other attributes such as color, shininess, or transparency can also be incorporated as separate entities

```
1    #VRML V1.0 ascii

2

3    DEF Color_1 Material {
4        ambientColor 0.5 0.5 0.5
5        diffuseColor 0.5 0.5 0.5
6        transparency 0
7    }

8

9    DEF object_1 Separator {
10       Coordinate3 {
11           point [
12                      0   0 10,
13                     10 0 10,
14                     10 0  0,
15                      0   0  0,
16           ]
17       }
18       USE Color_1
19       IndexedFaceSet {
20           coordIndex [
21                   0, 3, 2, 1, -1,
22           ]
23       }
24   }
```

Figure 10-9 shows the results.

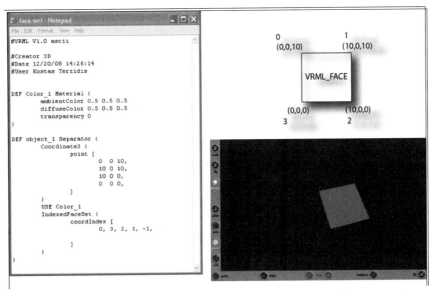

**Figure 10-9:** File (left), schematic (upper right), and 3D view (lower right) of a VRML file using the Cortona plug-in.

can also see the coordinates of all points and the connections of the points. For example the line

0, 3, 2, 1, -1,

refers to a sequence of points that start at point index 0 then go (or draw) to 3, then go to 2, then go to 1, and stop when you encounter a –1. So to read the geometry of an object you need to collect the x,y,z coordinates and then connect them in the given order. You can use the keywords `point` and `coordIndex` to find the beginning and end of these sections. You see how to export or import text files containing simple geometrical objects in the VRML format in the next two sections.

## 10.2.8 Writing VRML Files

Writing a VRML file is a matter of taking the internal representation of the `MyPoint-MyFace-MySolid-MyGroup` structure and exporting it into the `object-coordinate-coorindex` structure of VRML. In the following code you learn one way of writing out the VRML's geometry. The color of the object is hard-coded here as 50% gray.

```
 1 void writeVRML(String filename) {
 2    PrintWriter out = createWriter(filename);
 3
 4    out.println("#VRML V1.0 ascii");  //tag for hardware acceleration
 5    out.println("");
 6    out.println("#Creator My3D");
 7    out.println("#Date "+day()+"/"+month()+"/"+ year()+" "+
                          hour()+":"+minute()+":"+second());
 8    out.println("#User Kostas Terzidis");    // identification
 9    out.println("");
10    out.println("DEF Color_1 Material {");  //hard coded
11    out.println("      ambientColor "+red(solids[0].c)/256.
                                  +" "+green(solids[0].c)/256.
                                  +" "+blue(solids[0].c)/256.);
12    out.println("      diffuseColor 0.5 0.5 0.5");
13    out.println("      transparency 0");
14    out.println("}");
15    out.println("");
16
17    for(int k=0; k<nsolids; k++){
18      out.println("DEF " + "solid_" + k + " Separator {");
19      out.println("  Coordinate3 {");
20      out.println("         point [");
21      for(int j=0; j<solids[k].nfaces; j++)   {
22        for(int i=0; i<solids[k].faces[j].npoints; i++)   {
```

```
24        }
25      }
26      out.println("              ]");
27      out.println("    }");
28      out.println("    USE Color_1");   //hard coded
29      out.println("    IndexedFaceSet {");
30      out.println("              coordIndex [");
31      for(int j=0; j<solids[k].nfaces; j++)  {
32        out.print("          " );
33        for(int i=0; i<solids[k].faces[j].npoints; i++)  {
34          out.print((j*solids[k].faces[j].npoints+i) + ", " );
35        }
36        out.println("-1,");
37      }
38      out.println("              ]");
39      out.println("    }");
40      out.println("}");
41    }
42  out.flush();
43  out.close();
44 }
```

First, you define the procedure in line 1 and pass the name of the file you want to export. Then you create a `PrintWriter` to write out the VRML code. In lines 4 through 9, you write out information about the file (i.e., the version, creator, date, and user). In line 10, you define an object called `Color_1` of a `Material` type. This contains the ambient color, diffused color, and transparency values of a material that will be used later to color the geometrical objects. In this case, you are hard-coding (i.e., predetermining) the material information but that can be extracted from the color of the solid as in line 11. Once the material information is defined, you loop through all solids, all faces, and all points, and print out the coordinates. Note that coordinates are defined in the sequence as x, z, and y, and not in the standard x, y, and z. Then, for every face you print the sequence of points that define a face followed by a -1 to indicate the end of a face sequence (according to the VRML specification).

## 10.2.9 Reading VRML Files

Reading the geometry of an object in a VRML file requires two steps. First, you read the coordinates and then the point connections.

```
1  void  readVRML(String filename) {
2    String lines[] = loadStrings(filename);
3    if(lines.length==0)return;
```

```
 7   MyPoint [] ptemp = new MyPoint[0];
 8   boolean point_flag = false;
 9   boolean coordindex_flag = false;

10   for(int i=0; i<lines.length; i++){
11     if(match(lines[i],"point")!=null){point_flag=true; continue;}
12     if(match(lines[i],"coordIndex")!=null){
13        coordindex_flag=true; continue;
14     }
15   if(point_flag && match(lines[i],"]")!=null){
16      point_flag=false; continue;
17     }
18   if(coordindex_flag && match(lines[i],"]")!=null){
19        coordindex_flag=false;
20        solids = (MySolid[])append(solids,new MySolid(f));
21        nsolids++;
22        f = (MyFace[])expand(f,0);
23        ptemp = (MyPoint[])expand(ptemp,0);
24        p = (MyPoint[])expand(p,0);
25        continue;
26     }
27
28     String [] code = splitTokens(lines[i],", ");
29     if(point_flag)
30        p = (MyPoint[])append(p, new MyPoint(float(code[0]),
                                    float(code[1]), float(code[2])));
31     if(coordindex_flag){
32       for(int ii=0; ii<code.length-1; ii++)
33           ptemp = (MyPoint[])append(ptemp, new MyPoint(
                                     p[int(code[ii])].x,
                                     p[int(code[ii])].y,
                                     p[int(code[ii])].z));
34     f = (MyFace[])append(f,new MyFace(ptemp));
35     }
36   }
37 }
```

First, you load the file using the loadStrings command. This will populate
the lines[] array with all the lines of the file as text. Then, you initiate all arrays
that will be used to store the points, faces, and solids. You also define an array
ptemp[] that will be used to store the points of a solid temporarily until they
are used to create faces. Also, you define two boolean variables: point_flag
and coordIndex_flag that will be used to denote the presence of points or connections within a VRML file. In line 10, you loop through all the lines of the file
and you look for keywords. If the word points is encountered, you set the
points_flag flag to true. If the word coordIndex is encountered, you set

a "]" symbol is found, the reading of coordinates should stop. Similarly, when the `coordIndex_flag` flag is set and a "]" symbol is found, there is enough information to create a face and a solid. This is accomplished in lines 20 to 24. Specifically, in line 20 you create a new solid out of a series of faces, then in the next line you increase the counter that counts the solids, that is, `nsolids`. Then, you empty the arrays `f`, `ptemp`, and `p` (see lines 22, 23, and 24). This is accomplished by expanding each array to 0.

At this point, you have enough information to read the data from the file. First, you split each line into words separated by white spaces, making sure that no commas are included in any word. This is accomplished by using the `split-Tokens()` command, where you include a white space and a comma as separators. You then distinguish two cases: if the `points_flag` is set, you read triads of coordinate points that are used to construct `MyPoint` objects. Specifically, in line 33 you expand the `p[]` array by one element (note the cast `MyPoint[]`) and then create a new `MyPoint` by passing three numbers read from the file. Even though the data is read as strings, you cast them to floats in order to feed them to the `MyPoint` constructor. Also, note that the coordinate numbers are arranged in VRML as x, z, and y (not the usual x, y, and z).

In the second case, that is, if the `coordIndex_flag` flag is set, you construct faces out of points. These points are first added to a temporary array called `ptemp[]` and then passed to the face constructor to construct a face. So, line 33 is similar to line 30 discussed in the previous paragraph, and in line 34 you append a new face to the `f[]` array.

## 10.3 Client/Server Data Transfer

Processing is a programming language built upon yet another language called Java, which was developed primarily to be a network-oriented language. It was developed to work over the Internet and is, therefore, a good medium for transferring data or invoking graphics on remote computers. So far, all the graphics examples you've seen demonstrated were designed to work on a local machine. But what if you want to run something on a remote machine? For example, moving the mouse on one computer and seeing its movement on the screen of another computer.

The process of communication in Processing or Java is based on the client-server protocol: one computer plays the role of the client who asks for information and another computer plays the role of the server, which provides information in response to the client's request. The roles can be reversed, that is, both can send/receive information, but normally the server holds the information and serves requested HTML pages or files. A web client is the program that requests information from the server. A web browser is a client that requests HTML files from web servers.

Every computer that is connected to the Internet has an address, in order to be identified. This address is called an IP (Internet Protocol) address and is a 32-bit number. The IP address is usually expressed as four decimal numbers, each representing 8 bits, separated by periods. The format is "network.network.network.local". The number version of the IP address is represented by a name or series of names called the domain name. Here's an example:

```
130.5.5.25
```

Each number must be between 0 and 255 (i.e., a byte). The IP address 127.0.0.1 is the address of the local machine itself. Each of the decimal numbers represents a string of four binary digits. Thus, the above IP address really is this string of 0s and 1s:

```
10000010.00000101.00000101.00011001
```

As you can see, periods are inserted between each 8-bit sequence just as was done for the decimal version of the IP address. To establish a server in Processing is simple: you construct a server through the following statement:

```
Server MyServer = new Server(this, 5200);
```

A Server is a Processing class that waits for request over a network. The number 5200 is the port where the server is listening. Following is the code for establishing a server. The purpose of this server is to send to the client its mouse's x and y coordinates.

```
1     import processing.net.*; //get the net library
2
3     Server MyServer;          //define a server
4     void setup(){
5        size(300,300);
6        MyServer = new Server(this, 5200);
7     }
8     void draw(){
9         point(mouseX,mouseY);    //draw a point
10        MyServer.write(mouseX); //send x
11        MyServer.write(mouseY); //send y
12     }
```

In the first line of code, you import all the commands included in the net library of processing. Then you define a Server object called MyServer, which creates a server in line 6. You then draw points on the screen and use the server to send data out to the Internet (i.e., to whomever is receiving it), using the write() methods seen in lines 10 and 11.

A Client is a Processing class that sends requests over a network. To establish a client, you need to pass the address and port of the server to connect to. (Note that if you do not know the IP address's number you can use the ip() method of the client's class. It returns the IP address of the client as a string. As default value, we pass the address "127.0.0.1," which refers to the local computer itself). The number 5200 is the port where the server is listening. If you know the IP address of the server, you can type it here instead of the local number. To find the address of a machine you go to the command line prompt (in Windows), and type the command ipconfig:

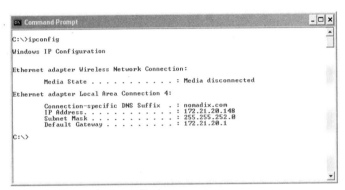

**Figure 10-10:** The ipconfig command

Following is the code for establishing a server. The purpose of this client is to receive the mouse's x and y coordinates of the server.

```
1    import processing.net.*; //get the net library
2
3    Client MyClient;              //define a client
4    void setup() {
5      size(300,300);
6      MyClient = new Client(this, "127.0.0.1", 5200);
7    }
8    void draw() {
9      if(MyClient.available()>0) { //if data are available
10       int x = MyClient.read();   //get the x-coordinate
11       int y = MyClient.read();   //get the y-coordinate
12       rect(x,y,5,5);             //draw a rect at xy
13       println(x+", "+y);         //print out coordinates
14     }
15   }
```

using the client() command that takes as parameters the parent object (indicated by the "this" expression), the server's IP address, and the specific port. In this case, you are using the IP address 127.0.0.1, which is the computer you are working on. In line 9 of the code you use the `available()` command to detect whether or not the server is sending data. If it is true (i.e., if it is not 0), then start to read the data values as they come in. In this case, you know that data comes in pairs, so you sequentially assign the odd data as x and the even as y. In more complicated cases, you may want to export an indicator on the server side to be used by the client as an identifier of what or how many data values are read in. For example, the server could be sending the string "x = 10" so the client would split the string based on the = symbol to determine that 10 is indeed the x coordinate.

To run a client/server program, you need to first run the server code to make sure that the server is up and waiting for clients. Then you run the client. As the server is waiting for connections, a client sends a request that is received by the server and the communication process begins. Once the first connection is established from a new client, a continuous communication stream is established by repeatedly sending/receiving information, allowing data to flow back and forth. In the example, the server is sending x and y mouse coordinates, and the client is seeing drawn on the screen small 5 × 5 rectangles that show the coordinates sent by the server.

The number 5000 stands for the port where the data will be sent or received. You can have multiple ports at the same time, since you can have multiple communications with other servers at the same time. In this case, you are using only one port, that is, the one numbered 5000.

Once you establish the connection with the server, you create an input stream and receive the data, that is, the mouseX and mouseY mouse coordinates. Remember that in the server's code, we used the `write()` method, which uses the output stream to send out data:

```
MyServer.write(mouseX);
MyServer.write(mouseY);
```

On the client's side a similar process is going on, except there you loop continuously, receiving data. The client needs to be in a constant state of waiting because it does not know when a request may come in. This is done through the line:

```
if(MyClient.available()>0)
```

```
int y = MyClient.read();
```

Input integers are assigned to the x and y variables that are used in the rect() method to draw a rectangle. The result of this process is shown in Figure 10-11.

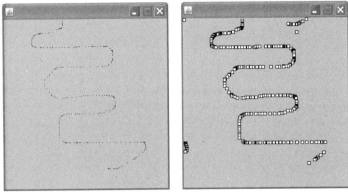

**Figure 10-11:** A client-server real-time interaction using graphics

For more information on the Java network objects and methods, look at the official Java site at http://java.sun.com.

## Summary

You have been introduced to the process of writing out and reading in files. Specifically, you have learned about the basic structure of two common graphics file formats called DXF and VRML. So, now you are able to import and export DXF and VRML files. This is an important task, because it allows you to interact with many computer graphics applications in their file format.

## Exercises

1. Find information about a file format called RIB. Write the import/export methods that would handle .rib files.

you will find in the DXF file.)

3. Find more information about the STL (Stereo Lithography) file format. Write the method that would allow to import and STL files.

4. Following are the contents of a text file called "positions.txt":

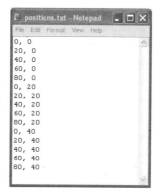

Write the code that will open the text file and draw on the screen a series of 10 × 10 rectangles each located at the file's data coordinates.

5. Write code that will open a text file and shuffle its contents as shown in the following figure:

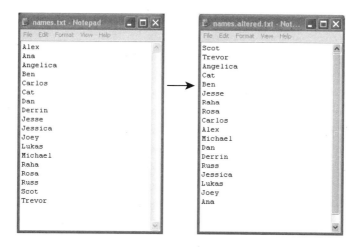

# 11

# Physical Computing

Physical computing is a term used to denote the use of physical devices to carry out computational processes. In its simplest form, it involves circuits with sensors and actuators driven by microcontroller boards.

*Sensors* are devices that sense information from the immediate environment, such as photocells that sense light intensity, thermistors that sense temperature, microphones that sense sound variations, and many more. One general classification of sensors is as either analog or digital, that is, whether they return a spectrum of variations or an on/off status. For example, a pushbutton is an on/off sensor that can sense whether it is being pressed or not. In contrast, a dial can reflect a spectrum of variations, depending on the rotation of the dial.

*Actuators* are devices that produce an action in their immediate environment, such as an LED (light emitting diode) a device that emits light, a motor that produces motion, or a speaker that vibrates sound. As in the case of sensors, one general categorization is as either analog or digital. For instance, an LED is a device that can either be on or off, whereas a motor can turn with variable degrees of speed or power output.

A *microcontroller board* is a computing device that allows, apart from arithmetic and logical operations, the input or output of information coming from sensors or actuators. In this chapter, we will examine the Arduino microcontroller, which runs a language similar to Processing. The objective is to mix Processing code with Arduino commands in order to extend the possibilities into physical computing. In this chapter, we will introduce the basics of electrical circuits and

The purpose is to show how to use, connect, and control devices in terms of responses, feedback, and multiple feedback systems.

## 11.1 Basics of Electrical Circuits

Electricity is the flow of electrons in a medium (i.e., copper wires). Electrons flow in one direction, which by convention, is defined from the positive to the negative pole of an electricity generator (i.e., a battery). The negative pole is also referred to as ground, for which we use the symbol GND. In some ways, the flow of electrons in a wire resembles the flow of water in a channel, and that analogy may be used occasionally in this chapter.

The number of electrons that pass through a medium per second is defined as *current*. Its conventional symbol is $I$ and it is measured in amperes. One ampere is equal to $6.28 \times 10^{18}$ electrons per second. This unit is quite large for 9V battery-based electrical circuits, so we will mostly use mA or milliamperes (i.e., 1/1,000 amp).

The potential to move electrons is defined as *voltage*. It is the ability of an electric source to send electrons through the medium and should remain constant. Its conventional symbol is V, and it is measured in volts.

A device that slows down the flow of electrons is referred to as a *resistor*. Its conventional symbol is $R$, and it is measured in ohms. The symbol for an ohm is the Greek omega letter $\Omega$. This unit is quite small for battery-based electrical circuits, so we will occasionally use $K\Omega$ or kilo-ohms (i.e., 1,000 ohms) or $M\Omega$ or mega-ohms (i.e., 1,000,000 ohms). Practically, resistors can be identified from the colors of the three strips on their body (see Figure 11-1). To identify the resistance, we use a code system: position the resistor so that the gold strip (or band) is on the right side, and then identify the code.

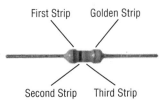

**Figure 11-1:** Color strips that indicate the value of resistance (in this case brown-black-orange, that is, 10K$\Omega$)

| COLOR | FIRST STRIP | SECOND STRIP | THIRD STRIP |
|-------|-------------|--------------|-------------|
| Black | 0 | 0 | x1 |
| Brown | 1 | 1 | x10 |
| Red | 2 | 2 | x100 |
| Orange | 3 | 3 | x1,000 |
| Yellow | 4 | 4 | x10,000 |
| Green | 5 | 5 | x100,000 |
| Blue | 6 | 6 | x1,000,000 |
| Purple | 7 | 7 | |
| Gray | 8 | 8 | |
| White | 9 | 9 | |

So, for instance, the resistance of the resistor in the figure above should be 1 (brown), then 0 (black), then ×100 (red), that is, 1,000 Ω or 1 KΩ.

The relationship between current, voltage, and resistance is referred to as Ohm's law and can be described in the following way: as the voltage remains constant, currency and resistance balance each other out to keep the voltage constant. This relationship is defined quantitatively as:

$$V = I * R \quad (\text{or } I = V/R \text{ or } R = V/I)$$

That is, the product of current and resistance is equal to the voltage. So, as the resistance increases (or decreases) the current decreases (or increases) correspondingly. For example, on a 5V voltage the following values of resistance and current will compensate for each other:11-KOhm resistor will allow 5/11,000 = 0.00045 or 0.4-mA current on a 5V voltage

- 16-KOhm resistor will allow 5/16,000 = 0.00031 or 0.3-mA current on a 5V voltage

- 21-KOhm resistor will allow 5/21,000 = 0.00023 or 0.2-mA current on a 5V voltage

A capacitor is a device that stores electrons that flow in a circuit. It functions similar to a tank of electrons, and its usefulness is in the fact that it can slow down temporarily until it is full and then stabilize the flow or count the time that it takes to fill up. This last feature is described quantitatively by the relationship:

Time = Capacity * Resistance

1 second because time = 1/1,000,000 F * 1,000,000 Ω = 1 sec.

Electrical circuits are usually created out of copper wires mounted on silicon boards. For practical purposes, there are temporary boards, called breadboards, where wires can be stuck in or pulled out to experiment with different circuit configurations. Figure 11-2 shows a typical breadboard on the left and on the right it shows the internal wiring underneath the holes.

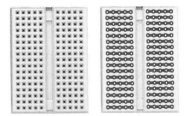

**Figure 11-2:** A typical breadboard (left) and the wiring underneath the holes (right).

## 11.2 Arduino Microcontroller Board

A microcontroller board is a computer hardware device that contains a micro-controller that can perform logico-arithmetic operations and a series of connec-tions that allows the controller access to external input/output devices. They are all welded as a circuit on a flat silicon plate, hence the term "board." Typically, they are small (hence the term "micro") and much less expensive than laptop computers. Their purpose is to allow the development of circuits using one or many microcontrollers that can sense and/or act within the physical environ-ment. In addition, many boards contain communication hardware for serial, Ethernet, or wireless networks.

Arduino is the name of a microcontroller board based on the Atmel AVR microcontroller. It contains a USB communication port, 8 analog i/o ports, 16 digital i/o ports, and a TX/RX serial port (see Figure 11-3). It can be connected to a computer's USB port and then establish communication between the com-puter and itself, also drawing power from the computer (there is a switch next to the Arduino's power plug that allows one to toggle between external and USB power).

grams. This software is also called Arduino, and it will be discussed in the next section.

**Figure 11-3:** Components of the Arduino microcontroller (left) and its connection to a computer via a USB cable (right)

## 11.3 Arduino Language

Arduino is a language designed to run on the Arduino microcontroller. Its structure is similar to Processing with a few minor differences. Arduino can be downloaded from the Processing web site (or directly from www.arduino.cc) and installed. In the next few paragraphs, we will introduce the basic elements, structure, and commands of Arduino, and then show how to use them in context of a circuit.

The main types of data variables are the following:

- boolean, which is 1 bit long and can take values of either true or false:

  ```
  boolean running = false;
  ```

- char, which is 1 byte (i.e., 8 bits) long and represents an ASCII character. Because of its size, 8 bits (compared to Processing's 16 bits), it can only hold 256 different characters. Each character is defined as an alphanumeric symbol enclosed within single quotation marks and that symbol corresponds to its ASCII index number. For example,

  ```
  char first = 'A';    //corresponds to 65
  ```

```
char name[] = "arduino";
```

- **byte**, which is an 8-bit element and, therefore, can store $2^0$ ($= 256$) different binary patterns. We use it to define integer numbers between 0 and 255.

```
byte b = 20;
```

- **int**, which is 16 bits long and holds integer numbers. Those would range from –32,768 to 32,767 (or $-2^{15}$ to $2^{15}$).

```
int analog_pin = 3;
```

- **long**, which is 32 bits long, can hold integer (whole) numbers. The range is between 2,147,483,648 and 2,147,483,647 or $-2^{31}$ to $2^{31}$.

```
long milliseconds= 60000;
```

- **float**, which is 32 bits long, can define real numbers (i.e., fractional numbers). The range is between $3.4028235 * 10^{38}$ and $-3.4028235 * 10^{38}$.

```
float pi = 3.1415927;   //8 number positions
```

- **double**, which is 64 bits long, can define real numbers with higher (i.e., double) precision:

```
double pi = 3.141592653589793;   //16 number positions
```

There are two more data types: unsigned integer and unsigned long, which correspond to only positive integers of longs. The basic variable data types can be seen in the following table.

| TYPE | SIZE | DESCRIPTION |
|---|---|---|
| boolean | 1 bit | True or false |
| char | 8 bits | 256 ASCII Codes |
| byte | 8 bits or 1 byte | Numbers between 0 to 255 |
| int | 16 bits | Integer numbers |
| long | 32 bits | Double-length integer numbers |
| float | 32 bits or 4 bytes | Floating numbers |
| double | 64 bits or 8 bytes | Double-precision floating numbers |

The structure of Arduino is similar to Processing code, as it is divided into two main processes: setup() and loop(). The setup() process is used to define initial environment properties (mainly the pin mode and the serial initiation)

```
void setup(){   //area to set up the variables or procedures to be used
    in the loop below
}
void loop(){    // in constant loop waiting to receive or to send
    information
}
```

The word `void` means that the process does not return any value, that is, it returns void. The term `setup()` is the name of the default "setup" process, and the parentheses are there in case one needs to insert parameters for processing; here they contain nothing, that is, `()`. The curly brackets `{` and `}` denote the beginning and end of the process and normally should include the commands to be executed. Comments are represented by either double slash (`//`), where everything after `//` is ignored by Processing until the end of the line, or by `/*` and `*/` where multiline comments use the `/*` to start and the `*/` to end.

In brief, all of the casting, logical, and arithmetic operations as well as loops, arrays, methods, procedures, and library imports are essentially the same and can be reviewed in Chapter 1, sections 1.1 to 1.8. Also, all mathematical, trigonometric, and random commands are exactly the same.

The main commands used to control the Arduino board are grouped in the categories of digital, analog, time, and serial communication. The first group includes three commands:

- `pinMode(int pin, boolean mode)`: This command defines the mode of a digital pin (0–13) to be either INPUT or OUTPUT. Note that INPUT is a constant equal to 0 or false, and OUTPUT is equal to 1 or true.

- `digitalWrite(int pin, boolean value)`: This command defines the value to be sent out from a digital pin (0–13) to be either HIGH or LOW. Note that HIGH is a constant equal to 1 or true, and LOW is equal to 0 or false. HIGH also corresponds to a +5V signal, whereas LOW corresponds to an almost 0V signal.

- `int digitalRead(int pin)`: This command receives a signal from a digital pin (0–13) that is either HIGH or LOW.

The next set of commands relate to the analog capabilities of the board. Those are:

- `analogWrite(int pin, byte value)`: This command defines the value to be sent out to the digital pins (3, 5, 6, 9, 10, and 11), which can vary between 0 and 255. While this appears as an analog output (i.e., set the speed of a motor), in reality it is the frequency for sending out digital signals that analog pin (0–5) that would vary between 0 and 1024 (corresponding from to 0V to +5V).

The next set of commands relates to the control of time. Those are:

- `long milliseconds`: This defines the number of milliseconds as a long (32-bit) integer. The maximum value can be about 9 hours and 32 minutes.

- `delay(long ms)`: This defines the number of milliseconds to halt the Arduino's loop.

The next set of commands relates to the serial communication capabilities of the board. Those are:

- `Serial.begin(int speed)`: This starts the serial communication at the specified speed, in data bytes per second. These rates can be 300, 1200, 2400, 4800, 9600, 14400, 19200, 28800, 38400, 57600, or 115200.

- `int Serial.available()`: This returns 0 if a serial communication is not established. Otherwise, it will return the number of bytes available to read from the serial buffer (1–128).

- `int Serial.read()`: This reads data bytes coming in through the serial port. If none is coming through, it will return -1.

- `Serial.flush()`: This clears the serial buffer of data.

- `Serial.print(data)`: This sends data to the serial port. The data can be of type byte, binary, decimal, hex, or string. You can use `println` instead to include a carriage return.

There are more specialized commands available for the Arduino board, which can be viewed on Arduino's web site at www.arduino.cc. However, for the purposes of this book, we will use only the ones outlined above. The next sections demonstrate the use of these commands in the context of circuits and as used as a reference for more complex electronic explorations.

## 11.4 LED

An LED is a light-emitting device. It consists of semiconductor material that, when electricity passes through it in a specific direction, emits light (or infrared/ultraviolet radiation). The word LED is an acronym for light emitting diode. The schematic symbol for an LED is shown on the left in Figure 11-4. For practical applications, we use the typical LED shown to the right in the figure.

**Figure 11-4:** Schematic symbol for an LED (left) and a typical LED (right)

In order to use the 13th digital pin of the Arduino to turn an LED on and off continuously every second, we employ the following code:

```
1    void setup(){
2       pinMode(13, OUTPUT);        // set the pin as output
3    }
4
5    void loop(){
6       digitalWrite(13, HIGH);     // sets the LED on
7       delay(1000);                    // wait a second
8       digitalWrite(13, LOW);      // sets the LED off
9       delay(1000);                    // wait a second
10   }
```

The second line of code sets Arduino's 13th pin to output mode. Then in the main loop, we send a high voltage of 5V using the `digitalWrite()` command (see line 6) and then a low voltage of 0V (see line 8). In between we delay the loop by 1,000 milliseconds, or 1 second. This code must be typed in the Arduino editor (shown in Figure 11-5).

**Figure 11-5:** The Arduino editor of the integrated development environment (IDE) application

an LED what the long leg in pin is and short leg into the GND (see Figure 11-6).
It should be blinking every second. If not, then look at the troubleshooting section at www.arduino.cc/en/Guide/Troubleshooting.

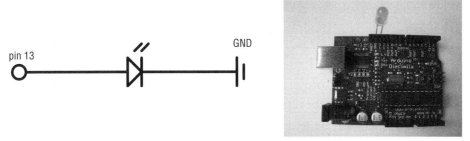

**Figure 11-6:** Schematic diagram of circuit (left) and actual appearance (right)

## 11.5 Photocell

A photocell (or photo-resistor) is a device used to measure light intensity. It consists of a semiconductor material that increases its resistance as light increases.
Unlike an LED, the direction of electricity flow does not matter. The schematic
symbol for photocell is shown to the left in Figure 11-7. For practical applications
we use typical photocells as shown to the right in the image.

**Figure 11.7:** Schematic symbol for a photocell (left) and
a typical photocell (right)

In order to use a photocell to measure light intensities that will be shown
as changes in the brightness of the computer's screen consider the following
code:

```
1    void setup(){
2      Serial.begin(9600);   //start serial at 9600 bits per second
3    }
4
```

This code is written for the Arduino board and it reads photocell intensities which then sends them to the computer through the serial stream. To do this we first initialize the serial communication at 9600 bits per second (see line 2). Then we read input data from the photocell from analog pin 5. This data is transferred over the serial line out to the computer (see lines 6 and 7). In order for this code to work, we need a circuit that captures data from a photocell. This circuit is shown in Figure 11-8 in schematics (left) and as a physical manifestation (right).

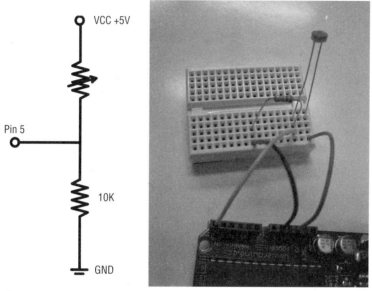

**Figure 11-8:** Schematic diagram of circuit (left) and actual appearance (right)

Note that the Serial.println() command sends data out through the serial line as ACSII characters followed by a carriage return, not as numbers. So we will need to convert the ASCII characters to numbers every time we encounter a carriage return. The following code in Processing reads the data coming in from the serial port and then converts them into integer numbers which are then used to change the background color of the window.

```
1    import processing.serial.*;
2
3    String buff = "";
4    int val = 0;
```

```
9        port = new Serial(this, Serial.list()[0], 9600);  // Use the
    first available port
10   }
11
12   void draw(){
13     while (port.available() > 0)
14       serialEvent(port.read());   //look for data
15       background(val);   //change background clr based on input data
16   }
17
18   void serialEvent(int serial) {
19     if(serial != NEWLINE) {
20       buff += char(serial);   //add on bytes until a newline is found
21     } else {
22       buff = buff.substring(0, buff.length()-1);
23       val = Integer.parseInt(buff)/4;   // Parse the String to int
24       println(val);
25       buff = "";   // Clear the value of "buff"
26     }
27   }
```

As we discussed earlier, Serial.println() sends out characters (i.e., bytes) over the serial line, so the main task of this code is to extract integer numbers out of 2 bytes plus a carriage return ASCII character (which is equal to 10). So, we first define a string that will hold the incoming bytes (called buff). Next, we define an integer called var that will hold the parsed integers, and then we define the word NEWLINE as 10 (since 10 is the ASCII number that corresponds to a new line). In line 9 of the code, we open serial communication with the serial port. At this point, the Arduino code is still running sending the photocell values (see line 7 in the previous code). Next, in the draw() section we read the serial data using the port.read() command provided that it is available (see lines 13 and 14). Then we parse the incoming data, using the procedure serialEvent(). In this procedure, we read characters as they come in, concatenating them in the buff string. If the incoming byte is a new line (i.e., ASCII code 10), we take the concatenated buff string minus the last byte (which is the new line) and cast it into an integer (see lines 22 and 23). This is the value of the light intensity that was sent out through the serial stream. The reason we divide by four is that the Arduino sends values between 0 and 1024, but we can only pass values from 0 to 256 to the background() procedure, so we need to divide by 4.

If the procedure was successful, the window should be changing color as the light intensities through the photocell change, as shown in Figure 11-9.

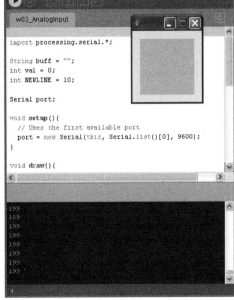

```
w03_AnalogInput

import processing.serial.*;

String buff = "";
int val = 0;
int NEWLINE = 10;

Serial port;

void setup(){
  // Uses the first available port
  port = new Serial(this, Serial.list()[0], 9600);
}

void draw(){
```

```
199
199
199
199
199
199
199
199
```

**Figure 11-9:** The Processing code that shows the changes in the window's background based on the serial input

# 11.6 Pushbutton

A pushbutton is a device that allows electricity to flow when it is pressed. In that sense, it can be viewed as a control switch. The schematic symbol for a pushbutton is shown to the left in Figure 11-10. The direction of electricity flow does not matter. For practical applications, we typically use a pushbutton with four legs, as shown in the image to the right.

**Figure 11-10:** Schematic symbol for a pushbutton (left) and a typical pushbutton with four legs (right)

```
 2      Serial.begin(9600);    //start the serial port in order to write
 3        pinMode(2,INPUT);    // set the pin 2 to input
 4    }
 5
 6    void loop(){
 7        int val = digitalRead(2);      //read from the pin 2
 8        if(val==LOW)          //if the current is low (i.e. pressed) then
 9            Serial.println("LOW");      //let me know
10    }
```

First, we establish a serial connection with the computer, and then we set the pushbutton's pin to input mode. Using the `digitalRead()` command within the main loop, the button's activity is monitored. If the button is pushed, an interruption in the flow occurs, which results in a low signal value (i.e., an interruption). Then we send a signal back to the computer to notify it of the event. The circuit (shown in Figure 11-11) requires a 10-KOhm resistor on the 5V power supply (VCC) and two connections to the pin (2 in this case) and the ground.

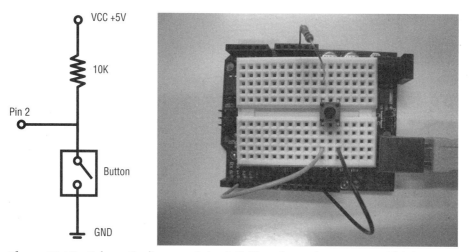

**Figure 11-11:** Schematic diagram of circuit (left) and actual appearance (right)

## 11.7 Servo Motor

A servo motor is a motor that pulses at a certain rate moving its gear at a certain angle. It has three connections: the black (ground), the red (connected to 5V), and the white or yellow wire here, which is set to the digital pin (5 in our case).

So, every degree corresponds to 2,000/180 = 11. So to move to 20 degrees we need to send a vibration of 500 + 11 * 20.

The following code demonstrates the full range of motion for nine divisions of 180 degrees:

```
1   void setup(){
2       pinMode(5,OUTPUT);   //set the pin to output
3       Serial.begin(9600);     //open the serial to print
4       Serial.print("Ready"); //write a message
5   }
6   void loop(){
7       int val = Serial.read();        //read the serial to see
8       if(val>'0' && val <= '9'){  //which key was pressed
9         val = val - '0';    //convert the character to an integer
10        val = val * (180/9);     //9 divisions of 180 degrees
11        Serial.print("moving servo to ");
12        Serial.print(val,DEC);
13        Serial.println();
14        for(int a=0; a<50; a++){
15          int pulseWidth = (val*11)+500; // See the formula above
16          digitalWrite(5,HIGH);
17          delayMicroseconds(pulseWidth);
18          digitalWrite(5,LOW);
19          delay(20);
20        }
21      }
22  }
```

In the preceding code, we first set up the motor's digital pin as output and then establish a serial connection with the computer. Then, in the main loop, we wait for keys to be pressed on the computer's keyboard. If a key is pressed between 1 and 9, then that keystroke character needs to be converted into an integer value to be processed. Since the keystrokes come in through the serial port as ASCII characters, we subtract the ASCII character for zero to get the actual number value (see line 9). For example, if the keystroke was 2, which corresponds in ASCII code to decimal value 82, we subtract the ASCII code for zero (which is 80) and we get 2, which is the integer value for the character "2". Once we have the decimal value for the keystroke, we multiply it by the length of one of the nine divisions of 180 (i.e., 180/9). That value is sent back to the computer through the serial port to be printed (see lines 11 to 13) and is also used to move the motor. Specifically, we pulse out the digital pin at a frequency that corresponds to the servo motor's specifications. In this case, we need values between 500 and 2,500. We convert these values into pulses by sending them in groups of 50 high/low signals delayed by 20 milliseconds (see lines 16 to 19). The circuit that connects the Arduino board to the servo motor is shown in Figure 11-12.

GND

**Figure 11-12:** Schematic diagram of a Fukuda servo motor circuit (left) and actual appearance (right)

## 11.8 Sound

A piezo element is a device that can produce or respond to vibrations of sound. It is able not only to produce sounds but also to measure pressure, acceleration, strain, any other force apply to it. The word "piezo" is Greek, and it means "press." A piezo that produces sound is also referred to as a piezo speaker. A typical piezo speaker looks like a drum and has two pins (a positive and a negative) to be connected in a circuit. The schematic symbol for a piezo speaker is shown to the left in Figure 11-13. For practical applications, we typically use a piezo speaker like that shown on the right in Figure 11-13.

**Figure 11-13:** Schematic symbol for a piezo speaker (left) and a typical piezo speaker (right)

Suppose that we want to construct a primitive musical instrument that will produce melodies through keystrokes on the keyboard. Consider the following code:

```
1    //                  "do", "re",  "mi", "fa","sol","la", "si", "do"
2    int  freqs[] = {   1915, 1700, 1519, 1432, 1275, 1136, 1014, 956};
3
4    void setup(){
5      pinMode(11,OUTPUT);
6      Serial.begin(9600);    //open the serial to print
7      }
8    void loop(){
9      int val = Serial.read();       //read the serial to see
10     if(val>'0' && val <= '9'){  //which key was pressed
11       val = val - '0';   //convert the character to an integer
12       Serial.print(val,DEC);
13       Serial.println();
```

```
16              delayMicroseconds(freqs[va..]);    //the tone's frequency
17              digitalWrite(11,LOW);
18              delayMicroseconds(freqs[val]);
19          }
20      }
21  }
```

In line 2 of the preceding code, we construct an array with the values of the frequencies that correspond to the octave tone scale. Next, we set pin 11 as an output pin and open the serial communication. Then, in the main loop, we wait for keys to be pressed on the computer's keyboard. If a key is pressed between 1 and 9, then that keystroke character needs to be converted into an integer value to be processed. Since the keystrokes come in through the serial port as ASCII characters, we subtract the ASCII character for zero to get the actual number value (see line 9). For example, suppose that the keystroke was 2, which corresponds in ASCII code to decimal value 82. If we subtract the ASCII code for zero, which is 80 then we get 2, which is the integer value for the character "2." Once we have the decimal value for the keystroke (stored in the variable val), we used that value to invoke the corresponding index of the array freqs[]. This produces a tone in that frequency for half a second, using the digitalWrite() command altering 500 times between high and low. The circuit is shown in Figure 11-14.

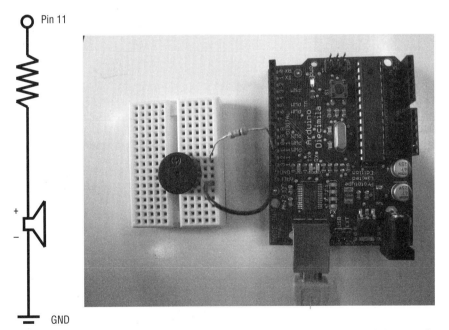

**Figure 11-14:** Schematic diagram of a piezo sound element (left) and the actual appearance (right)

in numbers that are taken from the Arduino `analogRead()` command. This, however, displays the absolute values of the input data as, for example, light intensity in a room (i.e., values such as 800, 800, 801, 800, 799, etc.). The problem is that when we change the room conditions or run the experiment on a different time of the day we may be getting values that are different from the ones in the original experiment (i.e., 500, 500, 501, 500, 499, etc.). So, we then need to readjust (or calibrate) the experiment to match the new conditions. However, if we modify the input data to show not their absolute value but rather their difference over time then we may be able to avoid readjustments. Consider the following code:

```
1    void setup(){
2      Serial.begin(9600);
3    }
4
5      int value2;
6      void loop(){
7        int value1 = analogRead(0);
8        Serial.println(value2-value1);
9        value2 = value1;
10   }
```

Here, the input data is displayed as the difference of before and after, not their absolute values. So for the same experiment (above) the values would be 0, 0, 1, 0, -1 regardless of the conditions of the experiment.

## 11.10 Responsive System: Photo-Sound

A response is a reaction to a specific stimulus. It is a tendency to revert to a former state. The minimal definition of a response involves at least two consecutive moments of time as a measure of comparison. However, apart from time, a formal configuration is necessary in order to manifest responsiveness. In that sense, a response cannot only be conceived directly through physical change but also indirectly through visual interpretation.

A responsive form may imply indirectly the existence of a living organism. Responsiveness is associated with living, vital, animated, and soulful organisms. What distinguishes a living animal from a dead, stuffed, or artificial one is not its form or its movements but rather in its response to external stimuli.

In the following paragraph, we will look into a simple responsive system that uses a photocell connected to a piezo speaker to produce sounds based on light intensities. In other words, shadows cast on the surface of a photocell will produce different musical tones. Consider the circuit shown in Figure 11-15.

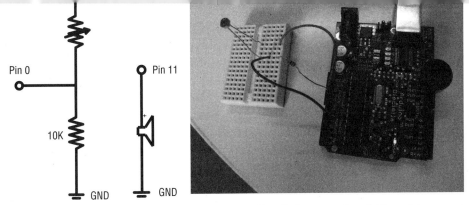

**Figure 11-15:** Schematic diagram of a photocell and piezo speaker (left) and the actual appearance (right)

Now, consider the following code:

```
1    //                      do    re    mi    fa    sol   la    si    do
2    int  freqs[] = {   1915, 1700, 1519, 1432, 1275, 1136, 1014,  956};
3
4    void setup(){
5        pinMode(11,OUTPUT);
6        Serial.begin(9600);
7    }
8    void loop(){
9        int value = analogRead(0);
10       int tone = (value/100)%8;
11       Serial.println(tone);
12       for(int i=0; i<100; i++){
13         digitalWrite(11,HIGH);
14         delayMicroseconds(freqs[tone]);
15         digitalWrite(11,LOW);
16         delayMicroseconds(freqs[tone]);
17       }
18   }
```

In line 2 of the preceding code, we construct an array with the values of the frequencies that correspond to the octave tone scale. Next, we set pin 11 as an output pin and open the serial communication. Then, in the main loop, we first receive a value from the analog port (i.e., the photocell's value for the light intensity). Then we convert that value in a range between the number 0 and 7. This is done assuming that we know in advanced the range of light intensity values returned by the photocell. In the next section, we will show a case where we do not know the range, but we use instead the differential. In this case, however, once we have the integer value between 0 and 7, we use it

# 11.11 A Feedback System: Photo-Motor

In simple terms, a feedback system is one that connects input to output. A sensor that feeds its sensed information to an actuator is a responsive system. For example, a photocell that receives light intensities and feeds them as angles to rotate a servo motor is responsive. Consider the circuit shown in Figure 11-16.

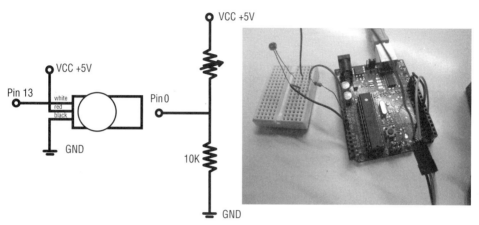

**Figure 11-16:** Schematic diagram of a photocell with a servo motor (left) and the actual appearance (right)

A photocell is connected at analog pin 0 and a motor is connected through digital pin 13. When the light changes, the motor moves in response. The code below describes this process:

```
1    void setup(){
2      pinMode(13,OUTPUT);
3    }
4
5    int degrees = 90;
6    int value2;
7    void loop(){
8        int value1 = analogRead(0);
9        int diff = value2 - value1;
10       degrees += diff;
11       degrees = constrain(degrees, 0, 180);
12       servoMove(13,degrees);
13       value2 = value1;
14   }
15
```

```
18      digitalWrite(pin,HIGH);
19      delayMicroseconds(pulseWidth);
20      digitalWrite(pin,LOW);
21      delay(20);
22   }
```

In line 2 of the preceding code, we set pin 13 to output mode. Then we read the input data from the sensor and convert it to degrees of an angle that is used to rotate the servo motor. Here, we use the differential of input sensor values to move the motor. This is done by getting a value called value1 and then subtracting it from the value that was previously received, called value2. This is done in lines 8 and 13. Once a differential is established (line 9), we use that value to control the angle of the servo motor. That variable is called degrees, and it represents the angle for rotating the motor. This is initiated at 90 and can increase or decrease based on the differential. For example, if value1 is 203 and value2 is 200, then the differential is -3 so the angle becomes 87. After we calculate the angle, we send it the procedure called servoMove(). There, given the pin and the angle, we calculate the pulse width, which is based on the formula (angle*11)+500. This is used as the time to delay the pulsing of the servo motor, using the digitalWrite() command altering between high and low.

The circuit shown above is responsive in the sense that when shadows are cast on the photocell, the motor moves by a certain angle clockwise or counterclockwise. However, if we physically connect the photocell and the motor into a system where the input of the photocell affects the output of the motor, which in turn affects the input to the photocell, then we have created a simple feedback system that behaves quite differently from a simply responsive one. This configuration can be seen in Figure 11-17. In fact, the overall behavior is a struggle to balance input and output in a system that can react not only to external actions but also to itself. Further, multiple feedback systems can be brought into contact, creating a series of behaviors that may result in a collective emergent behavior.

 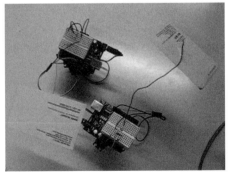

**Figure 11-17:** A simple feedback system with a motor and a photocell (left) and the interaction of two feedback systems (right)

order to control the Arduino board. The language is similar to Processing and data values can be communicated back and forth through the serial port. The electronic circuits presented in this chapter showed generic versions of input, output, responsive, and feedback systems that use photocells, buttons, servo motors, and piezo speakers.

## Exercises

**NOTE** Answers to the exercises are provided in Appendix B.

1. The following code reads serial input as a variable *in* and uses it to play one of the eight music tones on a piezo connected at the digital pin 11 (see the following circuit).

```
void setup() {
  Serial.begin(9600); // opens serial port, sets data rate to 9600 bps
  pinMode(11,OUTPUT);
}
int in=0;
void loop() {
  if (Serial.available() > 0)
    in = Serial.read();

  for(int i=0; i<500; i++){   //duration of the tone (.5 seconds)
    digitalWrite(11,HIGH);
    delayMicroseconds(freqs[in]);   //the tone's frequency
    digitalWrite(11,LOW);
    delayMicroseconds(freqs[in]);
  }
}
```

Write the corresponding code in Processing that will draw a 400 × 100 window with a vertical line such that, when the mouse moves back and forth, it will export through the serial port numbers between 0 and 8 that will play the music tones with the preceding Arduino code.

2. Consider the following Arduino code that gets data from a photocell and send it to the serial output:

```
void setup(){
  pinMode(11,OUTPUT);
  Serial.begin(9600);
}
void loop(){
  int value = analogRead(0);
  Serial.println(value);
}
```

Now consider the following Processing code that reads the data from the serial port:

```
import processing.serial.*;
```

```
int val = 0;
int NEWLINE = 10;
Serial port;

void setup(){
  port = new Serial(this, "COM6", 9600);
  output = createWriter("positions.txt");
}

void draw(){
  while (port.available() > 0)
    serialEvent(port.read());
  background(val);
}

void serialEvent(int serial) {
  if(serial != NEWLINE) {
    buff += char(serial);
  } else {
    buff = buff.substring(0, buff.length()-1);
    // Parse the String into an integer
    val = Integer.parseInt(buff)/4;
    println(val);
    // Clear the value of "buff"
    buff = "";
  }
}
```

Modify the Processing code so that you can open a file called "data.txt" to write the serial input data to that file.

3. Write the code using an Arduino that will snap to increments of 5 as the counter changes:

| VALUE | ROUNDIT |
|-------|---------|
| 0 | 0 |
| 1 | 0 |
| 2 | 0 |
| 3 | 0 |
| 4 | 0 |
| 5 | 5 |
| 6 | 5 |
| 7 | 5 |

| | |
|---|---|
| 8 | 5 |
| 9 | 5 |
| 10 | 10 |
| 11 | 10 |
| 12 | 10 |
| 13 | 10 |
| ... | ... |
| 245 | 245 |
| 246 | 245 |
| 247 | 245 |
| 248 | 245 |
| 249 | 245 |
| 250 | 250 |
| 251 | 250 |
| 252 | 250 |
| 253 | 250 |
| 255 | 255 |
| 256 | 260 |
| 257 | 260 |
| 258 | 260 |
| ... | ... |

```
void setup(){
  pinMode(11,OUTPUT);
  Serial.begin(9600);
}
void loop(){
  int value = analogRead(0);
  int roundit = _____
;
  Serial.println(roundit);
}
Answer: _____
```

5. Project: Passage

A passage is a movement from one place to another (as by going by, through, over, or across). While a passage signifies a process of flow, transition, and movement, it also implies the existence of a barrier, an obstruction, or an impediment. A passage is about the notion of a path, road, channel, trench, alley, or route, yet it is also about a cut, gash, incision, slash, slice, or slit on a barrier. In architecture, passages are typically addressed through doors that connect rooms. A door is a movable structure used to close off an entrance, typically consisting of a panel that swings on hinges or that slides or rotates.

   **Site**: Two spaces separated by a wall

   **Program**: A passage that disconnects the two spaces

Satisfying the above requirements, create a contraption(s) that will address the notion of a passage. The mechanism that operates the access to the passage must be responsive to someone or something.

# Equations of Lines and Planes

## Equation of Lines

Given two points $(x_1, y_1)$ and $(x_2, y_2)$ the equation of the line they define is $Ax + By + C$ where

```
A = (y₂-y₁)/(x₂-x₁)
B = -1
C = y₁ - A*x₁
```

The slope of the line is given by $m = -A/B = A$.
For example, assume points (110, 20) and (30, 70). Then

```
A = (70-20)/(30-110) = (50)/(-80) = -6.25
B = -1;
C = 20-(A*110) = 20-(-6.25*100) = 88.75
```

The equation of the line is $A * x + B * y + C = 0$ or $-6.25*x - y + 88.75$

Note that for $x = 0$, $y = C$, the value of C represents the point where the line intersects the y-axis.

Note also that for $y = 0$, $x = -C/A$ The value of the ratio $-C/A$ represents the point where the line intersects the x-axis.

$(x_4, y_4) = (100, 80)$.

The equation of the line is $7.5*x - y + 5 = 0$.

Its intersection with the previous line (the equation of which was $-6.75*x - y + 88.75 = 0$) is given by:

```
x' = (C2-C1)/(A1-A2) = (88.75 - 5) / (7.5 + 6.25) = 60.91
y' = A1*x + C1 = 7.5*60.91 + 5 = 50.68
```

One should always watch for parallel lines, which do not intersect (or intersect at infinity).

Two lines are parallel when $A = 1/A_2$.

Two lines are perpendicular to each other when $A1 = 1/A_2$.

One should also watch for vertical lines (lines parallel to the $y$-axis) since their slope is infinite.

The following code shows a simple case of line creation, intersection, and perpendicularity:

```
//suppose that given points we have two lines
float x1 = 110;
float y1 = 20;
float x2 = 30;
float y2 = 70;

float x3 = 20;
float y3 = 20;
float x4 = 100;
float y4 = 80;

//line 1 equations
float A1 = (y2-y1)/(x2-x1);
float B1 = -1;
float C1 = y1 - A1 * x1;

//line 2 equations
float A2 = (y4-y3)/(x4-x3);
float B2 = -1;
float C2 = y3 - A2 * x3;

//the intersection point is
float xint = (C2-C1)/(A1-A2);
float yint = A1*xint+ C1;

noFill();
ellipse(round(xint),round(yint),6,6);
```

```
//two lines are perpendicular when A1 = 1/A . A2,
circle:
float radius = 40;
float xc = 20;
float yc = 20;
ellipse(xc,yc,radius*2,radius*2);   //radius is the bounding box
dimensions

//the circle's equation is: pow(xc,2)+pow(yc,2) = pow(radius,2)
//take a point on the circle's periphery

float xp = 15;   //should be between -40 and 40
float yp = sqrt(pow(radius,2)-pow((xp),2));

ellipse(round(xp+xc),round(yp+yc),6,6);

//So a line from the center to xp,yp will be
stroke(255,0,0);
x1 = xc;
y1 = yc;
x2 = xp+xc;
y2 = yp+yc;
line(x1,y1,x2,y2);

//of course the equation is (see above)

//line 1 equations
 A1 = (y2-y1)/(x2-x1);
 B1 = -1;
 C1 = y1 - A1 * x1;

//A perpendicular line would be when A2 = -1/A1
//So line 2 should be

 A2 = -1/A1;
 B2 = -1;
 C2 = y2 - A2 * x2;

//so for
x3 = 100;   //arbitrary
y3 = C2 + (A2*x3);

line(x2,y2,x3,y3);
```

$I_3 = (x_3, y_3, z_3).$

The equation of a plane is $Ax + By + Cz - D = 0$, where the coefficients A, B, and C are calculated as follows:

1. Find the coefficients of the lines defined by pairs of points on the plane:

$$A_1 = x_2 - x_1; \quad B_1 = y_2 - y_1 \quad \text{and} \quad C_1 = z_2 - z_1$$
$$A_2 = x_3 - x_1; \quad B_2 = y_3 - y_1 \quad \text{and} \quad C_2 = z_3 - z_1.$$

2. Find the coefficients of the plane based on the coefficients of the lines:

$$A = b_1 c_2 - c_1 b_2; \quad B = c_1 a_2 - a_1 c_2; \quad C = a_1 b_2 - b_1 a_2 \quad \text{and} \quad D = Ax_1 + By_1 + Cz_1$$

For example, assume that $P_1 = (4, 10, -2)$, $P_2 = (10, 5, 0)$ and $P_3 = (-2, 6, 10)$.

Then $a_1 = 6$, $b_1 = -5$, $c_1 = 2$, $a_2 = -6$, $b_2 = -4$, $c_2 = 12$

$A = -5 * 12 - 2 * (-4) = -6 -+8 = -52$

$B = 2 * (-6) - 6 * 12 = -12 - 72 = -84$

$C = 6 * (-4) - (-5) * (-6) = -24 - 30 = -54$

$D = -52*4 + (-84) * 10 + (-54) * (-2) = -208 - 840 + 108 = -940$

The equation of the plane is $-52x - 84y - 54z + 940 = 0$

or $52x + 84y + 54z - 940 = 0$

or $26x + 42y + 27z - 470 = 0$

## Intersection of Planes

Suppose that you also have a second plane defined by points $P_4 = (-1, 12, 4)$, $P_5 = (3, 2, -2)$, and $P_6 = (5, -2, 8)$.

Its equation is $31x + 13y - z - 121 = 0$.

The simplest way to find the intersection of the two planes is by assigning arbitrary values to any of the unknowns (the 0 value simplifies the calculations) and calculating the values of the others. In this way, we can find two points, which suffice for the definition of the intersection line.

(for plane $P_1$, $P_2$, $P_3$).

Solving the equations, we have $y = 9.509$ and $z = 2.617$.

So, the first point of the intersection line is $P'_1 = (0, 9.509, 2.617)$.

Similarly, for $y = 0$, we find that $x = 4.330$ and $z = 13.230$, or $P'_2 = (4.330, 0, 13.230)$

# Answers to Exercises

## Chapter 1

**NOTE** Question 1 is a memorization exercise and does not have an answer.

2. Variable names cannot start with a number and cannot contain any arithmetic operation (+, -, *, /). The correct answer is D.

3. One bit that can be turned either on (true) or off (false). The correct answer is B.

4. For all the integer numbers between 0 and 99, there are only 10 numbers that, when divided, have a remainder of 0. These numbers are 0, 10, 20, 30, 40, 50, 60, 70, 80, and 90. The correct answer is C.

5. The correct answer is D because all the others either affect the values of $x$ and $y$ or do not assign anything to $x$ and $y$.

6. The algorithm is:

```
for(int i=0; i<15; i++){
        int x = i%5 * 20;
        int y = i/5 * 20;
rect(x,y,10,10);
}
```

```
    float x1 = sin(radians(i))*30;
    float y1 = cos(radians(i))*30;
    float x2 = sin(radians(i))*40;
    float y2 = cos(radians(i))*40;
    line(x1+50,y1+50,x2+50,y2+50);
}
```

8. The answer is:

```
rect(20,20,(1+sqrt(5))/2*40,40);
```

9. The algorithm is:

```
for(int i=0; i<20; i++){
    int x =(i%4)/3 *(-1) +1;
    print(x);
};
```

10. The answer is:

```
float x = round(mouseX/10.)*10.;
```

11. The answer is:

```
int x = int(random(-50,50))*2;
```

12. A staircase.

13. Pattern 1. The algorithm is:

```
size(500,100);
float x = 0;
for(int i=0; i<5000; i+=10){
   x += abs(sin(radians(i)))*10;
   line(x,0,x,100);
}
```

Pattern 2. The algorithm is:

```
size(300,300);
  float x = 0;
  float y = 0;
  for(int i=0; i<5000; i +=10){
      x += abs(sin(radians(i)))*10.;
      for(int j=0; j<5000; j +=10){
          y += abs(cos(radians(j)))*10.;
          line(0,y,500,y);
```

```
size(200,200);
for(int x =0; x<width; x++)
  for(int y = 0; y<height; y++){
     if(y%2==0)continue;
```

```
size(200,200);
for(int x =0; x<width; x++)
 for(int y = 0; y<height; y++){
    if(x%2==0)continue;
    rect(x*10,y*10,8,8);
}
```

## Pattern 5. The algorithm is:

```
size(200,200);
for(int x =0; x<width; x++)
  for(int y = 0; y<height; y++){
    rectMode(CENTER);
    if(y%2==0)continue;
    if(x%2==0)
       rect(x*10,y*10,8,8);
    else
     rect(x*10,y*10,4,4);
}
```

## Pattern 6. The algorithm is:

```
size(200,200);
for(int x =0; x<width; x++)
   for(int y = 0; y<height; y++){
      rectMode(CENTER);
      if(y%2==0)continue;
      if(x%2==0)
         rect(x*10,y*10,10,10);
      else
         rect(x*10,y*10,4,10);
 }
```

## Pattern 7. The algorithm is:

```
size(200,200);
for(int x=0; x<width; x++)
   for(int y= 0; y<height; y++){
     rectMode(CENTER);
     if(y%2==0)continue;
```

Pattern 8. The algorithm is:

```
size(200,200);
for(int x=0; x<width; x++)
  for(int y= 0; y<height; y++)
    rect(x*random(-10.,10.),y*random(-10.,10.),random(20.),random(20.));
```

Pattern 9. The algorithm is:

```
size(200,000);
for(int x=0; x<width; x++)
  for(int y= 0; y<height; y++)
    rect(x*random(-10.,10.),y*10,10,10);
```

Pattern 10. The algorithm is:

```
size(200,200);
for(int x=0; x<width; x++)
  for(int y= 0; y<height; y++)
    rect(x*10,y*10, random(-10.,10.),10);
```

Pattern 11. The algorithm is:

```
size(200,200);
for(int x=0; x<width; x+=10)
  for(int y= 0; y<height; y+=10){
      beginShape();
      vertex(x+random(-10.,10.),y+random(-10.,10.));
      vertex(x+random(-10.,10.)+10, y+random(-10.,10.));
        vertex(x+random(-10.,10.)+10, y+random(-10.,10.)+10);
        vertex(x+random(-10.,10.), y+random(-10.,10.)+10);
        endShape(CLOSE);
  }
```

Pattern 12. The algorithm is:

```
void setup(){
  size(200,200);
}
void draw(){
  background(255);
  noFill();
  float xx=0, yy=0;
```

```
            float xx = mouseX;
            float xpos = (x/20.)*xx;
            float ypos = y+(x%2)*mouseY;
      vertex(xpos,ypos);
      }
      endShape();
 }
}
```

## Pattern 14. The algorithm is:

```
void setup(){
size(200,200);
}
void draw(){
 noFill();
 background(255);
 for(int y=0; y<height; y+=10){
   beginShape();
   for(int x=0; x<30; x++){
       float xx = mouseX;
       float xpos = (x/20.)*xx;
        float ypos = y+((y%20)*2-10)/10*(x%2)*mouseY;
        vertex(xpos,ypos);
        }
   endShape();
   }
}
```

1. The algorithm is:

```
beginShape();
for(int i=0; i<20; i++){
  float x = ((i+3)/4) * (((i+1)/2)%2*2-1) *10;
  float y = ((i+2)/4) * (((i)/2)%2*2-1) *10;
  vertex(x+50, y+50);
}
endShape();
```

2. The algorithm is:

```
float [] px = new float[0];
float [] py = new float[0];
void setup(){
  size(100,100);
}
void draw(){
  background(255);
  stroke(0,255,0);
  beginShape();
  for(int i=1; i<px.length; i++)
    for(int j=0; j<px.length-1; j++){
      vertex(px[i],py[i]);
      vertex(px[j],py[j]);
    }
  endShape();
  stroke(0);
  for(int i=0; i<px.length; i++)
    rect(px[i],py[i],3,3);
}
void mousePressed(){
  rect(mouseX,mouseY, 3,3);
  px = append(px,mouseX);
  py = append(py,mouseY);
}
```

3. The algorithm is:

```
float [] xp = new float[0];
float [] yp = new float[0];
void setup(){
  size(200,200);
}
```

```
for(int x=0; x<width; x+=20)
    for(int y=0; y<height; y+=10){
        if(y%20!=0 && x==0)rect(x,y,8,8);
        if(y%20!=0 && x>width-21)rect(x+10,y,8,8);
        else
        rect(x+(y%20),y,18,8);
    }
```

5. The algorithm is:

```
size(200,100);
int step_height = 8;
int step_width = 10;
int n_steps = height/step_height;
for(int i=0; i<n_steps; i++){
  float x = i*step_width;
  float y = -i*step_height;
  rect(x,y+height,step_width,3);
}
```

6. The algorithm is:

```
size(200,400);
int step_height = 8;
int step_width = 10;
int dir = 1;
int n_steps = height/step_height;
int k=0;
float x=20,y=0;
for(int i=0; i<n_steps; i++){
    x += step_width*dir;
```

```
}
```

7. The algorithm is:

```
size(220,220);
noFill();
beginShape();
for(int i=2000; i>0; i-=10){
  float x = sin(radians(i))*(i/20);
  float y = cos(radians(i))*(i/20);
  vertex(x+110,y+110);
}
endShape();
```

8. The algorithm is:

```
size(220,440);
noFill();
beginShape();
for(int i=2000; i>10; i-=10){
  float x = sin(radians(i-20))*(i/20);
  float y = cos(radians(i-20))*(i/20);
  vertex(x+110,y+330);
}
for(int i=10; i<2000; i+=10){
  float x = sin(radians(i-20))*(i/20+10);
  float y = cos(radians(i-20))*(i/20+10);
  vertex(x+110,y+330);
}
for(int i=2000; i>10; i-=10){
  float x = sin(radians(i-210))*(i/20);
  float y = cos(radians(i-210))*(i/20);
  vertex(x+120,y+120);
}
for(int i=10; i<2000; i+=10){
  float x = sin(radians(i-210))*(i/20+10);
  float y = cos(radians(i-210))*(i/20+10);
  vertex(x+120,y+120);
}
endShape(CLOSE);
```

its pixels' values). Note that the generation of a `MyScreen` requires first the allocation of memory (line 7) and then the generation of $x$ and $y$ coordinates from the counter $p$ (lines 8 and 9).

```
1     class MyScreen{
2        MyPixel [] pixelGrid;
3
4        MyScreen(int xgrid, int ygrid){
5          pixelGrid = new MyPixel[xgrid*ygrid];
6           for(int p=0; p<pixelGrid.length; p++){
7             pixelGrid[p] = new MyPixel();
8             pixelGrid[p].x = p%xgrid;
9             pixelGrid[p].y = p/xgrid;
10   }
11       }
12
13       void plot(){
14          for(int p=0; p<pixelGrid.length; p++)
15            pixelGrid[p].plot();
16       }
17       }
```

The main code contains simply a call to the generation of a `MyScreen` object called $c$ that contains $80 \times 50$ pixels (line 1). Then in lines 4 and 5 we randomly assign gray values to the pixels.

```
1    MyScreen s = new MyScreen(80,50);
2    void setup(){
3       s.randomPattern();
4       for(int i=0; i<s.pixelGrid.length; i++)
```

```
5        s.pixelGrid[i].c = color((int)random(255));
6      s.plot();
7    }
```

2. Memory for the points was not allocated. In other words, after allocating memory for the array of points, we also need to allocate memory for each individual point, as in the following code:

```
for(int i=0; i<10; i++)
  p[i] = new MyPoint();
```

3. The problem is the same as with exercise 2, except it is harder to detect because there is no compilation error generated. The assignment of point p as a member of seq should been preceded by the allocation of memory for p as shown in the following code:

```
p = new MyPoint();
seg.a = p;
```

# Chapter 4

1. Sample Java classes

   a. Button class

```
Button b = new Button("Click Here");
add(b);
b.addActionListener(new ActionListener() {
  public void actionPerformed(ActionEvent e) {
    println(b.getLabel());
  }});
void mouseDragged(){
    int xoff = mouseX - pmouseX;   // get the offset
    int yoff = mouseY - pmouseY;
    MyPoint ref = new MyPoint(0.,0.);
    for(int i=0; i<group.numShapes; i++)
      if(group.shapes[i].isSelected){
        ref = group.shapes[i].centroid();   //this can be constrcted
        if(control.status.equals("Move"))   //Move
          group.shapes[i].move(( float)xoff, ( float)yoff);
        if(control.status.equals("Rotate"))   //Rotate
          group.shapes[i].rotate(( float)xoff, ref);
        if(control.status.equals("Scale"))   //Scale
          group.shapes[i].scale((float)mouseX/(float)xfirst,
                                 (float)mouseY/(float)yfirst, ref);
      }
    }
```

```
        add(coordsDisplay);
        add(input);

        input.addActionListener(new ActionListener() {
                public void actionPerformed(ActionEvent e) {
                        println("textfield = " + input.getText());
                    }
            });
```

### d. Choice class

```
Choice transform;   //definition
transform = new Choice();
transform.addItem("Move");
transform.addItem("Rotate");
transform.addItem("Scale");

 add(transform);
 transform.addItemListener(new ItemListener() {
   public void itemStateChanged(ItemEvent e) {
     status = transform.getSelectedIndex();
     }
   });
```

2. `setLayout(null);` is missing.

3. `MouseUp()` is not supported.

```
size(MyImage.width,MyImage.height);
image(MyImage,0,0);
for(int x=0; x<width; x+=5)
  for(int y=0; y<height; y+=5){
     float b = brightness(get(x,y))/50;
     fill(255);
     rect(x,y,5,5);
     fill(0);
     ellipse(x,y,5-b,5-b);
}
```

The code can be also exported as dxf to produce a 3D effect, as shown in the following code. The result is shown in the figures following the code. In the first figure, the original face image is shown to the left and its perforated version is superimposed in the image to the right. The second figure shows the modeling of the face's pattern perforation.

```
import processing.dxf.*;
PImage MyImage;
noStroke();
MyImage = loadImage("face.jpg");
size(MyImage.width,MyImage.height,P3D);
image(MyImage,0,0);
beginRaw( DXF, "out.dxf");
for(int x=0; x<width; x+=5)
  for(int y=0; y<height; y+=5){
     float b = brightness(get(x,y))/50;
     fill(0);
     ellipse(x,y,5-b,5-b);
  }
endRaw();
```

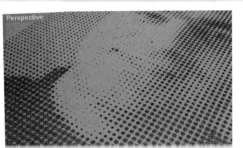

4. The algorithm is:

```
color c = get(x,y);
if(red(c)==0)
   set(x,y,color(255,255,255));
else
   set(x,y,color(255,0,0));
```

5. The algorithm is:

```
1   int [] xd = {0,1,1, 1, 0,-1,-1,-1,0};
2   int [] yd = {1,1,0,-1,-1,-1, 0, 1,1};
3   PImage MyImage;
4   int [][] MyCopy;
5   void setup(){
6     MyImage = loadImage("stockholm white.jpg");
7     size(MyImage.width,MyImage.height);
8     MyCopy = new int[width][height];
9     image(MyImage, 0,0);
10    filter(THRESHOLD);
11    for(int x=0; x<width; x++)
```

```
17  void skeletonize(){
18    for(int x=1; x<width-2; x++)
19      for(int y=2; y<height-1; y++){
20        int b=0;
21        int a=0;
22        for(int i=0; i<8; i++){
23          if(getBinary(x+xd[i],y+yd[i])==1)b++;
24          if(getBinary(x+xd[i],y+yd[i])==0 &&
25            getBinary(x+xd[i+1],y+yd[i+1])==1) a++;
26        }
27        int a2=0;
27        for(int i=0; i<8; i++)
29          if(getBinary(x+xd[i],y+1+yd[i])==0 &&
30            getBinary(x+xd[i+1],y+1+yd[i+1])==1) a2++;
31        int c2 = getBinary(x,y+1)*getBinary(x+1,y)*getBinary(x-1,y);
32        int a3=0;
33              for(int i=0; i<8; i++)
34              if(getBinary(x+1+xd[i],y+yd[i])==0 &&
35                getBinary(x+1+xd[i+1],y+yd[i+1])==1) a3++;
36          int c3=getBinary(x,y+1)*getBinary(x+1,y)
                 *getBinary(x,y-1);
37          if((2<=b && b<=6) && a==1  &&
38            (c2==0 || a2!=1) && (c3==0 || a3!=1))
39          if(getBinary(x,y)==1)MyCopy[x][y]=0;
40      }
41    for(int x=1; x<width-1; x++)
42      for(int y=1; y<height-1; y++)
43        if(MyCopy[x][y]==1)
44          set(x,y,color(0,0,0)); //black
45        else
46          set(x,y,color(255,255,255));   //white
47    }
48
49    int getBinary(int x,int y){
50      return((brightness(get(x,y))>128) ? 0 : 1);
51    }
```

The preceding algorithm is also referred to as Hilditch's algorithm. It
is a skeletonization process that progresses in steps. In each step, every
pixel in the image is evaluated based on its neighboring pixels for the
satisfaction of certain conditions. There are two neighboring conditions
for a pixel p1:

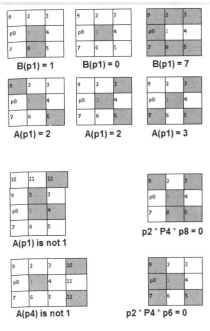

The algorithm above addresses all these conditions in lines 20 through 39.

```
void setup(){
size(300,300);
}
void draw(){
  noFill();
  background(255);
  float xn=0,yn=0;
  for(int i=0; i<30; i++){
    float x = (i/20.)* mouseX;
    float y = 50+(i%2)*mouseY;
    line(x,y,xn,yn);
    xn = x;
    yn = y;
  }
}
```

2. Pattern 2.1 can be produced through the following algorithm:

```
noFill();
size(300,300);
for(int i=1; i<20; i++){
  pushMatrix();
  translate(width/2,height/2);
  rotate(radians(i*45));
  scale(1./i,1./i);
  rect(0,0, 100,100);
  popMatrix();
}
```

Pattern 2.2 can be produced through the following algorithm:

```
noFill();
size(300,300);
background(255);
rectMode(CENTER);
for(int i=1; i<20; i++){
  pushMatrix();
  translate(width/2,height/2);
  rotate(radians(i*45));
  scale(1./i,1./i);
  rect(0,0, 100,100);
  popMatrix();
}
```

```
void setup(){
  noFill();
  size(500,500);
}
void draw(){
  background(255);
  for(float i=1; i<20; i++){
    pushMatrix();
    translate(width/2,height/2);
    scale(1/(i/mouseY*90),1/(i/mouseY*90));
    rotate(radians(i*mouseX));
    rect(0,0, 200,100);
    popMatrix();
  }
}
```

Pattern 3.2 can be produced through the following algorithm:

```
void setup(){
  noFill();
  size(500,500);
}
void draw(){
  background(255);
  for(float i=1; i<20; i++){
    pushMatrix();
    translate(width/2,height/2);
    scale(1/(i/mouseY*90),1/(i/mouseY*90));
    rotate(radians(i*mouseX));
    ellipse(0,0, 200,100);
    popMatrix();
  }
}
```

Pattern 3.3 can be produced through the following algorithm:

```
void setup(){
  noFill();
  //rectMode(CENTER);
  size(500,500);
}
void draw(){
  background(255);
  for(float i=1; i<20; i++){
    pushMatrix();
    translate(width/2,height/2);
    scale(1/(i/mouseY*90),1/(i/mouseY*90));
    rotate(radians(i*mouseX));
    line(250,0,250,500);
    popMatrix();
  }
}
```

# Chapter 7

1. Use the code provided in section 7.3 and replace the generator and base with the following data:

```
float [] gx = {0,0,20,20,10,10,20};    //generator data
float [] gy = {0,-20,-20,-10,-10,0,0};
float [] bx = {225,225,275,275,225};   //base data
float [] by = {275,225,225,275,275};
```

2. The problem here is to use two generators: all even segments will be replaced with generator 1 and all odd segments with generator 2. This algorithm uses the existing code in section 7.3, except that you define two generator arrays:

```
float [] gx1 = {0, 0, 10, 10,20 };    //generator1 data
float [] gy1 = {0, 10, 10, 0, 0 };
float [] gx2 = {0, 10, 10, 20,20 };   //generator2 data
float [] gy2 = {0,  0, -10, -10, 0 };
float [] bx = {100  ,200,300};   //base data
float [] by = {200, 300,200};
```

Then you replace lines 26, 27, and 28 with the following code:

```
float dg=0,x=0,y=0;
if(j%2==0){
dg = dist(0,0,gx1[gx1.length-1],gy1[gy1.length-1]);
```

```
  size(530,400);
  background(255);
  for(int i=0; i<colors.length; i++)
     colors[i] = color(random(255),random(255),random(255));
}
void draw(){
}
void mousePressed(){
  index = 0;
}
void keyPressed(){
  if(index==35)return;
  int done=0;
  background(255);
  index = 0;
  //All spaces with constraints
  int xr = (int)random(7);  //get a random integer 0 to 5 for x to
start
  int yr = (int)random(5);  //get a random integer 0 to 7 for y
  int xp = xr; int yp = yr;
  for(int i=0; i<space.length; i++){
    int numCubes=0;
    int k=0;
    while(numCubes < space[i]){
      xp = xr;
      yp = yr;
      if(random(1)<.5)
        xr = xr + (int)random(-2,2);  //get a random integer
increment of 1 in x
      else
        yr = yr + (int)random(-2,2);  //get a random integer
increment of 1 in y
      xr = constrain(xr, 0,6);
```

```
yr = constrain(yr, 0,4);
boolean exists = false;
for(int j=0; j<index; j++)
  if(cube[j].equals("MyCube" + xr + "x" + yr))
    exists = true;
if(exists==false){ //if there is nothing there
  cube[index] = ("MyCube" + xr + "x" + yr);
  //show the newly created cube
  fill(colors[space_name[i]-1]);
  rect(70+xr*50, height-(100+yr*50),50,50);
  numCubes++;
  index++;
}//if
else{
  xr = xp; yr = yp;
}
if((k++)>100){done = 1; break; }  //safety valve
}//while
if(done==1)break;
}//for
}
```

# Chapter 8

**NOTE** The answer to question 2 is not provided.

1. The algorithm is:

```
size(500,500, P3D);
camera(-20,20,-20,0,0,0,0,0,1);
for(float x=-10; x<10; x+=0.3)
  for(float y=-10; y<10; y+=0.3)
    for(float z=-10; z<10; z+=0.3)
      if((x*x + y*y + z*z)>100 && (x*x + y*y + z*z)<110)
        point(x,y,z);
```

3. The algorithm is:

```
size(500,500, P3D);
camera(-5,5,-20,0,0,0,0,0,1);
  for(int phi=0; phi<360; phi+=10){
    float x = 10*cos(radians(phi));
    float y = 10*sin(radians(phi));
    pushMatrix();
```

}

5. The algorithm is:

```
size(500,500, P3D);
camera(-10,10,-20,0,0,0,0,0,1);
beginShape();
for(int i=0; i<40; i++){
   float x = ((i/2)%2)*2-1;
   float y = (((i+1)/2)%2)*2-1;
   float z = 30-i;
   curveVertex(x,y,z);

}
endShape();
```

6. The projection algorithm is:

```
int xP(float eye){
   float t = 1.0/(1.0+((float) z / eye ));
   int px = int( x * sin(t) + y*cos(t));
   return(px);
}

int yP(float eye){
   float t = 1.0/(1.0+((float) z / eye ));
   int py = int( y * sin(t) - x*cos(t));
   return(py);
}
```

The resulting project for a cubical line arrangement is shown here.

# Chapter 9

1  First, create a class called MyGrid.

```
class MyGrid{
  float unit = 10;
  int span = 50;

  void plotXY(){
    for(int x=-span; x<span+1; x+=unit)
      for(int y=-span; y<span+1; y+=unit){
        line(x,-span,0,x,span,0);
        line(-span,y,0,span,  y,0);
      }
  }
    void plotZX(){
    for(int x=-span; x<span+1; x+=unit)
      for(int z=-span; z<span+1; z+=unit){
        line(x,0,-span,x,0,span);
        line(-span,0,z,span,  0,z);
      }
  }
  void plotYZ(){
    for(int y=-span; y<span+1; y+=unit)
      for(int z=-span; z<span+1; z+=unit){
        line(0,y,-span,0,y,span);
        line(0,-span,z,0,span,z);
      }
  }
}
```

This class contains the size of the grid's units and the span that the grid
will have. Then you create three methods each for every direction in space.
In each case, you loop in two directions and draw lines that correspond
to the XY, YZ, or ZX plane. In the setup() section of the main code, you
define a grid and then modify its members (optional). This is shown in
the following code:

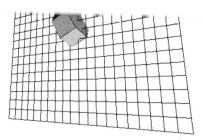

2. Creating a graphical user interface is quite simple. Simply extend the existing interface with one more choice, which we will call ColorChooser:

```
Choice ColorChooser;
    ColorChooser = new Choice();
    ColorChooser.add("Green");
    ColorChooser.add("Red");
    ColorChooser.add("Blue");
    ColorChooser.setLocation(200, 30);
    ColorChooser.setSize(100, 20);

    String color_name = "Green";
    ColorChooser.addItemListener(new ItemListener() {
      public void itemStateChanged(ItemEvent e) {
    color_name = ColorChooser.getItem(ColorChooser.getSelectedIndex());
        }});
```

Then in the main code, you modify the selection of a solid to also include a change in color:

```
    if(control.level_type.equals("Solid")){
        for(int i=0; i<group.nsolids; i++)
```

```
if(group.solids[i].pick(mouseX,mouseY)){
    group.solids[i].setSelected(true);
    if(control.color_name=="Green")
        group.solids[i].setColor(color(0,255,0));
    if(control.color_name=="Blue")
        group.solids[i].setColor(color(0,0,255));
    if(control.color_name=="Red")
        group.solids[i].setColor(color(255,0,0));
    return;
}
}
```

3. A converging extrusion is essentially an extrusion to a point. This point can be either a single point or a face whose vertices have collapsed into a single position. You use the second case here. The method to obtain this algorithm is to add one more line of code in the constructor of the MySolid class that will scale all points of the top face into a single position. Use the following line of code:

```
faces[ nfaces].scale(0,0,0,new MyPoint(0,0,height));
```

In such a case the constructor of a solid will be modified to include two cases: extrusion or convergence:

```
MySolid(MyPoint[] inPoints, float height, int type){

    nfaces = 0;
    faces = new MyFace[inPoints.length + 2];

    //bottom
    faces[0] = new MyFace(inPoints);
    nfaces++;

    //top
    faces[ nfaces] = new MyFace(inPoints);
    faces[ nfaces].move(0., 0., height);
    if (type==1)faces[ nfaces].scale(0,0,0,new MyPoint(0,0,height));
    nfaces++;
```

The rest of the code remains the same.

```
String -

void setup(){
  PFont myFont = createFont("Verdana",10);
  textFont(myFont, 10);
  lines = loadStrings("names.txt");
  size(300,22*lines.length);

  int k = lines.length-1;
  String temp = "";
  //swap 50 times randomly
  for (int i=0; i < 50; i++) {
    int r1 = int(random(k));
    int r2 = int(random(k));
    temp = lines[r1];
    lines[r1] = lines[r2];
    lines[r2] = temp;
  }
  saveStrings("names.altered.txt", lines);
}

void draw(){
  background(255);
  fill(0);
  for (int i=0; i < lines.length; i++) {
    text(lines[i], 10, (i+1)*20);
  }
}
```

# Chapter 11

**NOTE**  As a project, Question 5 does not have an answer in this Appendix.

1. The algorithm is:

```
import processing.serial.*;
Serial port;
void setup(){
  size(400,100);
  port = new Serial(this, "COM6", 9600);
}

void draw(){
  background(255);
  line(mouseX,0,mouseX,100);
  int tone = mouseX/50;
  port.write(tone);
}
```

2. The algorithm is:

```
import processing.serial.*;

PrintWriter output;

String buff = "";
int val = 0;
int NEWLINE = 10;

Serial port;

void setup(){
  // Uses the first available port
  port = new Serial(this, "COM6", 9600);
  output = createWriter("positions.txt");
}

void draw(){
  while (port.available() > 0)
    serialEvent(port.read());
  background(val);
  println(val);
  output.println(val);
}
```

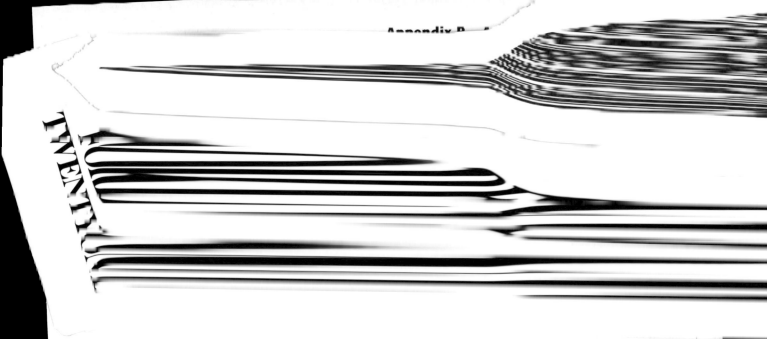

3. The answer is:

```
int roundit = (value/5)*5;
```

4. The algorithm is:

```
void setup(){
  pinMode(3,INPUT);    // set the pin 2 to input
}

void loop(){
  int val = digitalRead(3);      //read from the pin 2
  digitalWrite(13,!val);
}
```

# Further Readings

## Processing

Dawes, B. *Analog In, Digital Out: Brendan Dawes on Interactive Design*, Berkeley: New Riders, 2007

Fry, B. *Visualizing Data: Exploring and Explaining Data with the Processing Environment*, O'Reilly, 2008

Greenberg, Ira. *Processing: Creative Coding and Computational Art (Foundation)*, Apress.com, May 2007

Reas, C. and B. Fry *Processing: A Programming Handbook for Visual Designers and Artists*, Cambridge: MIT Press, 2007

Shiffman, D. *Learning Processing: A Beginner's Guide to Programming Images, Animation, and Interaction*, Burlington MA: Morgan Kaufmann Publishers, 2008

## Arduino

Banzi, M. *Getting Started with Arduino*, O'Reilly/Make Books, 2008

Igoe, T. *Making Things Talk: Practical Methods for Connecting Physical Objects*, O'Reilly/Make Books, 2007

O'Sullivan, D. and T. Igoe. *Physical Computing: Sensing and Controlling the Physical World with Computers*, Boston: Thomson Course Technology, 2004

## Java

Bloch, J. *Effective Java (2nd edition)* New York: Prentice Hall, 2008

Deitel, P. and H. Deitel. *Java: How to Program,* New York: Prentice Hall, 2007

Flanagan, D. *Java in a Nutshell,* O'Reilly, 2005

Flanagan, D. *Java Examples in a Nutshell,* O'Reilly, 2004

Horstmann, C. and G. Cornell. *Core Java, Volume I Fundamentals (8th Edition)* New York: Prentice Hall, 2007

## Computer Graphics

Ames, L, D. Nadeau, and J. Moreland. *VRML Sourcebook,* New York: Wiley, 1997

Angel, E. *Interactive Computer Graphics: A Top-Down Approach Using OpenGL (5th Edition),* Boston: Addison-Wesley, 2008

Foley, J., A. van Dam, S. Feiner, and J. Hughes. *Computer Graphics: Principles and Practice in C (2nd Edition),* Boston: Addison-Wesley, 1995

Maeda, J. *Design by Numbers,* Cambridge: MIT Press, 2001

Shirley, P., M. Ashikhmin, M. Gleicher, and S. Marschner. *Fundamentals of Computer Graphics,* Natick, MA: A. K. Peters, 2002

## Algorithms

Cormen, T., C. Leiserson, R. Rivest, and C. Stein. *Introduction to Algorithms,* Cambridge: MIT Press, 2001

Heineman, G. *Algorithms in a Nutshell,* O'Reilly, 2009

Kleinberg, J. and E. Tardos. *Algorithm Design,* Boston: Addison-Wesley, 2005

Terzidis, Kostas. *Algorithmic Architecture,* Oxford: Architectural Press/ Elsevier, 2006

Wolfram, S. *A New Kind of Science,* Champaign: Stephen Wolfram, 2002

## Digital Design

Agazzi, E. and L. Montecucco (eds.). *Complexity and Emergence,* New Jersey: World Scientific, 2002

Fishwick, P. (ed.). *Aesthetic Computing,* Cambridge: MIT Press, 2006

Johnson, S. *Emergence*, New York, Touchstone, 2001

Kwinter, Sanford. "The Computational Fallacy," *Cambridge Thresholds* 26, 2003, pp. 90–2

Latour, B., "Alternative Digitality," *Domus*, April 2004

Leach, N. "Swarm tectonics: a manifesto for an emergent architecture" in Hadid Z. and P. Schumacher P. *Latent Utopias: Experiments within Contemporary Architecture*, Vienna: Springer-Verlag, 2002, pp. 48–55

Lonsway, B. "The Mistaken Dimensionality of CAD," *Journal of Architectural Education* vol. 56 issue 2, November 2002, pp. 22–25

Novak, M. "Speciation, Transvergence, Allogenesis Notes on the Production of the Alien" in Spiller, N. (ed.). *Reflexive Architecture*, London: Wiley Academy, 2002, pp. 64–71

Saunders, Peter, "Nonlinearity: What it is and why it matters" in Di Cristina, G. (ed.). *Architecture and Science*, Wiley Academy, 2001, pp. 110–15

Serraino, P. "Form Follows Software," *ACADIA Proceedings*, 2003

Spiller, N. (ed.) *Cyber_Reader*, New York: Phaidon Press Ltd., 2002

Taylor, Mark. *The moment of Complexity: Emerging Network Culture*, Chicago: The University of Chicago Press, 2001

Terzidis, Kostas. *Expressive Form: A Conceptual Approach to Computational Design*, Spon Press–Routledge, 2003

Yessios, Chris. "A Fractal Studio," Proceedings of the Annual Conference of the Association for Computer Aided Design in Architecture (ACADIA), University of North Carolina, Nov. 1987, pp. 169–81

# Index